Communicating with Vulnerable Patients

Communicating with Vulnerable Patients explores ways to improve the communication process between highly vulnerable patients and the therapist, based on the assumption of the permanent presence of an 'outsider' or potential space in the communication field between them. In this space, the therapist and highly vulnerable patients can undergo transitional states of mind established between and within their relationship.

Leticia Castrechini-Franieck, also known as Maria Leticia Castrechini Fernandes Franieck, presents practical methods to overcome communication issues and engage therapeutically with highly vulnerable patients suffering from personality disorders, addiction, and trauma, as well as with deprived children. *Communicating with Vulnerable Patients* is presented in five parts, with Part one focused on building communication through a Transient Interactive Communication Approach (TICA) and Part two applying TICA in forensic settings with five case studies illustrating the approach in a range of contexts. Part three considers TICA in intercultural settings, including work with refugees, and Part four outlines adaptations of the approach, including T-WAS (Together We Are Strong), which aims to avoid an increase of antisocial behaviour in deprived children, and the use of TICA in the COVID-19 pandemic. The book concludes in Part five with reflections on outcomes and limitations of both TICA and T-WAS.

Communicating with Vulnerable Patients will be invaluable reading for professionals, psychotherapists, group therapists, and group analysts working with at-risk populations.

Maria Leticia Castrechini Fernandes Franieck, PhD, is a chartered counselling psychologist and a psychodynamic psychotherapist based in Germany. Her clinical practice is focused on working with highly vulnerable populations.

The Forensic Psychotherapy Monograph Series
Series Editor: Professor Brett Kahr

The Official Publication Series of the International Association for Forensic Psychotherapy

Selected titles in the series:

Violence: A Public Health Menace and a Public Health Approach
Edited by Sandra L. Bloom

Forensic Psychotherapy and Psychopathology: Winnicottian Perspectives
Edited by Brett Kahr

Dangerous Patients: A Psychodynamic Approach to Risk Assessment and Management
Edited by Ronald Doctor and Sarah Nettleton

The Mind of the Paedophile: Psychoanalytic Perspectives
Edited by Charles W. Socarides and Loretta R. Loeb

Violence in Children: Understanding and Helping Those Who Harm
Edited by Rosemary Campher

Murder: A Psychotherapeutic Investigation
Edited by Ronald Doctor

Psychic Assaults and Frightened Clinicians: Countertransference in Forensic Settings
Edited by John Gordon and Gabriel Kirtchuk

Forensic Aspects of Dissociative Identity Disorder
Edited by Adah Sachs and Graeme Galton

Playing with Dynamite: A Personal Approach to the Psychoanalytic Understanding of Perversions, Violence, and Criminality
Estela Welldon

The Internal World of the Juvenile Sex Offender: Through a Glass Darkly then Face to Face
Timothy Keogh

Disabling Perversions: Forensic Psychotherapy with People with Intellectual Disabilities
Alan Corbett

Sexual Abuse and the Sexual Offender: Common Man or Monster?
Barry Maletzky

Psychotherapy with Male Survivors of Sexual Abuse: The Invisible Men
Alan Corbett

Consulting to Chaos: An Approach to Patient-Centred Reflective Practice
Edited by John Gordon, Gabriel Kirtchuk, Maggie McAlister, and David Reiss

New Horizons in Forensic Psychotherapy: Exploring the Work of Estela V. Welldon
Edited by Brett Kahr

The End of the Sentence: Psychotherapy with Female Offenders
Edited by Pamela Windham Stewart and Jessica Collier

For further information about this series please visit www.routledge.com/The-Forensic-Psychotherapy-Monograph-Series/book-series/KARNFPM
The Forensic Psychotherapy Monograph Series

Communicating with Vulnerable Patients

A Novel Psychological Approach

Maria Leticia
Castrechini Fernandes Franieck
With Contribution from Niko Bittner

LONDON AND NEW YORK

Designed cover image: © Maria Leticia Castrechini Fernandes Franieck

First published 2023
by Routledge
4 Park Square, Milton Park, Abingdon, Oxon OX14 4RN

and by Routledge
605 Third Avenue, New York, NY 10158

Routledge is an imprint of the Taylor & Francis Group, an informa business

© 2023 Maria Leticia Castrechini Fernandes Franieck

The right of Maria Leticia Castrechini Fernandes Franieck to be identified as author of this work has been asserted in accordance with sections 77 and 78 of the Copyright, Designs and Patents Act 1988.

All rights reserved. No part of this book may be reprinted or reproduced or utilised in any form or by any electronic, mechanical, or other means, now known or hereafter invented, including photocopying and recording, or in any information storage or retrieval system, without permission in writing from the publishers.

Trademark notice: Product or corporate names may be trademarks or registered trademarks, and are used only for identification and explanation without intent to infringe.

British Library Cataloguing-in-Publication Data
A catalogue record for this book is available from the British Library

ISBN: 978-1-032-14041-4 (hbk)
ISBN: 978-1-032-14042-1 (pbk)
ISBN: 978-1-003-23208-7 (ebk)

DOI: 10.4324/9781003232087

Typeset in Times New Roman
by Apex CoVantage, LLC

To my twin sons Erick Franieck and Lucas Franieck, for making my life brighter

and

to my colleague Niko Bittner, for his valuable companionship

Contents

List of Contributors	ix
Series Editor's Foreword	x
BRETT KAHR	
Preface	xv
Acknowledgements	xvii
Introduction	xviii

PART ONE
On building communication   1

1 Handling, mastering, and integrating a personal and factual reality   3
2 On intercultural interactional communication   8
3 TICA – Transient Interactive Communication Approach   24

PART TWO
TICA in forensic settings   37

4 TICA in withdrawal therapy   39
5 TICA in pretrial detention   87

PART THREE
TICA in intercultural settings   113

6 TICA in short-term therapy with traumatized refugees   115
7 TICA in multicultural team supervision   138

PART FOUR
TICA adaptations (variations)   153

8 T-WAS – Together We Are Strong   155
WITH CONTRIBUTION FROM NIKO BITTNER

9 TICA in the COVID-19 pandemic   186
WITH CONTRIBUTION FROM NIKO BITTNER

PART FIVE
Reflections on TICA   203

10 Outcomes and limitations   205

Index   234

Contributor

Niko Bittner is a qualified pedagogue and Gestalt therapist. He works in youth social work and is a seminar leader at the Odenwald Institute, Germany, where he trains conflict coaches, among other things.

Forensic Psychotherapy Monograph Series
Series Editor's Foreword

In 1801, the English judiciary condemned a 13-year-old boy to death and then hanged him on the gallows at Tyburn, in the heart of London. But what crime had he committed? Apparently, this young lad had stolen merely a spoon (Westwick 1940). Tragically, during the early nineteenth century, such an infraction could actually result in capital punishment.

Throughout much of human history, our ancestors have performed rather poorly when responding to acts of violence. In most cases, our predecessors will either have *ignored* murderousness, as in the case of Graeco-Roman infanticide, which occurred so regularly in the ancient world that it acquired an almost normative status (deMause 1974; Kahr 1994); or they will have *punished* destructible behaviours with retaliatory sadism, a form of unconscious identification with the aggressor. Any history of criminology will readily reveal the cruel punishments inflicted upon prisoners throughout the ages, ranging from beatings and stockades, to more severe forms of torture, culminating in eviscerations, lynchings, beheadings, and electrocutions (e.g., Kahr 2020).

Only during the last 100 years have we begun to develop the capacity to respond more intelligently and more humanely to dangerousness and destruction. Since the advent of psychoanalysis, we now have access to a much deeper understanding of both the aetiology of aggressive acts, and to their treatment; and nowadays, we need no longer ignore criminals or abuse them – instead, we can offer forensic psychotherapeutic interventions with compassion and containment, as well as conduct research which can help to prevent future acts of violence. By *treating* aggressive patients, rather than by *punishing* them, forward-thinking mental health practitioners now possess the ability to draw upon the new discipline of forensic psychotherapy, designed to understand the causes of violence, in order to help rehumanize the dehumanized.

The discipline of forensic psychotherapy can trace its origins to the very early days of psychoanalysis. On 6 February 1907, at a meeting of the Wiener Psychoanalytische Vereinigung [Vienna Psycho-Analytical Society], Professor Sigmund Freud bemoaned the often horrible treatment of mentally ill offenders.

According to Otto Rank, Freud's secretary at the time, the founder of psychoanalysis expressed his sorrow at the "*unsinnige Behandlung dieser Leute*" (quoted in Rank 1907a, p. 101), which translates as the "nonsensical treatment of these people" (quoted in Rank 1907b, p. 108).

Many of the early psychoanalytical practitioners preoccupied themselves with forensic topics. Dr. Hanns Sachs, himself a trained lawyer, and the Princesse Marie Bonaparte, the French aristocrat, spoke fiercely against capital punishment. Sachs, one of the first members of Freud's inner circle, regarded the death penalty for offenders as an example of group sadism (Moellenhoff 1966); while Bonaparte (1927), who had studied various murderers throughout her career, actually campaigned to free the convicted killer Caryl Chessman, during his sentence on death row at the California State Prison in San Quentin (Bertin 1982).

Some years later, Melanie Klein (1932a), the Austrian-born, British-based clinician, concluded her first book, the landmark text *Die Psychoanalyse des Kindes* [*The Psycho-Analysis of Children*], with a truly memorable clarion call. Klein noted that acts of criminality invariably stem from disturbances in childhood, and that if young people could receive psychoanalytical treatment at an early age, then much cruelty would be prevented in later years. As she argued,

> If every child who shows disturbances that are at all severe were to be analysed in good time, a great number of these people who later end up in prisons or lunatic asylums, or who go completely to pieces, would be saved from such a fate and be able to develop a normal life"[1]
>
> (Klein 1932b, p. 374)

Shortly after the publication of Klein's transformative book, Atwell Westwick, a judge of the Superior Court of Santa Barbara, California, published a little-known, though highly inspiring, article on "Criminology and Psychoanalysis" in *The Psychoanalytic Quarterly*. Westwick may well be the first judge to have committed himself in print to the value of psychoanalysis in the study of criminality, arguing that punishment of the forensic patient remains, in fact, a sheer waste of time. With passion, Judge Westwick (1940, p. 281) queried,

> Can we not, in our well nigh hopeless and overwhelming struggle with the problems of delinquency and crime, profit by medical experience with the problems of health and disease? Will we not, eventually, terminate the senseless policy of sitting idly by until misbehavior occurs, often with irreparable damage, then dumping the delinquent into the juvenile court or reformatory and dumping the criminal into prison?

Westwick noted that we should, instead, train judges, probation officers, social workers, as well as teachers and parents, in the precepts of psychoanalysis, in order to arrive at a more sensitive, non-punitive understanding of the nature of criminality. As Westwick (1940, p. 281) opined,

> When we shall have succeeded in committing society to such a program, when we see it launched definitely upon the venture, as in time it surely will be – then shall we have erected an appropriate memorial to Sigmund Freud.

Although the roots of forensic psychotherapy stem back to the early years of the twentieth century (e.g., Kahr 2018), the discipline only became constellated more formally in the 1980s and 1990s, due, in large measure, to the pioneering work of the esteemed forensic psychiatrist and forensic psychotherapist, Dr. Estela Valentina Welldon (1988, 1996, 2002, 2011, 2015), and many of her colleagues, and, thankfully, the profession now boasts a much more robust foundation, with training courses available for young mental health workers in the United Kingdom and beyond. Since the inauguration of the Diploma in Forensic Psychotherapy, created by Dr. Welldon, hosted by the Portman Clinic in London, and sponsored by the British Postgraduate Medical Federation of the University of London, with the support and encouragement of its leader, Professor Sir Michael Peckham (Kahr 2021), students can now seek further instruction in the psychodynamic treatment of patients who act out in a dangerous and illegal manner. Dr. Welldon created not only the world's first training programme in forensic psychotherapy, she also launched the International Association for Forensic Psychotherapy in 1991, and hosted its first conference in 1992 at St. Bartholomew's Hospital in London. This passionate and devoted organization has certainly helped to develop the field globally.

Back in 1997, at the kind invitation of Cesare Sacerdoti, the owner of H. Karnac (Books) at that time, I had the privilege of commissioning a host of titles for a new book series, designed to promote this growing branch of forensic psychological assessment, treatment, and prevention; and the very first titles appeared several years later (Bloom 2001; Kahr 2001; Saunders 2001). Over time, this Forensic Psychotherapy Monograph Series, now published by Routledge, part of the Taylor and Francis Group, has endeavoured to produce a regular stream of high-quality titles, written by leading members of the profession, who share their expertise in a concise and practice-oriented fashion. We trust that this collection of books, which, in 2022, became the official monograph series of the International Association for Forensic Psychotherapy, will help to consolidate the knowledge and experience that we have already acquired, and will also provide new directions in the decades to come.

It gives me great pleasure that our colleague, Dr. Leticia Castrechini-Franieck, a highly experienced psychologist and group psychoanalyst, has written a groundbreaking tome, *Communicating with Vulnerable Patients: A Novel Psychological Approach*, as part of the Forensic Psychotherapy Monograph Series. Drawing upon years of work in detention centres, psychiatric hospitals and refugee/asylum-seeker camps, Dr. Castrechini-Franieck has examined the psychodynamics of the so-called "at risk" or "unbearable" patients, whose histories have contributed to her deeper understanding of the complex interplay between transgressor and victim.

I warmly remember meeting Dr. Castrechini-Franieck at the Freud Museum in London, and I became quite gripped as she told me about her important work. In the pages that follow, she describes how she first became involved in the forensic mental health community and how, with deep compassion and fine intelligence, she began to speak with these 'outsiders', through her unique and original method, known as TICA, namely the Transient Interactive Communication Approach. Moreover, in collaboration with colleague Niko Bittner, Dr. Castrechini-Franieck has also developed a special strand of TICA, known as T-WAS, namely Together We Are Strong, which, drawing upon the work of Dr. Donald Winnicott, endeavours to provide greater insight into collaboration with deprived and anti-social children, many of refugee backgrounds.

Indeed, the author has applied her expertise on communication not only to her patients but, also, to her colleagues in both forensic and intercultural settings, championing the ways in which we can all treat one another with greater honesty and respect. Readers will undoubtedly learn a great deal about the art and the science of forensic psychotherapeutic practice from this rich and compelling study.

As the new millennium begins to unfold, we now have an opportunity for psychotherapeutically oriented forensic mental health professionals to work in close conjunction with child psychologists and with infant mental health specialists so that the problems of violence can be tackled both retrospectively and, also, preventively. With the growth of the field of forensic psychotherapy, we at last have reason to be hopeful that serious criminality can be forestalled and perhaps, one day, even eradicated.

Professor Brett Kahr
Series Editor
Forensic Psychotherapy Monograph Series
International Association for Forensic Psychotherapy

Copyright © 2022, by Professor Brett Kahr.
Please do not quote without the permission of the author.

Note

1 The original German phrase reads:

> *Würde jedes Kind, das ernstere Störungen zeigt, rechtzeitig der Analyse unterzogen, dann könnte wohl ein großer Teil jener Menschen, die andernfalls in Gefängnissen und Irrenhäusern landen oder sonst völlig scheitern, vor diesem Schicksal bewahrt bleiben und sich zu normalen Menschen entwickeln*
>
> (Klein 1932a, p. 293).

References

Bertin, C., 1982. *La Dernière Bonaparte*. Paris: Librairie Académique Perrin.
Bloom, S.L., ed., 2001. *Violence: A Public Health Menace and a Public Health Approach*. London: Karnac Books.
Bonaparte, M., 1927. Le Cas de Madame Lefebvre. *Revue Française de Psychanalyse*, 1, 149–198.
deMause, L., 1974. The Evolution of Childhood. *In*: L. deMause, ed. *The History of Childhood*. New York: Psychohistory Press, 1–73.
Kahr, B., 1994. The Historical Foundations of Ritual Abuse: An Excavation of Ancient Infanticide. *In*: V. Sinason, ed. *Treating Survivors of Satanist Abuse*. London: Routledge, 45–56.
Kahr, B., ed., 2001. *Forensic Psychotherapy and Psychopathology: Winnicottian Perspectives*. London: Karnac Books.
Kahr, B., 2018. 'No Intolerable Persons' or 'Lewd Pregnant Women': Towards a History of Forensic Psychoanalysis. *In*: B. Kahr, ed. *New Horizons in Forensic Psychotherapy: Exploring the Work of Estela V. Welldon*. London: Karnac Books, 17–87.
Kahr, B., 2020. *Dangerous Lunatics: Trauma, Criminality, and Forensic Psychotherapy*. London: Confer Books.
Kahr, B., 2021. Professor Sir Michael Peckham: A Memorial Tribute. *International Journal of Forensic Psychotherapy*, 3, 163–165.
Klein, M., 1932a. *Die Psychoanalyse des Kindes*. Vienna: Internationaler Psychoanalytischer Verlag.
Klein, M., 1932b. *The Psycho-Analysis of Children*. Alix Strachey, transl. London: Hogarth Press and The Institute of Psycho-Analysis.
Moellenhoff, F., 1966. Hanns Sachs 1881–1947: The Creative Unconscious. *In*: F. Alexander, S. Eisenstein, and M. Grotjahn, eds. *Psychoanalytic Pioneers*. New York: Basic Books, 180–199.
Rank, O., ed., 1907a/1976. Vortragsabend: Am 6. Februar 1907. *In*: H. Nunberg and E. Federn, eds. *Protokolle der Wiener Psychoanalytischen Vereinigung: Band I. 1906–1908*. Frankfurt aM: S. Fischer Verlag, 97–104.
Rank, O., ed., 1907b/1962. Scientific Meeting on February 6, 1907. *In*: H. Nunberg and E. Federn, eds. and transl. *Minutes of the Vienna Psychoanalytic Society: Volume I: 1906–1908*. New York: International Universities Press, 103–110.
Saunders, J.W., ed., 2001. *Life Within Hidden Walls: Psychotherapy in Prisons*. London: Karnac Books.
Welldon, E.V., 1988. *Mother, Madonna, Whore: The Idealization and Denigration of Motherhood*. London: Free Association Books.
Welldon, E.V., 1996. Contrasts in Male and Female Sexual Perversions. *In*: C. Cordess and M. Cox, eds. *Forensic Psychotherapy: Crime, Psychodynamics and the Offender Patient. Volume II. Mainly Practice*. London: Jessica Kingsley Publishers, 273–289.
Welldon, E.V., 2002. *Sadomasochism*. Duxford, Cambridge: Icon Books.
Welldon, E.V. 2011. *Playing with Dynamite: A Personal Approach to the Psychoanalytic Understanding of Perversions, Violence, and Criminality*. London: Karnac Books.
Welldon, E., 2015. Forensic Psychotherapy. *Psychoanalytic Psychotherapy*, 29, 211–227.
Westwick, A., 1940. Criminology and Psychoanalysis. *Psychoanalytic Quarterly*, 9, 269–282.

Preface

This book in essence deals with ways to improve the communication process between 'highly vulnerable' and/or 'unbearable' patients and the therapist (in individual as well as in group context), based on the assumption of the permanent presence of an 'Outsider' in the communication field between them. Although, who is actually the 'Outsider'?

1   The 'Outsider' may refer to the 'highly vulnerable' and/or 'unbearable' patients per se, as frequently, due to their peculiar actions, they are placed beyond society. This happens because they do not fit in with expected social behaviour patterns.
2   The 'Outsider' may also refer to the therapist per se – a stranger that comes from a different background compared to the 'highly vulnerable' and/or 'unbearable' patients. In an overseas therapist, owing to cultural and language issues, the patients might perceive a newcomer to their well-established social environment. Hence, like the 'highly vulnerable' and/or 'unbearable' patients, a therapist from overseas may be metaphorically placed out of 'beyond society' as a stranger. Therefore, the overseas therapist needs to be aware of his or her permanent 'Outsider' role, as well as be able to accept this as a cross-cultural fact.
3   The 'Outsider' may represent the therapist's role as an observer of 'the analytic triad', as referred by Segal (Caper 1997). More simply, as an observer of the communication field created between the therapist and the client.
4   The 'Outsider' may also represent the idea of a third area, of the intermediate area as perceived by Winnicott's conception – in-between the two, as a potential space (Winnicott 1953, 1967). In this potential space, the therapist and 'highly vulnerable' and/or 'unbearable' patients can undergo transitional states of mind established between and within their relationship.
5   The 'Outsider' may, finally, refer to the 'analytic triad' as perceived by Ogden (2004/1994). The 'analytic triad' is a product of the two members of the analytic pair, in this case, a product of the therapist and the 'highly vulnerable' and/or 'unbearable' patients.

References

Caper, R., 1997. Symbol Formation and Creativity: Hanna Segal's Theoretical Contributions. *In*: D. Bell, ed. *Reason and Passion: A Celebration of the Work of Hanna Segal*. Tavistock Clinic Series. London: Routledge, 37–56.

Ogden, T.H., 2004/1994. *Subjects of Analysis*. 1st ed. Rowman & Littlefield [online]. Available from: http://gbv.eblib.com/patron/FullRecord.aspx?p=1061129.

Winnicott, D.W., 1953. Transitional Objects and Transitional Phenomena: A Study of the First Not-Me Possession. *The International Journal of Psycho-analysis*, 34, 89–97.

Winnicott, D.W., 1967. The Location of Cultural Experience. *The International Journal of Psycho-analysis*, 48 (3), 368–372.

Acknowledgements

I am indebted to Estela Welldon and Kahr Brett, whose enthusiasm first encouraged me to start writing this book, together with Brett's generosity in agreeing to write the Foreword.

Most particularly, I wish to thank all deprived children and adolescents, individuals in the forensic setting and traumatized refugees who allowed me to come into contact with them, without whom I could not have written this book.

I wish to acknowledge my gratitude to all my employers for their consent to publish the cases I managed while working in their organizations. I owe thanks to all my colleagues who provide me their written appreciation and/or criticisms of this book.

I also extend my warmest appreciations to Roosevelt Smerke Cassorla, Tim Page, and Michael Günter for their remarkable contributions to my work over the past years, and above all for their friendship, and to Heather McClelland for smoothing out my English.

I have expressed my gratitude to my twin sons Erick and Lucas, and also to my colleague Niko in my dedication.

For the permission to reproduce material that has already appeared in print, thanks are due to the International Forum Psychoanalytic Education (IFPE).

Introduction

This book aims first to share my experience of searching for increasingly effective ways to engage therapeutically with extremely vulnerable populations in different settings; and second to trigger reflections on the communication process with these patients. The key ideas developed here emerged from my personal struggle with establishing a way to handle controversial issues at the beginning of my clinical work in a foreign country with 'highly vulnerable' and 'unbearable' patients in 'an alien clinical forensic setting'. At the time, I thought I would not be able to manage this, but on reflection I realized that establishing a sound communication field could bring me some 'Hope'.

> Hope is definitely not the same thing as optimism. It is not the conviction that something will turn out well, but the certainty that something makes sense, regardless of how it turns out.
> (Havel and Hvížďala 1991, p. 181)

Whenever I refer to the term 'Hope' in this manuscript, it will always be in this sense.

The approach presented in this book – the 'Transient Interactive Communication Approach' (TICA) – has been developed to assist communication between/among therapist and 'highly vulnerable' and 'unbearable' patients, despite their medical records or even their ICD-11/DSM diagnoses (the 11th revision of the International Classification of Diseases and the *Diagnostic and Statistical Manual of Mental Disorders* of the American Psychiatric Association, currently in its fifth edition). The focus should not be on the patients' symptoms, neither on their defence mechanisms, but rather on providing them with a new experience in the communication field with the therapist. The primary purpose of TICA is, in particular, to support 'highly vulnerable' and/or 'unbearable' patients in rediscovering their potential and their sense of 'self', since they had frequently experienced successive miscommunication in their past relationships (Castrechini-Franieck and Page 2017; Castrechini-Franieck *et al.* 2014). However, sometimes and in some cases, healing equates to false optimism, particularly for these patients (Welldon 2011). One needs to be aware that in the relationship between patient and therapist, the expectation of healing is more frequently felt by the latter. Indeed, we are not only trained to do this, but we are also paid for doing this (based on the traditional medicine approaches). The 'Other', in turn, accepts the relationship with us due to their desperation to understand themselves in their miscommunication experiences (principle of transference), but this does not imply that the 'Other' wants or is even ready for healing – in my view, this matter is the first great risk of miscommunication before a relationship with the patient has even started. In my experience, the cases that ended in 'no healing expectation' could not be defined as 'lost cases', as a new communication experience might have provided the clients with the sensitivity to be in contact with their 'dark sides', without fear or shame, even if only for a while. Furthermore, this might be to a certain extent therapeutic. To illustrate, I will provide the following two examples from two distinct settings I experienced.

A case in a forensic setting

When I was working in a pretrial detention centre, my job was to run weekly psychological anamneses with all new prisoners whilst assessing potential suicidal risks and aggressors, as well as carrying out crisis interventions and counselling those who wanted to talk to me voluntarily. One day, a new prisoner came into my office, a man over 30 years old, from a first generation of migrants and jailed for the first time, due to committing fraud. Before I could introduce myself, he told me he would like to be counselled by me, as he had problems. I was astonished that he could think about receiving counselling from me without even knowing me yet, even more so considering the forensic context whereby talking to a psychologist meant you were 'mad'. I simply calmy and in a friendly manner stated my initial thoughts to him:

T: "Well, I am very surprised indeed now . . . you do not even know me yet . . . how could you trust me and talk about your problem with me when I am still a stranger? Are you sure about that?"

In doing so, I was expressing in words the feelings he had roused inside me whilst giving verbal representation to them – reverie function (Bion 1984). Moreover, I was questioning whether his request was based on idealization or even on an attempt to control and manipulate me by trigging my narcissistic side and flattering me with the status of being a competent psychologist. His answer to my intervention was:

P: "It is true I don't know you, but there is 'someone' who knows you and he advised me to talk to you when I get here. He said that you were the only person with whom he could talk about everything without being judged, and he felt understood by you. To talk about my problems, I need someone like this!"

In short, 'P' had been transferred from another big prison. '*the someone*' he met before was a prisoner awaiting trial at another prison where I had also worked, and there I used to talk to this '*someone*' weekly. This '*someone*' had a very bad record, with many violent assaults against women, so the prosecutor petitioned for a life sentence. At the time the topic of our conversations was mostly about the power of his rage and hate, and how it could turn him into a wild animal. Our discussions were in German, although his mother tongue was English – he was an immigrant. In fact, he refused to talk to me in English, as he did not like his mother tongue – a rare phenomenon, as one's mother tongue is perceived as the language of belonging (Grinberg and Grinberg 1989). Therefore, the work with him was based on providing verbal representations to his violent acts – yet again the reverie function. After two months of weekly sessions, he needed to be transferred to a bigger prison near to the court, where he would stand his trial. There he met 'P' and shared the same cell with him. To conclude, this '*someone*' received a long sentence.

As regards the problem of 'P', he was homosexual and came from a culture where homosexuality is banned and one can be murdered for this (homosexuality is already a big issue in the prison, and in his case, he was at risk to being bullied by prisoners from his own culture). In addition, he was an only child and was not able to honour the name of his family by producing heirs. This brought great shame on him and his culture. The topic of our conversation was generally about his feelings of being a permanent 'Outsider' both in the prison and outside (in his family and in society on account of his shame of being homosexual). The discussions with him were intercultural (see details in Chapter 2), while his emotional experience was provided with word representations.

A case in an intercultural setting

In summer 2019, I started a short-term course of therapy with a traumatized male refugee. He was from Syria and had arrived in Germany with his family (six children and his wife) three years ago. He told me about his emotional pain and asked me for help. He was afraid that one day he might direct his frustration towards his children by hitting and hurting them; thus, he wanted me to help him to control his aggression. I offered him weekly individual sessions and a family session once a month. In the individual sessions the focus was on the source of his aggression and his anger, and in the family sessions, we discussed his frustration with his family. Once, during an individual session, he said:

P: "You know I really like to come here . . . do you know why?"
    I was surprised by his unexpected statement and answered:
T: "Really? Do you like to come here? No, I don't know why. Why?"
    When I asked this first question, "Really?", I showed that I was not expecting that someone would like to talk to me. To not expect this also means that I accept the idea that someone might not like to come and talk to me. This may be understood by the patient as being in a situation where he can talk freely. And he answered:

P: "You are not here to fix me or to make me a better person. You're here to understand me . . . to figure out who I am . . . you are very funny indeed . . . you don't behave like a doctor . . . the way you talk . . . You don't talk like a robot . . . you smile . . . you are not like someone who just asks questions and tries to say what I should do!"

Just like '*the someone*' P had previously mentioned, P also felt understood and relished the communication process established between us.

It may appear that TICA is understood and welcomed by the patients in different settings as a kind of communicative situation, free of a desire to heal and focused on new experiences, which might make more sense for them. Having the chance to talk about aggression, hate, love and fear without being morally judged by the 'Other', might, to a certain extent, have a 'therapeutic' side-effect for the patients or at least bring them 'Hope' (Havel and Hvížďala 1991). As stated by the staff from the forensic setting (see details in Chapter 10), the patients became calmer and more thoughtful about themselves after experiencing TICA – possibly two rare features in their lives.

The following chapters will describe all the steps of this novel approach. Hence, the book is divided into five parts, based on the chronological development of the "Transient Interactive Communication Approach" – TICA. Part one, "On building communication", describes the author's struggle to find sense where there was no sense, that is her search for 'Hope' (Havel and Hvížďala 1991). Part two, "TICA in forensic settings", describes the use of TICA with offenders placed in different settings: in withdrawal therapy and in pretrial detention. It is worth emphasizing in this part the need to adapt TICA from a therapeutic setting to an ephemeral one. Part three, "TICA in intercultural settings", shows how TICA can be suitable for intercultural settings as well how to deal with cultural noise along with cultural misunderstanding in this setting. Part four, "TICA adaptations (variations)", an extension of TICA, is introduced, namely T-WAS – Together We Are Strong. T-WAS has been developed for preventive group work against antisocial behaviour with deprived latency children. In addition, challenges in the work during the COVID-19 pandemic are also briefly addressed. As a final point, Part five, "Reflections on TICA", presents not only the outcome of TICA from the perspectives of staff and patients, but also its limitations.

References

Bion, W.R., 1984. *Learning from Experience*. London: Maresfield Reprints.
Castrechini-Franieck, M.L., Günter, M., and Page, T., 2014. Engaging Brazilian Street Children in Play: Observations of Their Family Narratives. *Child Development Research*, 861703.
Castrechini-Franieck, M.L., and Page, T., 2017. The Family Narratives of Three Siblings Living in a 'Street Situation' Since Birth. *Early Child Development and Care*, 189 (10), 1575–1587.

Grinberg, L., and Grinberg, R., 1989. *Psychoanalytic Perspectives on Migration and Exile*. New Haven and London: Yale University Press.

Havel, V., and Hvížďala, K., 1991. *Disturbing the Peace: A Conversation with Karel Hvížďala*. 1st ed. New York: Vintage Books.

Welldon, E.V., 2011. *Playing with Dynamite: A Personal Approach to the Psychoanalytic Understanding of Perversions, Violence, and Criminality*. London: Karnac.

Part one

On building communication

Chapter 1

Handling, mastering, and integrating a personal and factual reality

Old and new paths

My interest in the forensic field started many years ago when I was still a student on the psychology course at the University of São Paulo in Brazil. This criminal psychology course took a year to complete and included practical training in a juvenile prison. I remember well my feelings of fear on our first training day in the juvenile prison. Before entering, our teacher offered some advice, saying: "A rebellion is the worst that can happen. In this case you will be held hostage and you will have to act calmly until the situation can be resolved. Do you understand?" – a real-life forensic situation in Brazil.

During the training, I experienced several situations in which the prisoners made use of us and our inexperience as a means of achieving their aims. To illustrate, once, during a group session, a prisoner started to masturbate beside a colleague of mine, for the purpose of shocking and numbing us. Furthermore, our work was misinformed. The positive side of this was that being faced with such a chaotic, dangerous and real situation triggered my emotional ability to deal with extremely vulnerable and aggressive communities for the very first time.

After my graduation, I worked for many years as a psychodynamic clinical psychologist in a private practice in Brazil. When I moved to Germany, I was afraid of clinical work, owing to diverse cross-cultural issues; thus, I embarked on a new career path as a researcher. Years later, whilst I was carrying out a study on children living in 'street situations' (Castrechini-Franieck and Page 2017; Castrechini-Franieck *et al*. 2014) and whilst I was writing my book about the influence of parenting on cultural transmission (Franieck and Günter 2010), I became interested in the influences of parenting on antisocial behaviour and its significance on the development of criminality (Pinquart 2017). It is true that antisocial behaviour may be a normal part of growing up. Even so, it is also the beginning of a long-term pattern of criminal activity (Moffitt 2018; Moffitt and CASPI 2001; Rutter *et al*. 1998). The latter generally refers to the future of most children living in 'street situations'. I myself have had contact with neglected children, who, during my study's assessments, were very responsive in the relationship they developed with me, as well as being absorbed in play. Conversely, in residential care, they started

DOI: 10.4324/9781003232087-2

to demonstrate antisocial tendencies. For this reason, I was eager to find out more about the progression of antisocial behaviour into criminality, mainly the potential connections with: a) cultural issues; b) family representations; and c) communication. As a result, my inquisitive mind drove me back to clinical work, and I began a full-time maternity cover role in a German psychiatric prison hospital.

Facing a different clinical theoretical framework

As someone who comes from overseas and who has extensive psychodynamic clinical experience in a private practice milieu, coupled with research skills in child development, I found myself placed in a German prison hospital that provided addiction treatment, involving a 13-month cognitive behavioural–based withdrawal therapy – that is, I was located in a forensic milieu, in an alien culture. Without doubt, having to work clinically in a cognitive behavioural framework was a daunting challenge for me, since my experience with this framework dated back to the time of my graduation. Moreover, it was hard for me to understand the implementation of 'homework' as a therapeutic tool for a population experiencing severe failures in its school system. So, I was faced with controversial methodological issues, as well as with many doubts about being able to do a good job.

Encountering an alien milieu, in an alien culture

I can still clearly remember my first day at work in the prison, which in fact was a cross-cultural shock for me. The German prison seemed to me like a hotel since in my country, prison installations are quite poor. For example, prisoners have to share a prison cell with many other prisoners (circa 30 people) with just one toilet bowl. There is no privacy. There is no chance of receiving addiction treatment. There are no luxuries, such as a TV in their cells. I was really impressed.

As regards my role in the prison, the first thing I got was a heavy key chain and a mobile alarm. Then I was introduced to the staff – and shortly after, the prisoners. At that time, it seemed to me to be a large group of prisoners, although it was just 12 of them. I could not work out what was going on – they started talking whilst I began having wild fantasies about being locked in a cell with dangerous people. Indeed, I started to feel myself like an alien in this context and just wanted to get out of there (not to mention that I still had to drive more than an hour to get home, as the prison was 75 km away). These were my funny feelings on my first clinical workday in an alien culture, in an 'alien milieu'. There might possibly be a connection between my wild fantasies this day with my first training day in the juvenile prison. So, the second day was a little bit less scared, the third one better than the second, and in the end, I was able to manage things and worked there for 16 months.

Over the first month in this 'alien milieu', I had only one task, which was to observe the work of my colleague, a fellow psychologist – I was there just to learn. I was not supposed to express myself during the therapeutic process, and if a patient asked me any questions, I was supposed to just answer briefly, although in most cases my colleague intervened just after I had given my answers – this was also a huge cultural shock for me. As previously mentioned, in my country, I started working with the prisoners from my first day of training. In any case, from the beginning of my time in this 'alien milieu', I was clearly placed in the role of a passive 'Outsider' – that was a fact.

Dealing with language issues

Working with people who speak a German dialect (Schwäbisch – Swabian) instead of High German was a major challenge for me. At the beginning, I was not able to follow any of the conversations. Again, I was placed as a passive 'Outsider'. I was, at this time, more like an infant that just listens to sounds but is unable to communicate through words. On top of that, I had a terrible accent both in German and in English, so everyone was easily able to recognize that I was a 'foreigner' – that is a fact.

I can clearly recall the day when during a group therapy session (still as a spectator) one of the prisoners (Mr. T.) asked me directly:

"Mrs. Franieck, could you understand what 'Mr. X' was saying?"

The whole group smiled at me while waiting for my answer.
Then I asked him back:

"Why are you asking me that?"

At this point, I was interested in understanding the thoughts (possible fantasies) that had led him to pose such an embarrassing question.
He answered:

"Because he speaks a very difficult German dialect from Frankfurt, and it is already difficult for me as a German guy to follow him. I was wondering whether you as a foreigner could understand him . . . but you have not answered my question yet".

His answer to my question triggered a long silence in the room. Then as a way of moving the attention away from me, the other psychologist tried to introduce a new theme to the group, which I understood as her worry about discussing the issue that 'Mrs. Franieck is a foreigner and might not understand German'.

As an 'Outsider', I was impressed with his question. It is true that his question could have been understood as an expression of his aggression in the group through projective mechanism in order to interrupt the dynamic. It could also represent a transference of the group's feelings onto me, since all forensic patients are also placed at the border of society as outsiders – I should have been the person who felt insecure and not them – massive projective identification (Bion 1984). Still, it was a reasonable question – that is a fact. Thus, in my view, he did deserve to get a fair answer despite all possible defence mechanisms in play. One should not forget that in the forensic milieu, most of the patients had internalized a self that does not match with society's values, as the communication between their inner reality and their external one is disturbed (Welldon 1997, p. 16). He deserved a truthful reply instead of attempts to dissipate the group's attention (which incidentally would have been an example of his projective identification acting out). Hence, for the first time since I had started working in this 'alien milieu', I had the courage to be an active 'Outsider' and interrupted the psychologist to answer him:

> Mr. T. you are right! It is quite difficult to follow 'Mr. X', I cannot do this. However, I do not need to understand all of his words, nor all the words spoken by all of you in the group to figure out what is going on here and now.

Then I started describing my observation and perception of their non-verbal and primitive communication in the group dynamic, like the non-verbal signals of their resistance in the group, their frustration, their rage, and mainly as regards their doubt as to whether I would be competent enough to manage this group, since I was a foreigner (here I tried to give a verbal representation of the feelings evoked by his questions). As I finished answering, I noticed that my response had triggered a long silence in the room, which was broken by a friendly smile on his part, in a welcoming way. At this moment, I had won the respect of the prisoners. Later, I realized that what had compelled me to answer him by interrupting the psychologist was my desire to reach out to the patients and above all to be fair to them as well as to myself – to turn into an active 'Outsider', which implied initiating conversation.

Questions raised in my mind whilst a technique emerged from daunting challenges

During this period as a spectator, and hence as a passive 'Outsider', my mind was constantly preoccupied with concomitant and confusing thoughts and fantasies that had to be jointly handled, mastered and promptly integrated into the therapy in a forensic setting. Some of them were connected to my emotional inner world (personal reality), others to my earlier experience in the juvenile prison in Brazil, others to my language skills and finally to my apprehension concerning the current external environment (factual reality, which involves cross-cultural issues). My strongest fear was about being misinformed whilst the prisoners might take advantage of my language skills as well as any cross-cultural differences – at the time, the perception of my personal inner reality and my factual reality was blurred. Indeed, they moved interchangeably in my mind, bringing about a lot of questions, mainly about apparently meaningless work and whether such daunting challenges could ever lead to growth. I needed to find my identity as a therapist.

In searching for answers to my questions, I recognized my permanent role as an 'Outsider' and therefore that the difficult challenge to be dealt with was connected to communication. How could I build a common form of communication despite not sharing the same mother tongue and cultural background, whilst also facing something which for me was an unusual therapeutic approach? How could I work within this alien framework, integrating psychoanalytical thinking where appropriate? How could I achieve an understandable interplay between both sides, which was based on giving meaning to the treatment for the patients, as well as for the therapist? Needless to say, nothing would be achieved in our therapeutic work unless all communication was meaningful – grounded in shared meaning. Shared meaning means that people understand each other's perspectives well enough to accept them despite their differences or disagreements. Thus, before starting work on the patients' individual psychological problems, it was imperative to develop communication skills whilst bearing in mind that both parties were 'Outsiders', thus strangers to one another (similar to a mother with her new-born infant – two strangers in contact without a common language). Equally important, communication should also have to be turned into a therapeutic tool in an effort to improve a patient's individual psychological skills through this new interactive experience.

Without being aware of it, the daunting challenges turned into the main pillars of the Transient Interactive Communication Approach – TICA.

References

Bion, W.R., 1984. *Learning from Experience*. London: Maresfield Reprints.

Castrechini-Franieck, M.L., Günter, M., and Page, T., 2014. Engaging Brazilian Street Children in Play: Observations of Their Family Narratives. *Child Development Research*, 861703.

Castrechini-Franieck, M.L., and Page, T., 2017. The Family Narratives of Three Siblings Living in a 'Street Situation' Since Birth. *Early Child Development and Care*, 189 (10), 1575–1587.

Franieck, L., and Günter, M., 2010. *On Latency: Individual Development, Narcissistic Impulse Reminiscence, and Cultural Ideal*. London: Karnac Books.

Moffitt, T.E., 2018. Male Antisocial Behaviour in Adolescence and Beyond. *Nature Human Behaviour*, 2, 177–186 [online]. Available from: https://pubmed.ncbi.nlm.nih.gov/30271880.

Moffitt, T.E., and Caspi, A., 2001. Childhood Predictors Differentiate Life-Course Persistent and Adolescence-Limited Antisocial Pathways Among Males and Females. *Development and Psychopathology*, 13 (2), 355–375.

Pinquart, M., 2017. Associations of Parenting Dimensions and Styles with Externalizing Problems of Children and Adolescents: An Updated Meta-Analysis. *Developmental Psychology*, 53 (5), 873–932.

Rutter, M., Giller, H., and Hagell, A., 1998. *Antisocial Behaviour by Young People*. Cambridge: Cambridge University Press.

Welldon, E.V., 1997. Forensic Psychotherapy: The Practical Approach. In: E.V. Welldon and C. van Velsen, eds. *A Practical Guide to Forensic Psychotherapy*. London: Jessica Kingsley, 13–19.

Chapter 2

On intercultural interactional communication

I could compile an extensive list of authors that have provided major stimulus on my work related to communication issues in the interplay between an outsider therapist and 'highly vulnerable/unbearable' patients. However, I would like to highlight in particular that the greatest contribution has come from my personal training analysis combined with the supervised analysis of patients. Of course, one can improve one's knowledge by learning through books. Rather engaging in interaction with 'highly vulnerable/unbearable' patients and building 'shared meaning communication' with them requires resources that go beyond the books. It requires one's ability to allow oneself to undergo a primitive emotional state in the interaction with these patients, without the fear of losing oneself and without being dominated by patients' wishes, phantasies or trauma whilst still keeping one's own sanity in addition to one's professionalism.

For years I, attended seminars on psychoanalysis whilst undergoing personal training analysis and supervised analysis of patients with training analysts from the Brazilian Society of Psychoanalysis São Paulo, though I am not a trained psychoanalyst, nor am I the master of any psychoanalytical school of thought. Consequently, it is true that I might be at risk of diluting the comprehension of some psychoanalytical concepts, and therefore forcing artificial integrations among different psychoanalytical theoretical systems (Da Barros 1989). Nevertheless, the seed of every psychoanalytic theory/concept, as well as assertions of patients and analysts, are together representations of one's emotional experience (Bion 1965). That is, my understanding of some psychoanalytical concepts is based on the representations of my emotional experiences from personal training analysis and supervised analysis of patients, as well as from my clinical and research work with more than 3,000 prisoners, 300 traumatized refugees and 250 deprived children. By sharing the representations of my emotional experiences with the reader, I wish to be able to build on a feasibly 'shared meaning communication'.

Once more, I must highlight the fact that my work has merely aimed to establish communication with 'highly vulnerable/unbearable' patients mostly placed outside of society's border. Simply put, I borrow the psychoanalytical concept from some psychoanalytical authors with the aim of getting in touch with people that cannot afford typical consultations in common mental health settings. Indeed, healing is not my primary concern. Naturally, what I do cannot be considered as psychoanalysis or even as psychoanalytical based psychotherapy – without doubt, it is just a Transient Interactive Communication Approach (TICA).

Interactive communication has been a dominant and also a common subject matter in the work of several psychoanalytical and contemporary psychoanalytical authors. Despite their diverse psychoanalytic schools of thought and fields of work, each of them has emphasized particular features of it that, in my opinion, should be taken into serious consideration. At this point, I will briefly outline their contributions without clarifying their meanings. In the following chapters, the implementation of these concepts will vividly illustrate their meanings.

- 'the analytic triad'; 'counter-transference', and 'symbol formation', of Segal (Caper 1997; Segal 1993, 1957);
- 'concomitant analysis past and present' of Riesenberg-Malcolm (1999);
- 'primitive communication' of McDougall (1993);
- 'projective counter-identification' and 'psychoanalysis and migration' of Grinberg (1993, 1990) and Grinberg and Grinberg (1989);
- 'maternal reverie', 'container-contained model', and 'α and β elements' of Bion (1984b, 1984a);
- 'transitional object and transitional phenomena', 'mutuality', 'holding', 'deprived child', and 'cultural experience' of Winnicott (1953, 2005, 2018);
- 'analytic triad' of Ogden (2004/1994);
- 'analyst's daydreaming' of Cassorla (2018) and Katz et al. (2017);
- 'affect attunement' and 'parents' representation' of Stern (1995, 2000);
- 'the five basic feelings' of Casriel (1972);
- 'matrix', 'communication and culture', 'resonance', and 'group conductor' of Foulkes (2018) and Foulkes and Foulkes (1990).

Despite a lack of literature on the development of an interactive communication between a psychological therapist and a forensic patient (or prisoners) in the forensic area, several studies have been carried out with the aim of either assessing the impact of the interactional characteristics on the forensic inpatient (Gildberg et al. 2010) or improving staff's interactive communication with forensic inpatients (Hörberg 2018; Marshall and Adams 2018; Živanović and Ćirić 2017).

In the broad field of psychology, several authors have been raising some significant theories on interactive communication issues, namely: the 'four ears model' and 'inside team' by Schulz von Thun (1981), 'five basic axioms of the communication theory' by Watzlawick et al. (2011), 'four forms of incongruent communication' by Satir (Moore and Kramer 1999), and 'the nonviolent communication' by Rosenberg (2015). However, they might not fully address the issues on cross-cultural communication, as in this field not only cross-cultural linguistic skills are required, but also intercultural interactional competences in a wider context.

Before going any further, it might be worth clarifying briefly the meaning of the terms 'multicultural', 'intercultural', and 'cross-cultural communication'.

> Multicultural refers to a society that contains several cultural or ethnic groups. People live alongside one another, but each cultural group does not necessarily have engaging interactions with each other.
>
> (Schriefer 2016)

When interactions between people in different cultures occur in a solely multicultural context, they are rarely rich learning experiences for anyone involved. Particularly in my work, I have been repeatedly confronted with this context, such as in prisons (especially when working with those awaiting trial) and refugee camps. In the private sphere, since I am a Brazilian national living in Germany, multiculturalism is part of my everyday life.

Like the term 'multicultural', the term 'intercultural' acknowledges the coexistence of multiple cultures in a single space.

> Intercultural describes communities in which there is a deep understanding and respect for all cultures. . . . Intercultural communication focuses on the mutual exchange of ideas and cultural norms and the development of deep relationships. In an intercultural society, no one is left unchanged because everyone learns from one another and grows together.
>
> (Schriefer 2016)

'Cross-cultural' is often confused with 'intercultural', yet they are not synonymous.

> Cross-cultural deals with the comparison of different cultures. In cross-cultural communication, differences are understood and acknowledged, and can bring about individual change, but not collective transformations. In cross-cultural societies, one culture is often considered 'the norm' and all other cultures are compared or contrasted to the dominant culture.
>
> (Schriefer 2016)

The challenge of being an immigrant in a foreign country is a good example of this context.

To return to the previous point, I have been placed and I have been operating in a culture that is not my own – my daily work routine involves cross-cultural communication training, and this continuous practice helps me to embody and adopt multiple cultural dimensions whilst improving my intercultural communication skills, thus making me more mindful when communicating with any other 'Outsider' or stranger. Establishing a cross-cultural community can be considered 'a skill' that one learns and develops as one gets to know and interacts with people from different cultures. Particularly, the cross-cultural studies carried out in business/organizational working settings, concerning miscommunication triggered by cultural peculiarities, are quite intriguing (House 2004; Hofstede 2001; Trompenaars and Hampden-Turner 1997; Hall 1973). Apparently, their outcomes can be extended to the clinical field, as they provide a revealing insight to the dynamics of the patient's matrix as referred to by Foulkes and Foulkes (1990, p. 213) – and also that of the therapist's, as in my case. That is, they afford a broader understanding of the sociological and cultural milieu, embedded in which the patient and therapist grew up – a crucial matter for mastering intercultural interactional communication skills.

As referred to in the previous chapter, as a direct result of the daunting challenges I faced as a migrant clinical psychologist in a foreign country, TICA becomes, culturally, an accurate approach for use in intercultural communication, as its prime aim and objective is to build a 'shared meaning communication'. Two distinct perspectives on interactive communication promoted the development of TICA, namely: the business/organizational perspective and the psychoanalytical one. The first one served as a guideline and helped me learn to respect the diversities rooted in cultural values, especially with regard to the obstacles encountered in communicating with German nationals. Through this learning process, it was possible to accept more easily my permanent role as an 'Outsider' in German society. The latter, in turn, served as a basis for reflection in risky situations when intercultural interactional communication was imperative, and my mind could be preoccupied by questions, doubts, and fears. At these times, they were very useful for organizing my ideas, but nonetheless, I was aware of their limitations.

In what follows, I briefly summarize my literary research of these perspectives and also illustrate what, in my view, could be their intersections.

On culture: from a business/organizational perspective to a genetic one

Maude (2016) asserted that culture is like a kaleidoscope (with multiple definitions), thus to date there is no universally accepted definition of it. According to him, culture can be briefly described as a system of values, beliefs, practices, and communication norms, with different surface levels and deep levels among them. While surface level is related to the basic function of a culture, which is universal, the deep level is connect to aspects that are not directly visible, rather to a culture's prevailing values and beliefs. In addition, culture is simultaneously a pervasive influence on the actions of individual members of the culture, as well as a product created by these individuals' actions.

It is true that during recent decades, several authors of different subjects have been running studies on national cultural values and intercultural communication, with the purpose of finding out ways of handling cultural diversities. However, it is difficult to cross-reference or compare them, as they frequently adopt different dimensions, although to a certain extent, with similar meanings. In what follows, two well-known studies (one on intercultural communication and the other on national cultural values) will be summarized for illustration.

The anthropologist Edward T. Hall, who has run studies on intercultural communication, stresses that "culture is communication and communication is culture" (Hall 1973, p. 186). Intercultural communication can be understood as belonging either to a high-context culture or to a low-context culture. In a higher-context culture, words carry implicit meanings with more information than what is actually spoken. The focus of communication is more on the way words are said than on the words themself. Thus, part of the communication is unexpressed and depends on the context of the moment and the culture as a whole. Conversely, in a lower-context culture, the communicator must be very explicit with their words in order to be fully understood. Furthermore, cultures can differ in terms of time orientation, more simply monochromic versus polychromic time orientation. While the former is based on the concept of 'one thing at a time', the latter focuses on multiple tasks being handled at any one time, and time is subordinate to interpersonal relations (Maude 2016; Blom and Meier 2004).

Hofstede, a Dutch social psychologist who has run studies on national cultural values, has in turn developed the internationally well-known 'cultural dimensions theory', which describes national cultures according to five main dimensions (Hofstede 2001), namely:

1   Power Distance (PDI), which focuses on how a society deals with inequalities among its people – in other words, with hierarchy.
2   Uncertainty Avoidance (UAI), which focuses on the level of tolerance with uncertainty and ambiguity within the society – in other words, how a society deals with an unknown future.
3   Masculinity vs. Femininity (MAS), which focuses on the degree to which 'masculine' values – like aggressiveness, competitiveness, acquisition of means, and success – are valued more highly than 'feminine' values like cooperation, nurture, care-giving, relationship building, modesty, and quality of life.
4   Individualism vs. Collectivism (IDV), which refers to cultural ways of understanding and structuring independence and interdependence. Independence refers to aspects of human functioning that include being physically and mentally separate individuals, whereas interdependence refers to aspects of human functioning that involve being connected to others. People in individualist cultures select, with high probability, elements of the personal self that are characterized by autonomy and independence – their consciousness is based on 'I' and tasks prevail over relationships. People from collectivist cultures tend to mostly select elements of the collective self, which is characterized by interdependence between the members of the group, as well as group acceptance – their consciousness is based on 'we', and relationship prevails over task.

5   Long-term vs. Short-term Orientation, which focuses on the degree to which people attach importance to a future-oriented way of thinking, rather than to a short-term-oriented one.

Despite all criticism on a number of grounds, Hofstede's dimensions have been internationally useful for understanding how members of various societies are likely to behave in different ways in a given situation. Indeed, to date, further studies on national cultural values have not refuted Hofstede's dimensions; on the contrary, they have provided supplementary information (Maude 2016; Thomas 2016; Gellert and Nowak 2014; Blom and Meier 2004; Schlippe *et al.* 2003).

To illustrate, Trompenaars and Hamden (1997) described national cultures according to seven main dimensions, expressed as couples of contrasting attitudinal dispositions that can be identified in each culture. The dimensions are divided into three criteria:

1   Relationship to other people (dimensions 1 to 5): (1) universalism-particularism (rules vs. relationships); (2) individualism-communitarianism (individual vs. group); (3) neutral-emotional (the degree and range of expression of feelings); (4) specific-diffuse (involvement degree); (5) achievement-ascription (the way that status is noticed and accorded).
2   Relationship to time (dimension 6): (6) sequential – synchronous – how people apprehend and manage the passage of time.
3   Relationship to environment (dimension 7): (7) internal – external control – the interplay between people and their natural environment.

(Trompenaars and Hampden-Turner 1997, pp. 8–10)

In 2004, the GLOBE survey, House et al. expanded Hofstede's framework by identifying nine dimensions, namely: [1] power distance; [2]uncertainty avoidance; [3]humane orientation (the degree people encourage and reward others for being altruistic, fair and generous); [4] in-group collectivism (the degree of peoples' loyalty towards organizations, groups, families); [5] institutional collectivism (the degree social institutions promote collective distribution of resources and collective action); [6] assertiveness (the degree people are assertive, confrontational, and aggressive in their relationships with others); [7] gender egalitarianism (the degree to which a society minimises gender inequality); [8] future (the degree to which people engage in future-oriented behaviours such as planning and investing) and [9] performance orientations (the degree to which people encourage and reward the performance of others) (House 2004, p. 30).

Despite all supplementary dimensions identified by recent studies on national cultural values in the business field, the dimension of 'individualist and collectivist' is widely perceived as an essential one (House 2004; Trompenaars and Hampden-Turner 1997; Hofstede and Bond 1984). Intriguingly, several genetic studies have suggested the existence of a robust relationship between the cultural construct 'individualism-collectivism' and the prevalence of alleles at several polymorphisms with apparent psychological effects. For instance, collectivism may have developed and prevailed in populations with a high proportion of putative social sensitivity alleles (Sapolsky 2017; Chiao et al. 2013; Chiao and Blizinsky 2010; Way and Lieberman 2010). Phrased more simply, genetic predispositions may interact with environmental and social factors to influence psycho-cultural differences.

On culture: relating the psychoanalytical perspective to the previous perspectives

From a psychoanalytical point of view the dimension 'individualism and collectivism' can be perceived in what Andre As-salome (1962, p. 4) referred to as the "dual orientation of narcissism": one is the sense of achieving individuality and the other, on the contrary, aims towards fusion, which remains embedded in our psyche throughout our development – an unconscious primitive ego function termed 'narcissism impulse reminiscence' (Castrechini-Franieck 2016; Castrechini-Franieck and Günter 2014; Franieck and Günter 2010).

Franieck and Günter (2010) highlight the importance of cultural ideal (cultural identity) as a feature of personality. In other words, 'cultural ideal' is understood as a model that must be offered and must represent the 'ego ideal' of each member of the group in tandem, in order to be taken in and to become part of a single self. As a result, each individual is able to identify him or herself as a member of a group while subsuming individual needs and interests in favour of those of the group (Freud 2001c, 2001b, 2001a).

> To put in another way, all cultural ideals are rooted in the 'narcissistic impulse reminiscence'. What each culture esteems as being the best way to keep the group under control is based on the choice for just one side of the 'dual orientation of narcissism' – either in the achievement of individuality or in a movement towards fusion.
>
> (Franieck and Günter 2010, p. 79)

Whereas the former will place more emphasis on the independent self (being independent is how I will sense the feeling of 'belonging to'; thus, I need to be in charge of myself), the latter will display a more interdependent self (to look for as well as to gain support from others is how I will sense the feeling of 'belonging to'; thus, I not only need to depend on a group but I also need to rely on them for guardianship). From this perspective, the emotional basis for the understanding of being 'excluded from' and 'being included in' a group may vary greatly. To illustrate, cultural ideals based on 'the sense of achieving individuality' will understand the group as a union of people who have their own identity and responsibility, and who came together to achieve a goal. In contrast, cultural ideals based on 'towards fusion' understand the group as a unit, since individuals have turned into a group, as a single body that aims to achieve a goal (Castrechini-Franieck 2017a, 2016; Castrechini-Franieck and Günter 2014; Franieck and Günter 2010). For this reason, the features of the projective mechanisms displayed by the latter are more likely to be refined and intrusive over the external objects than the former (in a multicultural team or in a group constellation, the interplay of this psychological mechanism can be clearly observed). Beyond the identification mechanism process permeates the refined projective mechanism (Castrechini-Franieck 2017c).

The idea of cultural issues relating to personality building is nothing new. Winnicott (1967) had already defined 'cultural experience' as an extension of the intermediate area of human experience between inner reality and the outside world – that is, an extension of the idea of transitional phenomena. Cultural experience is located in the potential space between the individual and society (or the world) and is first manifested in play. Although the potential space between baby and mother, between child and family, and between individual and society (or the world), depends on experience which leads to trust.

As will be illustrated in the following chapters, Winnicott's concept of 'cultural experience' is perceived as one of the main pillars of TICA, which is to provide patients with a neutral and intermediary room for new experiences, in which trust might be built, and thus communication might be established.

On communication

Communication is a vital link with the 'Other' and consists of the desire to inform someone of something – a way of conveying and discharging emotions in a direct manner, with the purpose of affecting and arousing reactions in the 'Other', and hence communication has crucial symbolic functions (McDougall 1993, pp. 116–117). Communication, however, is comprised of pre-language and language levels.

Language communication level

This is related to verbal/non-verbal information generated by mother tongue development and acquisitions. Therefore, it presumes the already present possession of an advanced individual ability for symbolization and representation.

> The capacity to communicate with oneself by using symbols is, I think, the basis of verbal thinking – which is the capacity to communicate with oneself by means of words. Not all internal communication is verbal thinking, but all verbal thinking is an internal communication by means of symbols – words.
> (Segal 1957, p. 396)

Winnicott *et al.* (2012) emphasized that symbols are needed not only in communication with the external world, but also in internal communication.

Castrechini-Franieck (2017b) asserted that symbolization naturally arises when separation from the object, ambivalence, guilt, and loss can be experienced and tolerated. Hence, symbolization is used to overcome loss.

In essence, verbal language should be the major factor in communication. Nevertheless, verbal languages differ in their content, which may cause controversy. To illustrate, the content of the Arabic language is more focused on metaphors (more ambiguous in meaning) than on descriptive content, as found in the German language, or even on relational content, as found in the Japanese language. For this reason, one needs during intercultural communication to avoid language domination (or imperialism), as it may trigger unequal communication in addition to the sense of having one culture imposing not only its language but also its values and civilization on the other culture, while devastating the language content of this culture.

Non-verbal communication in a cross-cultural context is particularly important. Non-verbal communication is defined as an attempt to express several intentions (i.e., emotions, interpersonal attitudes, self-presentation, and social interactions) in a way that cannot be expressed in words, due to a lack of language fluency and/or because, culturally, speakers have learnt not to express those intentions in words. To illustrate, while smiling expresses embarrassment to the Africans, to the Japanese, it is more likely to express anger or an attempt to mask distress, and, conversely, to the Chinese, it expresses an apology. Without doubt, non-verbal communication is not only more versatile but also expresses more truthfully the veracity of feelings and attitudes than the words in a verbal exchange. Hence, mutual miscommunication is a common risk in cross-cultural communication (Maude 2016; Thomas 2016; Blom and Meier 2004).

> Miscommunication occurs when there is a mismatch between what the speaker intends his words to mean and how the hearer interprets them.... As a result of people from different cultures sending and interpreting messages in culturally-influenced ways.
>
> (Maude 2016, p. 19).

In cross-cultural encounters, it is presumed that sender and receiver do not belong to or come from similar cultural and linguistic backgrounds, and therefore communication might be continuously affected by cultural noise. Cultural noise refers to impediments to successful communication between people of different cultures at the language level. Sources of cultural noise include differences in language (e.g., the same words having different meanings), values (e.g., the importance of being on time or setting work deadlines in a culture), non-verbal cues (e.g., the interpretation of body language), and many others. When a person is involved in cross-cultural communication, they should be aware of the various sources of cultural noise that may obstruct the communication process by triggering miscommunication and therefore posing an obstacle for the achievement of intercultural communication.

Pre-language communication level

Pre-language communication, also called primitive communication (Alexandris and Vaslamatzis 1993; McDougall 1993), refers to the communication that takes place during infancy. Thus, it is connected to a very individual physical sensation and a misrepresented/disorganized drive (Rappoport de Aisemberg 2017). That is, the infant is already in contact with the 'Other' (the mother or caregiver); however, their skills in symbolization and representation are yet to be developed in their interaction with the 'Other'. Therefore, at this point, communication is at the mercy of one's very individual, archaic, misrepresented/disorganized impulses.

Some psychoanalytical authors understand primitive communication as a daunting obstacle in the analytical setting, which should be overcome in countertransference (Rappoport de Aisemberg 2017; McDougall 1993; Segal 1993) or in projective counter-identification as referred to by Grinberg (1993).

Contemporary psychoanalytical authors perceive primitive communication as a natural part of the psyche's development. Hence, they also emphasize the importance of tolerating it as a crucial form of communication in the psychoanalytical setting, since it provides clues in the interpersonal field formed by the analyst and patient.

To illustrate, in 1962, Bion (1984b) described ‚maternal reverie'as the mother's capacity to contain her child's primitive communication whilst transforming sense information or misrepresented/disorganized experiences (beta elements) into creative thinking (alpha elements), which will provide the mind with a thinking apparatus. In other words, 'maternal reverie' can be perceived as the capacity to sense (and make sense of) what is going on inside the infant.

Katz *et al.* (2017) emphasized that like mothers perform with their babies, analysts bring in their skills in maternal reverie in the interaction with their patients.

> The analyst must let himself go adrift as he waits for reverie to make sense naturally. Untrained analysts often ignore their own reverie or imagine that it is a product of their own conflicts, without bothering to investigate them.
> (Katz *et al.* 2017, p. 95)

Cassorla (2018) termed this process as 'analyst's daydreaming' and explained it as follows:

> The analyst's daydreaming, or reverie, refers to the spontaneous emergence of images in his mind. This spontaneity refers to the necessity to curb memory and desire. For this to occur, an active exercise can be necessary on the part of the analyst, to go against the mental tendency to seek images, ideas, or past affects that make up part of the memory, or desired ideas and affects. In other words, to withstand the not knowing, the chaos, until something naturally takes shape. With practice, this active exercise tends to become automatic.
> (Cassorla 2018, p. 8)

In 1968/1969, Winnicott (1992/1987, 2018) emphasized that an infant's ability to play and symbolize precedes the period when the infant starts to use words. At this point, all ability to communicate relies on pre-verbal interaction instead of on language acquisition, and it takes place via the mutuality process. 'Mutuality' is described as the mother's ability to identify with her baby, whereas the baby feels himself to be understood – a product of unconscious communication and feelings shaped between the infant and his mother. Thus, the experience of mutuality can be perceived as an interdependent two-way process. On the one hand, there is the mother and her identification with her infant, and on the other side, there is the infant with his inner potential to grow (an achievement for the baby).

In 1985, Stern (2000/1985) presented the term 'affect attunement' as the immediate recasting of the emotional-behavioural state of the infant by his mother, using underlying behaviours. The emphasis lays on reciprocating the emotion and feelings, such as praise, joy, excitement, disappointment, and so on, that were projected by the infant onto his mother. As a result, the infant learns these affective attunements, along with their meanings. This process is based on a cross-modal imitation, in which infants understand emotion through the mother's recasting and restating of subjective states – thus a bond can develop between them. According to Stern, maternal attunement is "a partial and 'purposely' selective kind of imitation" (Stern 2010, p. 113).

> I proposed affect attunement, a form of selective and cross-modal imitation, as the path to sharing inner feelings state, in contrast to faithful imitation as the path to sharing overt behaviour.
>
> (Stern 2004, p. 84)

In a cross-cultural milieu, cultural noise brings about deep feelings of frustration due to the failure to inform the 'Other' about something, which in turn, frequently triggers a psychological regression similar to the one experienced during the pre-verbal level (Grinberg and Grinberg 1989). It is true that most communication between therapist and patient in a clinical setting must be focused on verbal language. However, if the therapist is able to remain aware of the interplay between the verbal, non-verbal, and pre-verbal levels, his intervention may resonate over the pre-verbal level and therefore be more effective (McDougall 1993; Casement 1991)

To work as a therapist in a cross-cultural milieu is an extremely complex and challenging task (regardless of who the 'Outsider' is, whether therapist or patient, or even both), as it requires unique communication skills that are not only linked to specific techniques, or even theoretical knowledge (i.e. cultural dimensions theory), but rather also involve a way of construing an intercultural encounter where communication can be reliably triggered (Sue 2003). Hence, in this milieu, therapists should embrace the ability to listen intently whilst promoting a neutral space, which represents a 'holding environment' as a form of management. Here, pre-verbal communication may have room to develop and may also be explored by both parties (Winnicott 1992/1987, 2018)whilst apprehending an internal and external reality and giving meaning to the emotional experience aroused from this encounter – 'container-contained model' as outlined by Bion (1984a). In doing so, 'shared meaning communication' can be achieved – a pathway for progress towards intercultural interactional communication.

In practice, as will be illustrated in the following chapters, one feasible way of handling intercultural interactional communication is by adopting (as well as offering) an external object as a core interactive tool throughout the first encounters with the patient. This external object may help with the avoidance of potential cultural noise and further miscommunication, as a great part of the discussion will be done, filtered and clarified through it, instead of a direct, face-to-face interaction with the therapist, who, after all, is an 'Outsider' (a stranger) to the patient. Thus, the therapist encourages the patient's capacity for play. A potential space is established, in which the patient's capacity for play can be developed, according to the patient's own pace (Winnicott 2005). In tandem, transitional states of mind can be undergone between and within their interactions, which may firmly resonate during the pre-verbal level.

The idea of encouraging a potential space in interactive communication is not completely innovative. Allcorn and Stein (2015) have been using storytelling as a potential space in supervision of organizational workplaces, mostly in group settings. However, in-group mental operations differ from those of dyads or individual settings. According to Foulkes and Foulkes (1990), the in-group mental operations are characterized by spontaneous unconscious verbal or non-verbal interaction between group members, which are similar to strings that vibrate and reinforce each other member of the group simultaneously and reciprocally, including the group conductor per se – this process was termed by Foulkes as 'resonance'. Indeed, resonance reactions also need a potential space to arise, so providing such a space is a task for the group conductor, as referred to by Foulkes and Foulkes (1990, p. 294). Whenever I refer to the term 'group conductor' or 'conductor' in this manuscript, it will always be in this sense raised by Foulkes.

Ogden (2004/1994), inspired by Winnicott's work, introduced what he calls an 'analytic third'. He emphasized that like the idea of the mother – infant unit, dynamic tension is synchronized with the mother and infant as separate subjects; in the analytic situation, the analyst and the patient experience the same dynamic tension. Thus, the interpersonal field formed by the analyst and the patient is at the core of communication in the analytic process.

> The analytic process reflects the interplay of three subjectivities: the subjectivity of the analyst, of the analysand, and of the analytic third. The analytic third is a creation of the analyst and the analysand, and at the same time the analyst and the analysand (qua analyst and analysand) are created by the analytic third. (There is no analyst, no analysand, no analysis in the absence of the third).
>
> (Ogden 2004/1994, p. 93)

In Winnicott's words (1955), the aim of analysis would be to become familiar with the process which the patient is going through, to understand the presented material and to communicate this understanding in words. To conclude this chapter, I would like to borrow his fifth aspect of the necessary setting for the holding environment in the analytical setting and adapt it to the needs of TICA. From this perspective, TICA's aims could be briefly termed as follows: to become familiar with the primitive communication of the patient, to encourage a potential space and the patient's capacity to play in tandem, and to develop 'shared meaning communication'.

References

Alexandris, A., and Vaslamatzis, G., 1993. Countertransferential Bodily Feelings and the Containing Function of the Analyst. *In:* A. Alexandris and G. Vaslamatzis, eds. *Countertransference: Theory, Technique, Teaching*. London: Karnac.

Allcorn, S., and Stein, H.F., 2015. *The Dysfunctional Workplace: Theory, Stories, and Practice*. Columbia: University of Missouri Press.

Andre As-salome, L., 1962. The Dual Orientation of Narcissism. *The Psychoanalytic Quarterly*, 31 (1), 1–30.

Bion, W.R., 1965. *Transformations: Change from Learning to Growth*. London: William Heinemann Medical Books Limited.

Bion, W.R., 1984a. *Attention & Interpretation*. London: Maresfield Reprints.

Bion, W.R., 1984b. *Learning from Experience*. London: Maresfield Reprints.

Blom, H., and Meier, H., 2004. *Interkulturelles Management: Interkulturelle Kommunikation; Internationales Personalmanagement; Diversity-Ansätze im Unternehmen*. 2nd ed. Herne: Verl. Neue Wirtschafts-Briefe.

Caper, R., 1997. Symbol Formation and Creativity: Hannas Segal's Theoretical Contributions. *In:* D. Bell, ed. *Reason and Passion: A Celebration of the Work of Hanna Segal*. London: Routledge, 37–56.

Casement, P., 1991. *Learning from the Patient*. New York and London: Guilford Press.

Casriel, D., 1972. *A Scream Away from Happiness*. New York: Grosset & Dunlap.

Cassorla, R.M.S., 2018. *The Psychoanalyst, the Theatre of Dreams and the Clinic of Enactment*. Abingdon, Oxon and New York: Routledge.

Castrechini-Franieck, M.L., 2016. Remarks on Latency: Onset in Different Cultures. *The Journal of Psychohistory*, 43, 214–227.

Castrechini-Franieck, M.L., 2017a. Wohin gehöre ich eigentlich? *JuKiP – Ihr Fachmagazin für Gesundheits- und Kinderkrankenpflege*, 6 (1), 36–39.

Castrechini-Franieck, M.L., 2017b. *Giving Deeply Traumatized Refugees the Space They Need in Which to Reconstruct the Boundary They Have Lost Between Reality and Fantasy, While They Face Language and Cultural Barriers* [online]. Available from: https://wp.me/pelHL-Ep [Accessed 2 May 2020].

Castrechini-Franieck, M.L., 2017c. Managing Narcissistic Impulse-Reminiscence and Cultural Ideal Under the Circumstances of Mass Immigration. *Psychoanalytic Review*, 104 (6), 723–734.

Castrechini-Franieck, M.L., and Günter, M., 2014. Die Transmission kultureller Ideale in der Latenz: Theoretische Überlegungen und empirische Befunde aus einer Untersuchung in zwei verschiedenen Kulturen. *In:* M. Endres, C. Salamander, and D. Bürgin, eds. *Latenz: Entwicklung und Behandlung.* Frankfurt aM: Brandes & Apsel.

Chiao, J.Y., and Blizinsky, K.D., 2010. Culture-Gene Coevolution of Individualism-Collectivism and the Serotonin Transporter Gene. *Proceedings: Biological Sciences,* 277 (1681), 529–537.

Chiao, J.Y., et al., 2013. Cultural Neuroscience: Progress and Promise. *Psychological Inquiry,* 24 (1), 1–19 [online]. Available from: https://pubmed.ncbi.nlm.nih.gov/239 14126.

Da Barros, E.M.R., 1989. *Melanie Klein. Evoluções.* São Paulo: Escuta.

Foulkes, S.H., 2018. *Therapeutic Group Analysis.* London: Routledge.

Foulkes, S.H., and Foulkes, E., 1990. *Selected Papers of S.H. Foulkes: Psychoanalysis and Group Analysis, Edited and with a Brief Biography by Elizabeth Foulkes.* London: Karnac Books.

Franieck, L., and Günter, M., 2010. *On Latency: Individual Development, Narcissistic Impulse Reminiscence, and Cultural Ideal.* London: Karnac Books.

Freud, S., 2001a. The Future of an Illusion. *In: The Standard Edition of the Complete Psychological Works of Sigmund Freud: Early Psycho-Analytic Publications.* London: Vintage, 1–57.

Freud, S., 2001b. Civilization and Its Discontents. *In: The Standard Edition of the Complete Psychological Works of Sigmund Freud: Early Psycho-Analytic Publications.* London: Vintage, 57–147.

Freud, S., 2001c. Group Psychology and the Analysis of the Ego. *In: The Standard Edition of the Complete Psychological Works of Sigmund Freud: Early Psycho-Analytic Publications. Vol. 18, 1920–1922, Beyond the Pleasure Principle, Group Psychology and Other Works.* London: Vintage, 65–145.

Gellert, M., and Nowak, C., 2014. *Teamarbeit, Teamentwicklung, Teamberatung: Ein Praxisbuch für die Arbeit in und mit Teams.* 5th ed. Meezen: Limmer.

Gildberg, F., Elverdam, B., and Hounsgaard, L., 2010. Forensic Psychiatric Nursing: A Literature Review and Thematic Analysis of Staff – Patient Interaction. *Journal of Psychiatric and Mental Health Nursing,* 17, 359–368.

Grinberg, L., 1990. *The Goals of Pschoanalysis: Identification, Identity and Supervision.* London: Karnac Books.

Grinberg, L., 1993. Countertransference and the Concept of Projective Counteridentification. *In:* A. Alexandris and G. Vaslamatzis, eds. *Countertransference: Theory, Technique, Teaching.* London: Karnac, 47–68.

Grinberg, L., and Grinberg, R., 1989. *Psychoanalytic Perspectives on Migration and Exile.* New Haven and London: Yale University Press.

Hall, E.T., 1973. *The Silent Language.* New York: Anchor Books.

Hofstede, G.H., 2001. *Culture's Consequences: Comparing Values, Behaviours, Institutions, and Organizations Across Nations.* 2nd ed. Thousand Oaks and London: Sage.

Hofstede, G.H., and Bond, M.H., 1984. Hofstede's Culture Dimensions: An Independent Validation Using Rokeach's Value Survey. *Journal of Cross-Cultural Psychology,* 15 (4), 417–433.

Hörberg, U., 2018. 'The Art of Understanding in Forensic Psychiatric Care' – From a Caring Science Perspective Based on a Lifeworld Approach. *Issues in Mental Health Nursing,* 39 (9), 802–809.

House, R.J., 2004. *Culture, Leadership, and Organizations: The Globe Study of 62 Societies.* Thousand Oaks and London: Sage.

Katz, M., Cassorla, R.M.S., and Civitarese, G., eds., 2017. *Advances in Contemporary Psychoanalytic Field Theory: Concept and Future Development*. London and New York: Routledge.

Marshall, L.A., and Adams, E.A., 2018. Building from the Ground Up: Exploring Forensic Mental Health Staff's Relationships with Patients. *The Journal of Forensic Psychiatry & Psychology*, 29 (5), 744–761.

Maude, B., 2016. *Managing Cross-Cultural Communication: Principles and Practice*. 2nd ed. London: Macmillan Education Palgrave.

McDougall, J., 1993. Countertransference and Primitive Communication. *In:* A. Alexandris and G. Vaslamatzis, eds. *Countertransference: Theory, Technique, Teaching*. London: Karnac, 95–134.

Moore, M., and Kramer, D., 1999. Satir for Beginners: Incongruent Communication Patterns in Romantic Fiction. *ETC: A Review of General Semantics*, 56 (4), 429–437 [online]. Available from: www.jstor.org/stable/42577981.

Ogden, T.H., 2004/1994. *Subjects of Analysis*. 1st ed. Lanham, MD: Rowman & Littlefield.

Rappoport de Aisemberg, E., 2017. About the Theory of the Analytic Field. *In:* R.M.S. Cassorla, G. Civitarese, and M. Katz, eds. *Advances in Contemporary Psychoanalytic Field Theory: Concept and Future Development*. Abingdon, Oxon and New York: Routledge.

Riesenberg-Malcolm, R., 1999. Interpretation: The Past in the Present. *In:* P.L. Roth, ed. *On Bearing Unbearable States of Mind*. London: Routledge, 38–52.

Rosenberg, M.B., 2015. *Nonviolent Communication: A Language of Life*. 3rd ed. Encinitas, CA: PuddleDancer Press.

Sapolsky, R.M., 2017. *Behave: The Biology of Humans at Our Best and Worst*. London: Vintage Digital.

Schlippe, A. von, Hachimi, M.E., and Jürgens, G., 2003. *Multikulturelle Systemische Praxis: Ein Reiseführer für Beratung Therapie und Supervision*. 1st ed. Heidelberg: Carl-Auer-Systeme-Verl.

Schriefer, P., 2016. *What's the Difference Between Multicultural, Intercultural, and Cross-Cultural Communication?* [online]. Available from: https://springinstitute.org/whats-difference-multicultural-intercultural-cross-cultural-communication/ [Accessed April 2021].

Schulz von Thun, F., 1981. *Miteinander reden: Störungen und Klärungen Psychologie der zwischenmenschlichen Kommunikation*. Reinbek bei Hamburg: Rowohlt.

Segal, H., 1957. Notes on Symbol Formation. *The International Journal of Psychoanalysis*, 38 (6), 391–397.

Segal, H., 1993. Countertransference. *In:* A. Alexandris and G. Vaslamatzis, eds. *Countertransference: Theory, Technique, Teaching*. London: Karnac, 13–20.

Stern, D.N., 1995. *The Motherhood Constellation: A Unified View of Parent-Infant Psychotherapy*. New York: Basic Books.

Stern, D.N., 2000/1985. *The Interpersonal World of the Infant: A View from Psychoanalysis and Developmental Psychology, with a New Introduction by the Author Daniel N. Stern*. New York: Basic Books.

Stern, D.N., 2004. *The Present Moment in Psychotherapy and Everyday Life*. New York: W.W. Norton.

Stern, D.N., 2010. *Forms of Vitality: Exploring Dynamic Experience in Psychology, the Arts, Psychotherapy, and Development*. Oxford and New York: Oxford University Press.

Sue, S., 2003. In Defense of Cultural Competency in Psychotherapy and Treatment. *The American Psychologist*, 58 (11), 964–970.

Thomas, A., 2016. *Interkulturelle Psychologie: Verstehen und Handeln in internationalen Kontexten*. 1st ed. Göttingen: Hogrefe.
Trompenaars, A., and Hampden-Turner, C., 1997. *Riding the Waves of Culture: Understanding Cultural Diversity in Business*. 2nd ed. London: Nicholas Brealey.
Watzlawick, P., Bavelas, J.B., and Jackson, D.D., 2011. *Pragmatics of Human Communication: A Study of Interactional Patterns, Pathologies, and Paradoxes, Paul Watzlawick, Janet Beavin Bavelas, Don D. Jackson; Foreword to the Paperback Edition by Bill O'Hanlon*. New York and London: W.W. Norton.
Way, B.M., and Lieberman, M.D., 2010. Is There a Genetic Contribution to Cultural Differences? Collectivism, Individualism and Genetic Markers of Social Sensitivity. *Social Cognitive and Affective Neuroscience*, 5 (2–3), 203–211.
Winnicott, D.W., 1953. Transitional Objects and Transitional Phenomena: A Study of the First Not-Me Possession. *The International Journal of Psycho-analysis*, 34, 89–97.
Winnicott, D.W., 1955. Metapsychological and Clinical Aspects of Regression Within the Psychoanalytical Set-Up. *The International Journal of Psycho-analysis*, 36, 16–26.
Winnicott, D.W., 1967. The Location of Cultural Experience. *The International Journal of Psycho-analysis*, 48 (3), 368–372.
Winnicott, D.W., 1992/1987. Communication Between Infant and Mother, Mother and Infant, Compared and Contrasted. In: D.W. Winnicott, *et al*., eds. *Babies and Their Mothers*. Reading, MA and Wokingham: Addison-Wesley, 89–104.
Winnicott, D.W., 2005. *Playing and Reality*. London: Routledge.
Winnicott, D.W., 2018. The Mother-Infant Experience of Mutuality. In: *Psycho-Analytic Explorations*. London: Routledge, 251–260.
Winnicott, D.W., *et al*., 2012. *Deprivation and Delinquency*. Milton Park and Abingdon, Oxon: Routledge.
Živanović, D., and Ćirić, Z., 2017. Therapeutic Communication in Health Care. *SciFed Nursing & Healthcare Journal*, 1, 2.

Chapter 3

TICA – Transient Interactive Communication Approach

The seed of TICA

Communication has always been at the heart of the matter in one's life, as there is no human life without communication. Therefore, I will start this chapter by reporting a period of my life that illustrates the primary value of interactive communication to me.

I believe this to be my earliest memory, to which I only had access via personal training analysis. I was a toddler, and I was walking on the footpath in front of my home, with my older brothers and my grandparents. At one point, I tried to walk along the footpath by myself, walking quickly. My grandparents ordered me to stop because according to them, I was going to fall. Not surprisingly as a toddler, my impulsiveness did not permit me to stop – maybe I was just playing in a potential space (Winnicott 1953) whilst testing my limits. My grandparents threatened me by saying that if I fell, they would take pictures of me sitting on the ground and crying due to the physical pain I would feel – the photo would be proof of my disobedience, so that I would not forget it. However, I continued walking off. Suddenly, I fell, as is expected of any toddler. My grandparents started taking pictures of me. I started crying and screaming because I was angry with my grandparents and not because I was in physical pain (but rather in emotional pain) – miscommunication alongside misapprehension. In reality, as adults, my grandparents were not able to deal with my impulsiveness, nor were they able to support me through the created potential space where I could experience my limits. Instead of this, they punished me. In the process of analysis, I was able to generate representations of this experience and was also to deal with feelings of being clearly abandoned and alone, followed by a great sense of loneliness. Years later, I asked my mother about this event, and she confirmed all the details and showed me the photos. Whilst I was writing this book, I asked her to send me the photos and she said she did not have them anymore; somehow, they had been lost. However, she sent me another photo, one of me walking with the help of my brothers (Figure 3.1). According to her, it had been taken minutes before the one I had asked for.

DOI: 10.4324/9781003232087-4

TICA – Transient Interactive Communication Approach 25

Figure 3.1 Toddler walking on the footpath

My goal in reporting this very personal moment is to underpin what I call 'the seed' of my desire to communicate with the 'Other', in search of a shared meaning in communication.

The roots of TICA: on learning to reach out to children living in 'street situations'

The roots of TICA are linked to the research I had carried out on deprived and maltreated children (Castrechini-Franieck *et al*. 2014; Castrechini-Franieck and Page 2017). The assessments of these children were always a major challenge, as the adopted communication approach used to reach out to these children needed to be accurate; otherwise, the potential risk of failing to assess them was high, in particular with those children living in 'street situations'. The contact with the children living in 'street situations' was mostly characterized by an expectation from their sides of a reward – due to their precarious situation – as well as by transience (Castrechini-Franieck 2014) – owing to their defence mechanism against attachment (Williams 2011). Therefore, I needed to learn how to articulate clearly. To illustrate an articulate form of communication and its influence on a fruitful interaction, I would like to introduce a vignette of the time when I was assessing three siblings living in 'street situations'. However, before presenting this vignette, it is essential to provide some background about the siblings' personal history in order to understand their context, their personal matrix (Foulkes and Foulkes 1990).

The three brothers – aged 5, 8, and 11 – had been living in the 'street situations' all their lives, having been born there to a mother who had also been living in this situation since she was 14. The short history of their mother that was known to me included that at the age of 8, she was placed in a care home operated by the church, as her mother had been sent to prison. However, during her adolescence, she got into trouble with the care home's rules. At 14, she was expelled from the care institution and adopted a lifestyle on the streets, which included drug addiction and prostitution. Her three children were fathered by two different men, both drug addicts. The eldest one never knew his natural father. However, their mother was described by every social worker as being an affectionate towards her children. At the time of the assessment, she was in hospital due to AIDS, and by this stage, her illness was terminal. Although the three boys wanted to be with their mother until her death, in accordance with child welfare policies, the children were removed from the care of their mother and placed in a residential care home. As the two older brothers fought a lot, the staff decided to separate them. The eldest one was sent to a different residential care home from his brothers. Their caregivers described them as being disruptive in their placements, and this was connected to their desire for their mother. They were also disruptive during assessment sessions. The eldest was observed yelling and refusing to take part minutes before beginning his assessment. The 8-year-old boy became disruptive after his assessment, attempting to break the door separating him from the room I was in, when a social worker tried to interrupt his game on a computer (the video game he was playing involved a baby in need of care, which may have been a contributing factor to his outburst). The youngest did not exchange a single word with me during the whole assessment, though he played in silence very attentively with me. Each child was assessed in individual sessions in different places and at different times – a control factor to avoid any interchange of information about their play time. The assessments took place a couple of days after the separation from their mother (Castrechini-Franieck and Page 2017).

The vignette refers to the communication approach used minutes before the assessment of the eldest one, John.

John should have been brought to me from his care home by a social worker. I was waiting for him in an office in the social work department of the town hall.

When he came into my office, he was furious and very disruptive. I could not understand what was going on. He did not say "hello" to me, conversely, he yelled at himself whilst punching the walls and walking around like a caged little lion. I was impressed with this 'caged little lion'. I clearly recall the moment when I tried to start a conversation with him by introducing myself:

ME: "Hi! I am Leticia and you – who are you? Are you John?"
Then he yelled:
J: "Here there is no John . . . NO John!"
At this point, I decided to follow his thoughts with the aim of getting more information and being able to understand what was going on, and I asked him the following.
ME: "Ok! Then who is here now? Do you have a name?"
The answer came in a crying tone.
J: "Here is just a boy! JUST a boy!" (Swearing and moaning in a low voice)
I decided to continue the communication on his terms, since I did have an aim, the aim of reaching out to him. So, I said:
ME: "OK, boy . . . I see you are really angry! I am sorry! I cannot understand what is going on now in your mind because I do not live inside your mind. I am sorry! Actually, I am here because I would like to play with you and also to get to know you better!"
Without thinking, he yelled at me:
J: "If you want to know me, just take my records and read them . . . here they have all my records . . . read them and you can see who I am!"

His answer moved me deeply. It was not clear to me why he was so angry, but it was evident that his anger and frustration turned him into a nobody, 'just a boy', 'a record'. It was both a sad and truthful answer at the same time. I was surprised how 'the caged little lion' was fully aware of his role as an 'Outsider' in the social system.

I was aware that if I could not communicate clearly with him, I would lose him. I understood that in order to make/maintain contact with him, I would have to match his anger level and respond to him according to his aggressive tone (Winnicott *et al.* 2012), in the 'Hope' (Havel and Hvížďala 1991) of reaching him.

In doing so, one should be aware and secure of one's own feelings. In other words, one should be aware that one is not under the control of one's own anger and/or frustration triggered by the other (the patient), whilst feeling comfortable in answering by setting boundaries – which also means being able to deal properly with one's own aggressive side. In short, as long as one is aware of one's own feelings and simultaneously has a clear understanding of the aim to be achieved, a situation of 'acting-out' will not be encouraged. On the contrary, this way of working will help the patient to realize the therapist's emotional control over himself or herself whilst introducing the boundary between them.

28 On building communication

So, I answered loudly and clearly to John:

ME: "Hey boy, I am not interested in your records! You know, I can assess your records anytime I want to read them. For that, I don't need to meet you, *but* I did want to meet you because I would just like to play with you. I was hoping we could perhaps have a fun time playing together. You know, it is your choice and not mine. Either you can stay here with your anger and it will not change anything in your day – only your anger will get worse – or you can give yourself a chance to do something different, like playing with me, and perhaps have a good time instead of keeping your anger. It is up to you! In case you find the game boring, and you decide to stop playing, you can go away anytime . . . you do not need to stay with me, not at all. I do want to play with you John, but I cannot force you to do this. Now it is your turn!"

What I tried to communicate to him was my genuine intention to initiate contact with him, along with all my limitations/impotence, to reach out to him; all the while, he kept his distance whilst ignoring me. Furthermore, I showed him my strength, my backbone, while giving him the freedom to make decisions at a moment when his freedom had been taken away from him.

He thought for some minutes. He seemed to be thinking about my words, and he calmed down. Then, he agreed to come with me and play, and we had a lovely and fun time together. At the end of the assessment, I accompanied him to the waiting room, where another social worker from his residential care home was waiting for him. Along the way we chatted and when the social worked met us, she said:

SW: "What has happened with you, John?"

I replied:

ME: "Sorry, I don't understand what you mean".
SW: "John has changed . . . he is not the same boy as before! He laughs now!"

John and I looked into each other's eyes and laughed.

Later, I received an explanation as to why he had been so angry at the beginning. In fact, the person who had picked him up at his residential care home to bring him to me had been the same social worker who had sent him and his brothers to the different residential care homes. At that time, fearing their rebellion on account of going into residential care, she had fetched them from 'their home' with the promise of taking them to see their mother in hospital. Instead of this, she had taken them to the residential care home. So, he had had every right to be furious – this was a real and painful experience he had gone through alone, minutes before we met. Despite all this, we did have a great time together and John had not only been able to accept my offer, but he had also been able to benefit from it. With this in mind, this is one of the strengths of TICA – one is able to develop communication with the other in freedom, despite all external variables and their burdens.

To conclude this vignette, I would now like to express here all my gratitude for having the chance to spend time with John. I have learnt a lot from him. From the 'caged little lion', he turned into a 'teacher' for me. From this day on, I have stopped reading patients' records before my first contact with them in interviews or assessments (see Chapter 5). All John's words from the beginning of our encounter have had great resonance for me. Metaphorically speaking, they have represented a lighthouse in the middle of the ocean every time I have felt lost in the process of communicating with a patient.

Some observations on TICA

TICA lays emphasis on 'just being with' the other person with an open frame of mind whilst searching for the achievement of 'shared meaning communication'. In other words, one allows oneself to become lost in a misrepresented/disorganized emotional state during the interaction with the other person, without the fear of losing oneself or being dominated by the other's wishes and phantasies. At the same time, one observes this process and tries to comprehend them and transform them into representations, by developing 'shared meaning communication'. Theoretically, it can be perceived as an integration of the following concepts: the experience of 'mutuality' (Winnicott 1992/1987, 2018) or 'attunement' (Stern 1995), the ability of 'reverie' combined with the 'container-contained model' (Bion 1959, 1984b, 1984a), and the 'analytic third' (Ogden 2004/1994).

TICA should not be mistakenly perceived as a technique, as healing is not its primary goal. However, its emphasis is on creating a potential space that may allow a new experience in communicating in relationships with others. Whether TICA might trigger a healing process or not will depend wholly on the communication with the patient per se – will the patient change? Is the patient ready for change? Hence, if one decides to consider TICA, one needs to be resilient, as failures in the therapeutic healing process may easily happen, since the basic idea is that the patients have freedom of choice.

To illustrate, in my work I have never made assertions like: "I can help you" or "We will find a solution" or "You will get better"; on the contrary, I have usually said "I am here to listen to you. I will try to understand you; however, I don't know if I will be able to" or when they ask me for my opinion, I usually reply like this, "Sorry, I cannot decide for you . . . we can talk about your issue and I can try to think together with you; however, the decision is yours . . ." Or even when I have been placed in the 'role of God' as an expression of their expectation of miraculous healing (when they are looking for quick answers or for someone who can be their guardian) and expect me to make decisions for them, I usually say: "I am sorry, but I am not God! And I am so happy I am not God! Please do not take this as an offence!" (The patients usually laugh with this intervention and accept the reality). To put it another way, my message is that I am not expecting my patients to be healed, but I am with them and I accept them as they really are. In addition, I also offer them freedom of choice. In particular, I make it clear that their relationship with me will not be based on a narcissistic level, in which I am the one who holds the knowledge and holds the power to heal. In my understanding this is the first step in initiating fruitful communication.

On building communication – first steps

To return to my previous point in Chapter 1, throughout my inner struggle, my inquisitive mind has driven me to the wish of creating 'shared meaning communication' with my patients. Despite the fact that I would surely have to cope with barriers caused by cultural noise and any consequent miscommunication, I was keen to experience this.

Hence, the first step in developing 'shared meaning communication' should start with what I call 'interpretation training'. Put more simply, in order to break down communication barriers, it is important to focus attention on how our brain processes information and builds a representation of our surroundings. 'Interpretation training' does not have the goal of achieving a single and common interpretation. Quite the opposite, it is an exercise in awareness of the countless forms of interpretation that may exist, while encouraging the welcoming of the 'different' or the stranger beyond oneself. For this reason, 'interpretation training' requires the creation of a potential neutral space and the existence of a neutral object at the same time for the process of being able to experience and play with different and/or similar meanings – similar to a transitional object and a transitional space (Winnicott 1953, 2005).

From a clinical perspective, the concept of a transitional object may basically be perceived as the object that not only permeates communication between inner and outer words, but also makes the transition between fantasy and fact (by accepting difference and similarity between both), whilst bringing about symbolism.

> When symbolism is employed, the infant is already clearly distinguishing between fantasy and fact, between inner objects and external objects, between primary creativity and perception.
>
> (Winnicott 1953, p. 92)

> The transitional objects and transitional phenomena belong to the realm of illusion which is at the basis of initiation of experience. This early stage in development is made possible by the mother's special capacity for making adaptation to the needs of her infant, thus allowing the infant the illusion that what the infant creates really exists. This intermediate area of experience, unchallenged in respect of its belonging to inner or external (shared) reality, constitutes the greater part of the infant's experience and throughout life is retained in the intense experiencing that belongs to the arts and to religion and to imaginative living, and to creative scientific work.
>
> (Winnicott 1953, p. 97)

TICA – Transient Interactive Communication Approach

To this end, cartoons could be used as improvement tools. My suggestion is to adopt optical illusion cartoons as an initial approach, as that there are several ways of viewing them that are identical in form, though different in meaning (Perls 1969). In order to interpret an optical illusion, the brain must function in ways which it is not familiar with. Thinking in ways that are creative and challenging to one's visual perception increases the brain's flexibility (Fliege and Torche 2013). In particular, I would strongly advise starting with the classical 100-year-old optical illusion, the "duck or rabbit" (Figure 3.2) as the first preferred tool, adopted to encourage communication in any context. The ambiguous image, in which a rabbit or a duck can be seen, is quite neutral but also captivating and thus has a very positive impact on the patients.

The "duck or rabbit" illusion cartoon may serve as a basis for discussion about the various ways in which people respond to misunderstandings in their lives, especially those in close relationships. Here, it also introduces the potential for misunderstandings to occur in therapeutic settings (including a cross-cultural one) and the necessity to resolve them – the transference work. Depending on the circumstances, patients spontaneously start talking about conflicts that they have experienced in their lives and are able to recognize the misunderstandings. Indeed, in moments of intense conflict, when this cartoon is presented for a second time, it can appease aggressive acts faster than words.

The following chapters refer to a detailed description of TICA's features, including all the steps in this approach, along with different settings, therapeutic outlines, and aims. I hope that by the final chapter, I will be able to encourage the reader to persist in trying to build 'shared meaning communication' with their patients despite all the daunting challenges the reader is likely to encounter.

Figure.3.2 Duck/rabbit head

In particular, Chapter 4 explores in detail the initial outlines and aims of TICA in a cognitive behavioural withdrawal therapy context. In short, the emphasis is placed on 'interpretation training' through the adoption of cartoons and films as useful means in group sessions, which could easily fit in with the therapeutic goals, namely: a) to encourage the patients to explore triggers for their offending behaviour; b) to reflect on the consequences of their behaviour; and c) to set goals for changing their behaviour in future. The cartoons and films supply a potential space whilst applying an interactive communication approach in the group dynamic. The latter intends to broaden the scope of reflection on how the patients might be thinking and feeling, especially in relation to love, frustration, disappointments, prejudice, anger, and aggression, occasionally linking this to earlier life experiences. The creation of a potential space through a 'transitional object' triggers several achievements in the group (and by the group) – e.g., a child sexual offender could be accepted as a member of the group. Indeed, 'the transitional object' also helped the patients to overcome the therapist's absence during her holidays, which is equally a prerequisite for their successful release, as it is expected that after their release, the patients will be able 'to stand on their own two feet'. Again, this is another strength of TICA – the therapist is able to build communication with patients without triggering any kind of dependence by the latter on former.

From withdrawal therapy to crises interventions in a pretrial detention centre

Although the difference in the psychological work in forensic withdrawal therapy and in a pretrial detention centre might be clear to everyone, when I started working in a pretrial detention centre, the use of TICA was still unclear to me (see Chapter 10). The principles of a pretrial detention are quite different from those of forensic withdrawal therapy. The latter presumes the existence of a verdict, a period of time associated with a sentence, awareness of aims to be reached, and regular contact with a psychologist. The former is characterized by no verdict and is therefore associated with both transient and uncertain situations, preventing any long-term future planning. Metaphorically speaking, it is like being placed in limbo while awaiting trial.

Once again, questions preoccupied my mind regarding daunting challenges.

What should be the communication approach in this new milieu? Indeed, how could I offer an opportunity for reasonable communication under the conditions found in pretrial detention centres, as described previously? How can daily transience and uncertainties in my work be dealt with and fitted into reality?

Since my tasks were restricted to: a) assessing suicide risks; b) intervening in crises; c) giving psychological support to prisoners that were emotionally unstable; and finally d) giving psychological support to sex offenders (who could not share their worries about their trial with anyone else due to their offence), I neither had much freedom of choice, nor much time to run 'interpretation training'. In order to cope with the limitations on my work in this milieu, I needed to go back to the time when I worked with the children living in 'street situations' and once again try to develop a new accurate approach. So, I started doing drawings on paper of a prisoner's current lifestyle through their 'lifetime' (Schauer and Ruf-Leuschner 2014). Hence, replacing verbal representations by drawn ones. Just as cartoons and films turned into transitional objects in 'interpretation training', the method of drawing is per se a transitional object and also triggers a potential space. Therefore, drawings are most useful in crisis intervention contexts (including work with those considered a suicide risk) when most of the 'highly vulnerable' and/or 'unbearable' patients act on impulse and lack focus on their capacity for abstract thoughts – in this situation, drawings have supremacy over words. More recently I also adopted the use of pendants in different colours, as a transitional object during discussions with potentially aggressive/violent patients (see details in Chapter 5)

From the tormentor to the prey

When I started working with traumatized refugees, I developed my understanding of the complex vicious circle of tormentor and prey. In fact, the latter may be understood as the negative consequence of the former's actions in this dynamic. Therefore, the focus of the psychological work was kept unaltered, though language issues proved to be the key challenge in work with traumatized refugees, since an interpreter had to be included in the therapeutic setting – a complex cross-cultural therapeutic setting. The features of this unique triangular setting will be discussed in Chapter 6. Therefore, TICA had to be adapted yet again to create a more effective and independent work setting, in which communication needed to be less verbal, briefer, and more concrete, with the aim of overcoming cultural noise. This could, for example, have been achieved by representing the therapist's understanding through a picture or even by representing the patient's speech through a picture (also the offer of a transitional object). The 'feelings wheel' (see description in Chapter 6) was a very appropriate tool indeed for working with traumatized refugees. All communication was carried out using this tool, which was readily accepted by the patient, and in most cases, after the therapist's verbal representation, the patients spontaneously started associating and talking about difficult and painful matters related to their trauma. Indeed, 'feelings wheels' are a tool that allows reapplication over a short period of time. Hence, it is likely to mirror the dynamic of the patient's emotional state.

In short-term multicultural team supervision

When I was requested to supervise a multicultural team in the presence of their new superiors in only six meetings, with the aim of improving communication among them, I was faced with a new daunting challenge. Once again, I felt as though I had been placed in an alien context. Unlike the clinical setting, communication in an organization's workplace needed to be highly focused on the organization's defined goals. How could I create a potential space in such a prescriptive und limited context as this? Hence, TICA had to be adapted to this alien context. The adoption of coloured cards in communication, along with homework tasks, encouraged the team's growth, and it was possible not only to open up communication, but also to improve communication among the group's members, including the new superiors. Chapter 7 illustrates the team's growth via session transcriptions.

Preventive work with deprived children

TICA turns into T-WAS, a wonderful metamorphosis that gives a shout-out to its roots in research with children at risk; however, it has now become preventive psychosocial group work with deprived latency children in an attempt to avoid an increase in antisocial behaviour.

Chapter 8 shows how T-WAS can be perceived as a fine-tuning of TICA. Achieving shared meaning communication here means laying emphasis on the group's ongoing experience of dealing with diversity in the group – starting with the diversity embodied by the 'group conductors' (Foulkes and Foulkes 1990) themselves – a couple made up of by a foreign female psychologist, with a contemporary psychoanalytic background, and a native male pedagogue and martial arts teacher with a Gestalt background – a vivid and concrete pathway for achieving 'shared meaning communication'. In addition, the conductors had to provide and assist the children with socially relevant experiences of parental representation models. Consequently, the emphasis of the potential space had to be on creating transference and counter-transference circumstances and object relation conditions that allowed corrective attachment experiences (Stern 1995). Communication was mostly established via diverse play activities.

COVID-19 time

Chapter 9 briefly presents the necessary adaptation of TICA as a consequence of the COVID-19 pandemic. Despite the need for isolation and/or the 2-metre distancing rules, the most important goal during this time has been to maintain a connection. The use of films, videos, letters, photos, and calls, combined with close cooperation with staff and interpreters, has highlighted the resilience of this Transient Interactive Communication Approach.

References

Bion, W.R., 1959. Attacks on Linking. *The International Journal of Psycho-analysis*, 40, 308–315.
Bion, W.R., 1984a. *Attention & Interpretation*. London: Maresfield Reprints.
Bion, W.R., 1984b. *Learning from Experience*. London: Maresfield Reprints.

Castrechini-Franieck, L., 2014. *We Were Born on the Street, How Do Experiences of Transience and Permanence Affect Us?* [online]. Available from: https://ifpe.wordpress.com/volume-3-winter-2014/ [Google Scholar].

Castrechini-Franieck, M.L., Günter, M., and Page, T., 2014. Engaging Brazilian Street Children in Play: Observations of Their Family Narratives. *Child Development Research*, 861703.

Castrechini-Franieck, M.L., and Page, T., 2017. The Family Narratives of Three Siblings Living in a 'Street Situation' Since Birth. *Early Child Development and Care*, 189 (10), 1575–1587.

Fliege, C., and Torche, J., 2013. *Brain Games: Optical Illusions, Lower Your Brain Age in Minutes a Day*. Lincolnwood, IL: Publications International, Ltd.

Foulkes, S.H., and Foulkes, E., 1990. *Selected Papers of S.H. Foulkes: Psychoanalysis and Group Analysis, Edited and with a Brief Biography by Elizabeth Foulkes*. London: Karnac Books.

Havel, V., and Hvížďala, K., 1991. *Disturbing the Peace: A Conversation with Karel Hvížďala*. 1st ed. New York: Vintage Books.

Ogden, T.H., 2004/1994. *Subjects of Analysis*. 1st ed. Lanham, MD: Rowman & Littlefield.

Perls, F.S., 1969. *Ego, Hunger and Aggression: The Beginning of Gestalt Therapy*. New York: Vintage.

Schauer, M., and Ruf-Leuschner, M., 2014. Lifeline in Narrative Exposure Therapy. *Psychotherapeut*, 59, 226–238.

Stern, D.N., 1995. *The Motherhood Constellation: A Unified View of Parent-Infant Psychotherapy*. New York: Basic Books.

Williams, A., 2011. *Working with Street Children: An Approach Explored*. Lyme Regis: Russell House.

Winnicott, D.W., 1953. Transitional Objects and Transitional Phenomena: A Study of the First Not-Me Possession. *The International Journal of Psycho-analysis*, 34, 89–97.

Winnicott, D.W., 1992/1987. Communication Between Infant and Mother, Mother and Infant, Compared and Contrasted. *In:* D.W. Winnicott, *et al.*, eds. *Babies and Their Mothers*. Reading, MA and Wokingham: Addison-Wesley, 89–104.

Winnicott, D.W., 2005. *Playing and Reality*. London: Routledge.

Winnicott, D.W., 2018. The Mother-Infant Experience of Mutuality. *In: Psycho-Analytic Explorations*. London: Routledge, 251–260.

Winnicott, D.W., *et al.*, 2012. *Deprivation and Delinquency*. Milton Park and Abingdon, Oxon: Routledge.

Part two

TICA in forensic settings

Chapter 4

TICA in withdrawal therapy

A substantial part of this chapter was presented at the 23rd Annual Conference of the International Association for Forensic Psychotherapy, in spring 2014 in Zeist, Utrecht, The Netherlands, under the title: "The promotion of a transitional space in which to overcome transference issues when treating personality disorder patients".

Withdrawal therapeutic community context

Features

The therapeutic community context involved addiction treatment with 13 months of cognitive behavioural–based withdrawal therapy in a specialist unit for 18 male offenders (their ages ranging from 21–45 years old), with histories of repeat and heterogeneous offending, severe alcohol and drug problems, and comorbid disorders (primarily personality disorders).

To get a place in the therapeutic community, one had to enclose a detailed biography, including addiction history, together with a motivational report. As a rule, most of the applicants had to be coming to the end of their sentence and/or had to hold the right to appeal for early discharge. Early discharge meant that after the applicants had already served two-thirds of their sentence, it may have been possible for them to get probation, based on good behaviour.

The three exclusion criteria for the treatment were as follows.

1 Mental disorders (such as mental/physical disability, acute psychosis, severe personality disorders, sexual abuse of children) that significantly hindered the patient in developing a therapeutic relationship and thereby made them unsuitable for therapeutic work.
2 Inability to do sport and work, as both activities were central pillars of the therapy.
3 Foreign applicants without German language fluency, and/or facing the prospect of deportation.

DOI: 10.4324/9781003232087-6

Goals

The core goal of the therapeutic community was abstinence. To this end, the therapeutic work was mostly focused on searching for one's own triggers for substance abuse while dealing with blocking attitudes, feelings and behaviours that led them to this addiction. At the same time, patients were encouraged to explore triggers for their offending behaviours and to reflect on the consequence in order to set goals for changing their behaviours in the future, as well as improving their quality of life and social competence. The latter was achieved via learning approaches that not only promoted abilities and creativities of the patients, but also rebuilt their self-esteem and self-confidence. Abilities in this context were perceived as concentration, perseverance, diligence, frustration tolerance and cooperation in teamwork. Simply put, the emphasis of the treatment was placed on the development of: a) social competence skills; b) the ability to set oneself apart from others, such as saying "no"; c) the ability to express one's own needs; d) the ability to maintain one's relationship with others, while expressing sympathy for others; and e) the ability to deal with their own feelings, particularly aggressive ones, mainly triggered by frustrations.

Pillars of the treatment

The four core pillars of the treatment were as follows.

1   Sport: this was an early morning, daily activity.
2   Work: the work available in the prison was restricted to the following areas: the library, the cleaning facilities, the garden, the chamber, and the kitchen, and prisoners were paid according to the usual rate of remuneration.
3   Group therapy: The patients were divided into two groups. Each one was given a Greek name, and each psychologist was responsible for a group. The two 90-minute sessions took place twice a week in the afternoon (after patients had finished worked) on the same day, at the same time and continued from the first to the last day of the withdrawal therapy. To achieve the treatment's goals, the following themes had to be addressed in the group: a) emotional training; b) anti-aggression training; c) training in social competence and self-assurance; d) relapse prevention; e) relaxation training; and finally, f) quality of life. In this context, the role of the group conductor was as a mediator in conflict situations and as a critical adviser along the way to finding solutions to problems. As the same time, there were also other group activities, such as occupational therapy and psychodrama, which were also expected to support the therapeutic objectives. However, these groups formed a temporary aspect of the treatment and did not feature continuously like the a–f list of themes described here.
4   Individual therapy: this took place at least once a week and was conducted by the psychologist who also led the group.

Table 4.1 Description of the daily activities

Time	Activities
5:30 am–06:30 am	Sport or jogging: an activity conducted by a nurse
6:30 am–07:00 am	Shower and breakfast
7:00 am–12:00 pm	Work
12:00 pm–1:00 pm	Lunch in a common room at the rehabilitation centre, together with the whole group of patients
	Lunch was cooked by the prison kitchen
1:00 pm–2:00 pm	Leisure time, e.g., playing cards, reading a book, sleeping, chatting.
	In exceptional cases, a patient might go back to work during this short time.
2:00 pm–6:30 pm	Group and individual therapy
6:30 pm–8:00 pm	Dinner time: they cooked their own dinner in small groups of two or three in the rehabilitation centre's kitchen.
8:00 pm–10:30 pm	Leisure time, the same as before. However, in the evening, they could watch TV programmes in a shared TV room.
10:45 pm	Bedtime. The bedrooms were mostly twin rooms with single beds. The few existing single rooms were intended for those patients who were close to being released.

Aside from the four pillars of treatment, the patients had to follow a tight daily schedule, as is illustrated in Table 4.1.

Treatment step programme

The 13-month treatment was made up of a step programme including the following three phases.

1. Trial Phase (lasted for a month): this served to scrutinize the motivation as well as the suitability of the applicant for the therapy. In the trial phase, the applicants took part in the collective therapeutic services of the station, i.e., the occupational therapy and informative groups. However, continuous individual therapy was not yet possible, as the applicant's right to take part in the therapy was still being assessed. In cases when the applicants were not suitable for therapy, it was necessary to transfer them back to their local prison, either during or at the end of the trial phase, depending on each case.
2. Admission Phase (lasted for three months): in the subsequent phase, the applicant turns into a patient and first, a differentiated diagnosis was conducted by the psychologists. Following this, the psychologist and the patient together defined the therapy's goals, along with an individual treatment plan. During this phase, the work in the occupational therapy had to be intensive. The patients were supposed to attend it three times a week (each for two hours), and they learnt to work with different materials, such as clay, colours,

wood, stone, and glass, whilst developing their concentration, stamina, diligence, frustration tolerance, failure, ability to handle criticism, and assertiveness. At the end of the admission phase, the patients should have dealt with possible damage caused by addictive substances. In addition, they should have worked out the root cause of their addiction and delinquency. This process of self-knowledge should have been developed both in the group and in individual therapy. For instance, before their inclusion in the next phase, a written explanation of their personal addiction and offence record had to first be presented to the psychologist in an individual therapy session and then presented in the group therapy for discussion in the group. Lastly the patients also had to be interviewed in the multidisciplinary team meeting in order to be assessed by all staff as to whether or not they were able to continue to the next phase – which meant undergoing 'the treatment phase'.

3   Treatment Phase (lasted for nine months): in this phase, issues such as problems, weaknesses, and strengths were addressed further and more deeply. To illustrate, after three months in the treatment phase, each patient should have been ready to listen to the feedback from all members of the group with regards to his good and bad qualities, as observed in the day-to-day life of the residential setting. In this phase, the goals were focused on getting the patients ready to live outside the prison; hence, one of the central features of this phase was for the prisoners to be given privileges. In other words, in this phase some rules were relaxed, and patients were allowed to start leaving the prison for a while. First, they were allowed to leave the prison for two hours, under the supervision of a member of staff. Then, a second time, for four hours, still under supervision. From the third time onwards, they were allowed to go out alone and the period outside increased, for example, eight hours, 24 hours, and finally 48 hours. Receiving privileges was, in particular, a daunting challenge for the patients, as it provided evidence as to whether what had been worked through in therapy had been taken on board by the patients and also it provided evidence as to whether they were able or not to handle risk situations by experiencing them in reality. In dealing with other people outside the prison, both social skills were able to be practised and self-esteem was able to be strengthened or increased. However, the privilege not only aimed to promote social skills but also to prepare the patient for release (such as finding housing and a job).

Team constellation and decision making

The therapeutic community was made up of a multidisciplinary team as illustrated in Table 4.2.

Bearing the treatment setting in mind, the core team was made up of the psychologists and nursing staff, as they had daily contact with the patients and worked very closely with them, thus being able to identify any kinds of progress or disruption in the community. One of the core points of the treatment was the early

TICA in withdrawal therapy 43

Table 4.2 Description of team members' roles

Multidisciplinary team	Role
The prison director	Allows or dismisses the appeals for privileges.
The hospital director – a forensic psychiatrist	Manages the therapeutic community.
A physician	Responsible for the prisoners' health in the rehabilitation centre.
Two psychologists	Each psychologist was responsible for a group of patients (N = 9) from their admission until their discharge. New applicants could be included in the group at any time. The psychologist's job included: conducting group therapy and individual therapy, attending daily team meetings and weekly therapeutic community meetings, writing reports for the court and patient records, and generating homework. In the treatment, the main role of the psychologist was to perform auxiliary ego functions, i.e., by giving personal advice, using role-play models of behaviour, etc. In other words, the patients had to work out their own insights and rules of behaviour, whilst the therapist should be as reserved as possible and encourage the patient to reflect. As part of the treatment, the psychologist had to provide weekly homework (also during holidays and other breaks) to further deepen the changes in attitude and behaviour developed in individual and in group therapy sessions and to test solutions to problems in everyday life.
A social worker	Motivate patients to take responsibility for their civil and social rights and duties and provide counselling and support for specific problems. The social worker offered support through information and assistance with correspondence, telephone calls, and the development of plans with regard to debt settlement, office visits, finding accommodation, job searches, and therapeutic aftercare.
Five in nursing staff	Responsible for providing daily structure to the therapeutic centre. Although they were trained on the same basis as for forensic settings, each one had a particular responsibility in the treatment, e.g., one of them was responsible for everything connected to developing links with wider society, another for running outside sports.
An occupational therapist	Leads groups focused on offering an opportunity for learning and rediscovering personal skills whilst expressing feelings and thoughts in self-designed products.
A psychodrama therapist	Leads group therapy focused on body language awareness, reduction of tension, and perception and handling of emotions. The group was scheduled once a month, for three intensive days over the weekend.
A pastor	Lead groups (usually weekly) focused on the development of the soul.

morning daily team meeting between the psychologists and the nursing staff – an important opportunity for information exchange. In this meeting, the nurses, who stayed overnight at the rehabilitation centre, handed the patients over to the psychologists and their colleagues. Evenings and nights were usually a time when conflict among patients took place. Therefore, this meeting was imperative for decision making. Certainly, there were frequently different views as regards the decisions being made, which could trigger tension among the members of the core team. Hence, an external forensic psychotherapist supervised the core team on a monthly basis, in an effort to remedy potential internal conflicts.

Another central point for the decision making related to the patients' future treatment was the weekly multidisciplinary team meeting. At this meeting, all appeals for privileges were assessed (relaxations of the rules), and whether a patient would or would not be admitted to the next phase (and if not, what was to be done or worked on for the patient to perhaps move to the next phase in future) was discussed. The regularly schedule of the multidisciplinary team meeting included a detailed discussion about each case, an interview with patients receiving treatment, and the introduction of new patients to staff, who did not have daily contact with them.

The Theseus group

Theseus was the group of patients for which I was responsible. Over the 16 months I worked in the therapeutic community, 15 patients were under my responsibility; however, I was unable to follow the treatment of all of them. For instance, of the 15, four gave up on the treatment during the trial phase, mostly due to their difficulty in facing a new environment with specific rules. Five were able to take part in the group for just a couple of months, as some patients were either close to their discharge date when I started working with them or had just been admitted as I was about to leave. Six underwent the 13 months of treatment and all had their appeals for probation allowed, due to their good behaviour. These patients can be described from a personal point of view as follows:

> Mr. M. was a well-built, reserved and very well-educated man, in his mid-30s. He came from East Germany and had experienced the end of communism during his adolescence (14 years old) with sadness and mourning and started at that point to consume alcohol and drugs. He was in prison for the second time due to drug trafficking, which apropos became his lifestyle as well as the source of his addiction (mostly marijuana and cocaine). With drug trafficking, he was able to lead an extremely luxurious lifestyle. At the beginning, his emotional interaction with others in the group (including the psychologist) was cold and distant. His motto was: "life is boring".
>
> Mr. T. was a cunning person who had learned to survive in a disruptive criminal family. Despite being in his later 30s, emotionally, in relationships, he could be described as an immature man, and due to this, he had often

experienced sentimental distress and easily got into trouble with his family and partners. To counterbalance the repeated failures in his life, he had started to take drugs on a massive scale (mainly heroin) at the age of 17. His criminal record included recurrent detentions due to multiple thefts (with weapons), fraud, drug trafficking, and armed robbery. Indeed, this was his second attempt to undergo treatment after relapsing back into drugs during his first treatment in another community, and hence being expelled. In the group, Mr. T. always tried to be very friendly and helpful towards the other members of the group, though he was very cheeky towards the psychologist. He was the one who had posed the question to me in the group about whether I could follow another patient's German dialect (see Chapter 1).

Mr. R., a man in his late 40s, was tall and big, and always in good humour. His criminal record included recurrent detentions due to drug trafficking. Like Mr. M., drug trafficking became his lifestyle as well as the source of his addiction. He started consuming heroin when he was 17 years old, and up to this point, had suffered two massive heroin overdoses. The last overdose left serious neurological damage in his arms, which made it difficult for him to write or to draw, for example. Ironically, his hobby was drawing (the cards in Chapter 10 were mostly made by him). His goal in the therapy was to develop 'alternatives to living with drugs'. At that time, he was fully aware that a new overdose would lead to death. In the group he was respected for being the eldest and the coolest member, but above of all, for having survived two heroin overdoses.

Mr. S. was a 25-year-old bedwetting patient, who grew up in a care home, and who had been expelled from school due to his dyslexia. His criminal record included theft and gang vandalism. This time he had been sent to prison for a major assault against a person. He started to use alcohol and marijuana when he was only 8 years old. The caregiver at the care home used to keep the children under control by giving them either alcohol or marijuana. From his adolescence onwards, he started to use other drugs (e.g., amphetamines, cocaine, heroin, Subutex), but not regularly. At first, he was often suspicious of everyone in the group, including the psychologist, and one could sense his aggressiveness in his eyes.

Mr. C. was a single man (and an only child) in his early 40s, with many debts. Since his 20s, he had consumed massive amounts of alcohol, and thus he had frequently been involved in pub fights but had escaped imprisonment. This was the first time he had been imprisoned due to assault, followed by the attempted rape of a woman. Integrating into the group presented Mr. C. with various difficulties, as he used to behave like a 'mummy's boy' (which did not match the penitentiary system).

Mr. B. was a 30-year-old reserved man also from East Germany who had attempted suicide twice in the past. Like Mr. M., he had also experienced the end of communism with sadness and mourning. At that point, he was at the end of his childhood and had begun to drink. Between the ages of 13 and 15, he had started to regularly consume massive amounts of alcohol.

His criminal record included theft, assault, and finally child sex abuse (of 13 year old girls) – a couple of incidents, though without using force. He had been waiting for this therapy for two years. In fact, he had been discounted due to the exclusion criteria. His inclusion in the group which I led was an exception. In the group, Mr. B. was always sociable towards the other members of the group when it came to practical issues, although he was distant and silent in group discussions on emotional issues.

In practice, the patients all also held the position of 'Outsider' – Mr. M. and Mr. B. were from East Germany, Mr. S. and Mr. C. were the sons of immigrants and Mr. T. and Mr. R. were estranged from their German family.

When I started my work with this group of patients, my mind was full of questions, such as the following. How could I address the treatment's themes properly in group therapy considering the diverse life experiences of the group's members? How could I get their attention, rouse their interest and ensure participation in treatment's themes? How could I make myself clear and understandable when talking to them, despite all the cross-cultural issues? How could I show them how important it is to reflect instead of acting impulsively? How could I convince them that the privileges actually mean a daunting challenge, instead of merely freedom? How could I gain their trust in the group? Finally, how would I be able to conduct a group, considering the pre-conditions for the formation of a group which according to Foulkes and Foulkes (1990, pp. 152–153) had failed?

After Mr. M.'s fair question, when he questioned my ability to understand a German dialect, as described in Chapter 1, I became well aware that the first step should be to offer them a space in the group for the exchange of ideas and thoughts in a playful way (Winnicott *et al*. 2012), while dealing concretely with problems caused by language and cultural matters. To put this another way, we needed to adjust our perceptions of a 'shared language/shared meaning', which meant developing one's ability to understand each other's perspectives well enough to accept them, even though one may not have agreed with them.

Creating a potential space – 'playing' with cartoons

As referred to in Chapter 3, the first step in developing 'shared meaning communication' should be 'interpretation training' based on optical illusion cartoons as a tool. At this initial level, the group conductor (Foulkes and Foulkes 1990, p. 292) must be directive, since 'interpretation training' involves providing themes and situations for the group to work on. By building 'shared meaning communication', a group identity can also be established. From there, non-directive work will be more effective.

The introduction of the cartoons was done as a new and playful activity, such as: "Let's talk about what we can see!"

I remember well that everyone in the Theseus group were very astonished with my idea. So far, the group sessions had been very demanding, as they had been focused on personal problems only. Hence, the new activity was more than welcome by the group.

Before starting with the cartoons, I made it clear that there were two rules in this 'game' that had to be followed, which were:

- each member of the group, including me as a member of the group, had to honestly relate their perceptions/interpretations of the cartoons in the group without any inhibitions, even if their response sounded weird – after all, there was no right or wrong answer, and our aim was just to 'play';
- I was to be the last person to share my perceptions/interpretations – here the goals were first to give the patients freedom to play with their own ideas, to take full advantage of the created potential space, and second, to provide them with a final gestalt of the issues trigged by the cartoons in the group. To put it another way, the goals were to provide patients with verbal representations of the experienced transitional states of mind they had undergone between and within the group interaction.

The latter was the apex of the 'interpretation training', as in this regard, the therapist held a space in which to collect the emotional movements that had occurred in the group at that point and introduce interpretations connected to them and also to the treatment (Riesenberg-Malcolm 1999; Foulkes and Foulkes 1990), which was more effective and vivid. The role of the therapist as group conductor was to embrace the group and the experience of its members by creating calming, smoothing and safe individual and shared experience – a 'holding environment' (Winnicot 1955) whilst undertaking the role of a temporary container, by absorbing disruptive/confusing thoughts, feelings and behaviours without losing self-integration – the 'container' (Bion 1970, 1959). Indeed, presenting a final gestalt also meant making sense of what was going on in the group – reverie concept (Bion 1984).

To return to the previous point, the work with the cartoons was organized in two steps, namely identifying basic optical illusions and establishing the therapeutic setting.

First step in building communication: basic optical illusions

I first selected three types of optical illusion cartoons that covered three basic matters respectively: a) ambiguity; b) experience; and c) genetic issues. These three basic matters usually have an enormous impact on our perceptions/interpretations. Hence, I strongly recommend introducing additional cartoons just after raising awareness of these matters in the group.

1. The **"duck and rabbit"**: The earliest known version is an unattributed drawing dating back to 23 October 1892, issued by *Fliegende Blätter*, a German humour magazine. It refers to an ambiguous optical illusion cartoon in which an image of a rabbit or a duck can be concomitantly seen (Figure 4.1).

48　TICA in forensic settings

Figure 4.1 Duck/rabbit head

I presented the "duck and rabbit" cartoon whilst asking them: *"Look at this picture! Could you tell me please what you see?"* Most of them could first see the duck and then they were surprised to also realize the existence of a rabbit. The 'duck and rabbit' cartoon has the potential to teach the acceptance of ambiguity, the existence of different points of view, and everyone's right to think differently. It is a vivid illustration of how a simple drawing can trigger two diverse and justified interpretations (Perls 1969).

Following the discussion, I asked further: "Can you relate this picture to situations in your life?" It could certainly be applied to ordinary issues in life, like a discussion between partners. In fact, just like the cartoon, both parties in a relationship have the potential to be right in their point of view – it is just that each party sees the same issue differently, which is quite different from interpreting things as 'the other is against me'. Indeed, it can also be extended to therapeutic settings, as when the therapist brings a new understanding of a situation that apparently could sound weird to the patient.

In the Theseus group, the "duck and rabbit" cartoon was presented every time a conflict took place and stubbornness commanded the group's discussions. At that time, there were no words from my side. As 'group conductor', I just covered my face with the cartoon, in an effort to remind them of the importance of understanding each other's perspectives well enough to accept them, even though one may not agree with them. The effect was always fascinating – a long silence usually fell in the room followed by a more understanding discussion. I also gave them a printed copy of this cartoon for the purpose of providing them with a concrete object to take away from the group therapy session, which they could look at any time they wanted to – akin to a transitional object (Winnicott 1953). However, this was only an offer, and they were free to take it or not. All of them did take it.

2   The **"Love Poem of the Dolphins"** optical illusion cartoon by Sandro del Prete incorporates a figure/ground perceptual reversal – dolphins and a couple in a sensual position (Figure 4.2).

When I presented this illusion cartoon and said: "Look at this picture! Could you tell me please what you see?" there was a long silence in the room. They were afraid to tell me what they saw. The "Love Poem of the Dolphins" cartoon is an intriguingly complex optical illusion – indeed, a controversial one, due to the erotic image of a couple. Therefore, its use might trigger aversion from some forensic colleagues, who think that a therapist should not raise sexualized issues in the group, since they might turn into very dangerous issues – would that amount to a kind of taboo? From my point of view, the therapist needs to consider their aim in introducing such an image, whilst recalling what was discussed in Chapter 3: "As long as one is aware of one's own feelings and simultaneously has a clear understanding of the aim to be achieved, a situation of 'acting-out' will not be encouraged".

This optical illusion cartoon is therefore an extremely vivid example of how one's perceptions/interpretations are primed through experience. Young and innocent children will most likely perceive a group of dolphins, as they cannot recognize erotic scenes. Instead, they see nine dolphins. Adults, in contrast, will possibly see a couple in a suggestive embrace, due to their sexualized experiences. Indeed, some might have trouble perceiving the dolphins, which can be discovered by reversing the image – what might constitute the ground (the dark areas) becomes a group of small dolphins (the figures). In the end, the patients were more fixed in finding the dolphins than being properly stimulated by the image of a sensual couple. They were astonished by this peculiar illusion. To conclude, I invited them to reflect on the picture and I asked: "Can you relate this picture to your life and treatment?"

In fact, the experience triggered by the use of this cartoon can be viewed on two different levels:

a   The patients' quotidian perceptions/interpretations of society, family members, and partners. Here, the core point is rather that their perception, interpretation, and understanding of the external world could have started to be primed through their earlier failed experiences in life.

b   The therapists' perceptions and interpretations, specifically as regards running patients' treatment based only on ICD-10/DSM categorization. This does not dismiss the importance of a diagnosis; nevertheless, the therapist should keep in mind that each patient should be considered unique. Metaphorically speaking, the therapist should not fail to recall the perception of the dolphins.

It is valuable to address these two levels in an open group discussion. Furthermore, it is crucial for the treatment that in the discussions, the attention

Figure 4.2 Couple in the bottle

TICA in withdrawal therapy 51

should not lie only with the patients' behaviour, but also on the therapist's behaviour. In this way, the therapist turns into an active member of the group, instead of just being the conductor of it (Foulkes and Foulkes 1990).

3   The **"Ishihara Test"** – The Ishihara test is a colour perception test for red-green colour deficiencies (Figure 4.3). It was named after its designer, Shinobu Ishihara, a professor at the University of Tokyo, who first published his tests in 1917.

I presented this cartoon whilst asking them: "Look at this picture! Could you tell me please which number you see?" "The Ishihara's Test for Colour Deficiency" is a remarkable example of how one's perceptions/interpretations can be under the influence of genetic issues. To illustrate, a primary and secondary colour-blind person will see the number 3 in the picture instead of the number 8, due to the nuances of the pastel tones on the left side. Again, this experience can be turned into a basis for a discussion about the interplay of genetic issues and environment, such as whether or not one has complete free will in their behaviour (Sapolsky 2017; Worthman *et al*. 2010). Despite

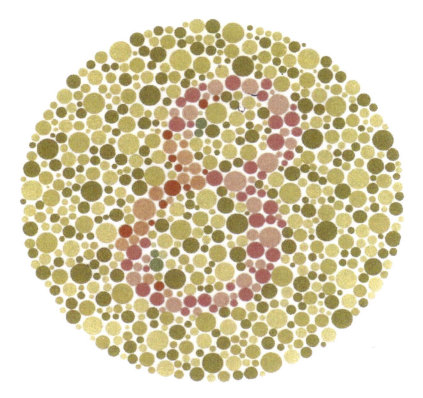

Figure 4.3 Platte with number 8

52 TICA in forensic settings

all genetic issues, one must cope with one's deficiencies over the course of one's life, while learning how to avoid trouble, like colour-blind people do. Acknowledging the significant impact of ambiguity, experience and genetic issues on our usual perception of the world can be defined as the prime source of interpretation training. From this moment onwards, it becomes easier to cope with different points of view in the group.

Second step in building communication: establishing the therapeutic setting

After the task involving the three optical illusion cartoons, it is essential to establish a therapeutic setting, which can be achieved through the introduction of two award-winning cartoon paintings. Evidently, one can also use other sorts of cartoons. In fact, the key point is to create a potential space in which the patients feel free to play with their own perceptions/interpretations in the group within a therapeutic setting (Winnicott *et al.* 1984, pp. 95–96; Winnicot 1971, pp. 38–52).

4   The **"Wallpaper"** award-winning cartoon painting by Mike Twohy (Figure 4.4).

   For the purpose of establishing a therapeutic setting, I presented the "Wallpaper" cartoon and said to the patients: "Look at this picture! Could you tell

Figure 4.4 Man wallpapering

me please what it means? What are your first impressions?" I received some quite interesting reactions. Some of them laughed at the situation, others said that the guy was weird, since he was wallpapering a false bookshelf, and some commented that actually the guy wanted to impress, demonstrating that he was a knowledgeable person. The discussion went further and deeper, as they ask themselves why someone would waste time by pretending. At this point, I invited them to look at the picture differently, then I asked:

> Can you relate this picture to the (your) treatment? What about pretending? The treatment is surely an optimal strategy for achieving a shortening of your sentence in a short period of time. Are you willing to learn anything from the treatment? Or is your aim focused just on shortening your sentence? Who are you trying to convince? Me, the therapist, the one who will write your reports for the court? What about trying to convince yourself? Why are you really here? Are you looking after your own (selfish) interests?

My questions trigged silence and, especially, reflections among the members of the group. In conclusion, the first step of the therapeutic setting was established – reflecting on the treatment's meaning whilst clarifying one's personal goal in undertaking it.

5. The **"Brennender Baum"** award-winning cartoon painting by Gehard Mester (Figure 4.5).

This cartoon is useful for establishing the second step of the therapeutic setting, which involves reflecting on the therapist's role, as well as on the patients' skills and tenacity. As soon as I presented this cartoon, most of the patients burst out laughing, then I asked them: "What does this picture mean? What do you think will happen? What do you think about the man? Is he crazy?" Some of the patients thought that the man was really crazy, as there was no sense in trying to save a tree that was already on fire, which indicated a hopeless situation. Others understood the man's behaviour as a sign of faith in a desperate situation, which also demonstrated similarities to a hopeless situation. Then, I introduced my usual question: "Can you relate this picture to the (your) treatment?". No one could answer me properly, other than comparing me to the crazy man in the cartoon due to my strange question. At this point, I invited them to listen to a few more details and told them:

> Yes, I look like the man in the picture . . . let's imagine this picture a little bit differently . . . let's think that you are the tree and the fire is your crime and addiction . . . they are consuming you . . . yes, I am here . . . I am the man . . . and I am watering your roots, because I believe in them . . . I believe that something good and strong inside you exists . . . but I cannot predict if your roots will be strong enough to bear the damage caused by the flames (crime and addictions) . . . but nonetheless, I do want to try!

Figure 4.5 Tree in flame

Silence fell in the room whilst some were close to tears. The second step of the therapeutic setting had been established – clarifying the roles and facing reality.

In conclusion, these five cartoons aroused the patients' own willingness to attend future sessions and play an active part. The persistent work with the cartoons was always based on enacting free association and fantasies ("What does this picture mean? What do you think will happen?"), whilst simultaneously connecting them with the 'here and now' ("Can you relate this picture to your treatment?") and lasted approximately one month. More award-winning cartoons are available online (https://sanalmuze.aydindoganvakfi.org.tr/competitions).

From cartoons to short films

The next stage of the 'interpretation training' involved exploring short films.

One needs to keep in mind that the act of watching a film is quite similar to the act of dreaming whilst awake, as films are mostly fantastical expressions. I usually refer to films as 'adult visual fairy tales'. However, the depth at which one can understand a film varies greatly. Indeed, one's understanding of a film will mostly be based on the representations of their own experience and fantasies – or metaphorically speaking, it will be connected to the kind of glasses one is wearing as to which grade of myopia one suffers. Therefore, watching a film and discussing it together afterwards in the group – like with the cartoons – yet again aimed to create a potential space to play with the patients' different fantasies. Another benefit of using films is that the emotions evoked by the films' plots can be discussed in depth in the group, without fear, since the discussion relates to an external object (the film) and not to me (the psychologist/therapist). However, with the help of the therapist (the group conductor), most of the emotional issues discussed in the film can also be transferred (or correlated) to the patients' real life in a much less threatening situation. Thus, the patients do not feel forced to start talking about their own emotions directly in the group.

The presentation of short films also lasted for a month. Table 4.3 illustrates 14 selected short films. Each film addressed a particular point to be discussed as a theme in the group, and the films were also ordered according to the sequence in which they were presented during the treatment.

I strongly suggest starting any work with films by highlighting the topic of aggression, since it is not only a controversial topic but it is also intrinsically connected to the patients' lives. I first selected films with plots dealing with aggression in the animal kingdom by highlighting, during the group discussion, the absence of revenge in their world, alongside the positive aspect and survival nature of their aggression. Then, films with plots handling contained/hidden human aggression were viewed – aggression which was capable of hurting whilst also firing the need for human revenge. Next, films with plots relating to a form of aggression that had been aroused from fear and low self-esteem, which can turn into self-destructive behaviour, were shown to the patients. Afterwards, films with plots focusing on children demonstrating aggression, which highlighted the importance and influence of a positive environment in their education, mainly as regards to adults as role models, were watched. Finally, films where the plots ended with children as victims of aggression were viewed. In this case, I selected one film in particular (see Table 4.3, Film 8) in which it was once more possible to relate the behaviour of wild animals to that of humans (as in the first film). I selected this film since this kind of comparison led to a livelier discussion. I highly recommend ending the topic of aggression by focusing on children, particularly on children as victims of aggression, since most forensic patients have experienced maltreatment and/or abuse in their childhood, and so they automatically transfer any feelings evoked by the film to their past memories and regressive experiences of aggression in their family, bringing these to the group for discussion. The discussion of this kind of shared experience creates a unique chance for the development of a group identity, since precisely at this moment, each member of the group feels welcomed and understood by the others, as they share the same pain from their past. This is a step forward in the group's communication (as the group is now more cohesive) and in the treatment. From this point onwards, the members of the group were ready to talk fearlessly about their own emotions in the group.

56 TICA in forensic settings

Table 4.3 List of films with internet links

Short film	Plot summary	General theme	Specific topics to be addressed in the group therapy
1 *Battle at Kruger* www.youtube.com/ watch?v=LU8DDYz68kM	Several buffaloes were grazing. Suddenly, lions came and all of them ran away, except the baby buffalo, who was easily caught as prey (by the lions). After some minutes, the buffalo returned with the entire herd. The herd did nothing against the lions until the baby buffalo got up and started walking by himself. Then several buffalo scattered the lions to rescue and protect the baby.	**Aggression:** raise awareness of aggression **Emotion:** control and purpose	The most important issue of the film is to draw attention to the natural aggression among animals, along with the wise reaction of the buffalo (the lack of revenge as well as their caution before defending the baby buffalo – they did not do anything as long as they were assured that the baby buffalo was alive). Reflection on the human need for revenge is crucial, as well as further reflection on the reasons for patients' offences (whether they were connected or not with feasible revenge).
2 *Elephant Birth in Bali* www.youtube.com/ watch?v=97CRwd_ U2FU&has_verified=1	The film shows a female elephant struggling to give birth to her baby. The scenes are compelling.	**Aggression:** raise awareness of aggression **Emotion:** emotion control and purpose	To point out the natural aggression towards life and growth instead of the aggression directed towards destruction and death is the central issue. Yet again, it is possible to reflect on the animal kingdom and human beings.

TICA in withdrawal therapy 57

| 3 | New McDonald's commercial www.youtube.com/ watch?v=G8AfZqK3Ur4 | A couple arrived at a lake by car. The wife was at the wheel and waited for her husband to get out of the car. He went fishing. Then she gave him a McDonald's paper bag with a very angry face. At the lake, the man then placed the McDonald's bag next to him while he was fishing. Suddenly, a monster appeared from the lake. The man just closed his eyes and expected to be devoured. However, the monster devours the McDonald's paper bag. The next day, the husband brought his wife with him to the lake. She looked very pleased to be with him. She held in her hands a new McDonald's paper bag and she was placed by her husband at the same place where the monster devoured the McDonald's paper bag the day before. | **Aggression:** raise awareness of the hidden aggression and further cold planned revenge
Social competence: the lack of communication in the relationship | The power of the cold and planned revenge, and avoidance of conflicts in the relationship and its consequences. |

(*Continued*)

58 TICA in forensic settings

Table 4.3 (Continued)

Short film	Plot summary	General theme	Specific topics to be addressed in the group therapy
4 *Suzuki Bikes Dog Walking* www.youtube.com/watch?v=WhKEGrPFsKE&list=UU7LrD103UaTxVcuNXny56uw&index=10&t=0s	The film starts with a couple leaving home early morning – the man is a budding motorcyclist who wants to go for a ride on his powerful motorcycle. Suddenly and before he was able to leave home, his wife comes to him and gives him the family's small dog which needed to be taken for a walk. The man is unable to say "No". He takes the dog and tries to drive the motorcycle very slowly so that the dog can accompany him. The woman watches his attempt with a happy face. However, when he turns the corner, we can hear him speeding up on the motorcycle while his wife starts screaming, due to the dog.	**Aggression:** raise awareness of the hidden aggression and further cold planned revenge **Emotion:** avoidance of conflict **Social competence:** fulfilling the expectations of the other person against one's own will	The film is an example of dark humour that promotes a very good discussion on two levels. The first level is connected to being in a relationship and the need to deal with fears, rage, expectations, frustrations, and also the consequence of a lack of communication in the relationship. The second level is the hidden aggression and disappointment.

TICA in withdrawal therapy 59

5	*Fly Bird Fly* www.youtube.com/ watch?v=9CgD8tIMSf4 	The film shows a school ceremony, in which a boy holds a dove tightly in his hands. The dove is meant to be released at the end of the ceremony, as a beautiful symbol of peace. At the release time, the dove falls dead to the ground.	**Aggression:** Feasible roots of aggression and involuntary aggression **Emotion:** the avoidance of fears. **Social competence:** fulfilment of the expectations of others	Going into detail about what the feelings of fear might trigger inside us, in the film's case the death of the dove – an involuntary form of aggression alongside the need to fulfil society's expectations are the central ideas for discussion about this film.
6	blz2 – www.youtube.com/ watch?v=2-xXDn0h0uM 	The film shows a number of young women, actresses, and models suffering from anorexia and/or bulimia in the name of beauty.	**Emotion:** fulfil external expectations, weak self **Aggression:** Self-injury, relapse, quality of life	To draw attention to the lack of self-reflection followed by the loss of self-awareness. The first scene shows an image of a fat girl in the mirror, then the focus is on of the anorexic girl in front of the mirror. This film allows a fruitful discussion about themes like self-injury (and its connection to drug consumption) and low self-esteem, always being related to patients' addiction.
7	*Child Friendly* www.youtube.com/ watch?v=3DmSFJkOtRU 	The film shows an adult always being followed by a child, who mimics all the adult's behaviour. Most of the behaviour is aggressive and covers a series of aggression levels, i.e., verbal, body, psychological, property damage, and addiction. At the end, a written message appears saying: "Children see . . . children do".	**Aggression:** The different types of aggression **Emotion:** anger, dissatisfaction, unhappiness, frustration, dependence **Social competence:** disrespect towards others, dominance over others	The film highlights not only the importance of keeping good and constructive role models for the children, but also the role of the environment in education. On the emotional level, this film might arouse the patients' childhood memories, and if they are verbalized in the group, they should be worked out.

(*Continued*)

Table 4.3 (Continued)

Short film	Plot summary	General theme	Specific topics to be addressed in the group therapy
8 Ministry of Social Affairs – Lebanon – Animals www.youtube.com/ watch?v=OzRI_m5gKWY	The film starts by showing a series of different animals caressing their young. The last animal to be shown is a panda, then the image of a little girl with a purple eye hugging a teddy bear appears (the girl was victim of aggression) and a written message: "Some kids wish their parents were animals".	**Aggression:** victim of aggression **Emotion:** affection, care, abandonment, loneliness, maltreatment **Quality of life:** comparison with animals and humans	Another moving film that leads to compassion for the hurt little girl – a victim of maltreatment. In the group, this film activates memories for those who were neglected or maltreated in childhood – an important moment in the group to be worked out.
9 Publi Tv – niños con cáncer www.youtube.com/ watch?v=T_i34m981-Y	The film shows a little girl waiting on a couch. Suddenly, she hears a noise and goes to the window and sees a car arriving. She runs to the bathroom, takes a pair of scissors and starts cutting her hair. The doorbells rings and she run to open the door. Her parents and her brother, who suffers from cancer, are standing at the door. Her parents look surprised to her, as she has a strange hairstyle. She gives her brother the hair she has cut, and her brother gives her the cap that covers his bald head.	**Emotion:** compassion, benevolence, generosity, love, loss **Social competence:** to put oneself in the other person's shoes, to care about the other person	The film is very moving – a brilliant exemplar to trigger discussion about emotion and social competence.

TICA in withdrawal therapy 61

| 10 | Graffiti – Pfizer commercial www.youtube.com/ watch?v=gVUkbRng7fo | The film starts with an adolescent walking on the streets at night whilst doing graffiti. When he arrives home early in the morning, his mother looks at the clock and seems to be unhappy with him, as he stayed the night away from home. He does not speak with his mother and goes to a bedroom and opens the bedroom windows. His sister, who is very sick, is lying on the bed in her bedroom. He opens the curtain in order to help her to look outside the window. Meanwhile, their mother comes into the bedroom and also looks outside the windows. The adolescent has graffitied some beautiful flowers on the walls in front of her bedroom. He also wrote "Be brave". The mother, who was angry with him, smiles and then says "Thanks" to her son. | **Emotion:** compassion, benevolence, generosity, love, expectation **Social competence:** to put oneself in the other person's shoes, to care about the other person, not to judge hastily | Like the previous film, this one is also very moving. However, the scene when the mother seems to be unhappy with her son because she has come to her own conclusions about his night away from home is an interesting point for discussion mainly as regards to pre-concepts and pre-ideas about the other person in the relationship. Also, the mother's silence as a way to avoid conflict is an interesting point to be addressed. |

(Continued)

Table 4.3 (Continued)

Short film	Plot summary	General theme	Specific topics to be addressed in the group therapy
11 Butterfinger commercial www.youtube.com/watch?v=9E8c5IYaO04	The film starts with an old man tasting a Butterfinger™ while an old woman observes him doing so, showing that she's hungry. The old man decides to share his Butterfinger™ and gives her half of it. The old woman looks at the Butterfinger™ on the table and still shows that she's hungry. Then the old man smiles and takes out his teeth and lends them to her. The old woman smiles, showing that she's pleased.	**Emotion:** compassion, benevolence **Social competence:** to put oneself in the other person's shoes, to care of the other person	The film also demonstrates a dark sense of humour in a disgusting way. However, it is so cute how the old man puts himself in the old woman's shoes that it opens a very good discussion. It is recommended to present this film just after films 3 and 4 in the table, as this allows for a discussion about the types of relationship between couples in all the films. It is also possible to connect the discussion to the ordinary problems in relationships in real life.
12. INPES Free Hugs www.youtube.com/watch?v=MDWL8z0_wBA	The film shows a man on the street holding a sign which reads "FREE HUGS" while waiting for people to come to him and give him a hug.	**Emotion:** shame, trust, affection, lack of affection, feeling of belonging **Social competence:** compassion	The key point of this film is the different reactions of people towards the man who is asking for a hug (asking for affection). Posing the question: "What is more difficult: showing anger or asking for affection?" evokes a very good group discussion.

TICA in withdrawal therapy 63

13. *Sand Art Love 2008* www.youtube.com/ watch?v=orLB-yzUntE 	A love story is presented through sand art.	**Emotion:** love, transformation, losses	This film is very expressive and triggers in the viewer the experience of transformations and transience, which can be related to the features of the treatment.
14. *Centre Stage TV CCTV9* www.youtube.com/ watch?v=OdWVgobALZc 	A 'physically impaired' couple of ballet dancers, (she without an arm and he without a leg) dance in a theatre.	**Social competence:** Self-assurance	This is a moving example of willingness, determination, and self-love, and is a very good piece to be related to the aims of the treatment.

The next step was to present film plots with more expressive emotional attachment, e.g., children's/adolescents' responses towards siblings who suffer from cancer, the companionship of old couples, people's attitudes towards a public request for affection, an ordinary love story and finally the willingness to go beyond one's personal limits. The latter was intended to relate to the patients' willingness to go beyond their addiction. In other words, the extent to which they were prepared to fight to achieve their aims. I can clearly remember that when addressing this issue, I highlighted the personal resilience involved in dealing with frustration, and I called upon my case as an 'Outsider' to illustrate. I said:

> Keeping clean involves a daily struggle . . . it is similar to my case . . . I am a foreigner . . . I cannot speak German well, as I was not born here and I only stared learning German at the end of my 30s . . . so, every day, when I get up, I need to tell myself . . . "You are not a German and you do not speak German well, thus today you will experience situations in which people will not understand what you are saying and they might also think that you are not able to understand them, even though you do. You might get angry, but you decided to live in this country . . . you need to be strong!" . . . We can transfer this situation to your case . . . You get up clean today, but you should be aware that you might experience frustrating situations in your day-to-day life that will not only annoy you but also might trigger your desire to take drugs again . . . but you decided to keep clean . . . you need to be strong!

Furthermore, the focus needed to be shifted to the situation in the here and now (Riesenberg-Malcolm 1999), so that patients could start appreciating the significance of 'shared meaning communication'.

After two months of 'interpretation training' with cartoons and short films, the members of the Theseus group became more patient, thoughtful, reflective, and analytical. They started arriving to the group's meeting room early, eager to learn more in (and with) the group, and also to develop a group identity. The most impressive illustration of the latter was their request to change the name of the group after two months.

From Theseus to Dalva

One day, Mr. M. posed a question to the group: "Why is our group called Theseus?" No one was able to answer his question properly and so I just explained what the name 'Theseus' means – a legendary Ancient Greek hero most famous for defeating the Minotaur in the labyrinth of Crete.

At that point, Mr. M. answered: "But this name has nothing to do with us".

The others immediately agreed with Mr. M. and I asked them: "OK! What would you like to do?" They were unanimous: "Let's change the group name! We want a name that represents us!" This was clearly part of a search for their identity. Then, they started discussing which name it could be. Mr. R. wanted the name

'Avatar', but the others did not want a name from a film – they wanted a unique one, one that belonged only to them. They were looking for a name that could represent hope for them, like when one looks at the sky and can see a star shining, bringing light and courage. At this point, I interrupted the discussion and asked them: "What is the German name of the star that appears on the east side, just before dawn, also called the dawn star? This star is the planet Venus and shines clearly just before the sunrise. I do not know its German name, but in Portuguese we call it the 'Dalva star'!"

Suddenly they said: "That is it! 'Dalva'! A nice name! We can call our group 'Dalva'. Why not?"

I replied saying: "Yes, you could; however, 'Dalva' is a female name". They were thoughtful for a few seconds, and then Mr. M. replied: "It doesn't matter! Actually, our psychologist comes from Brazil and speaks Portuguese! Why don't we have a female Portuguese name that could represent her?" They were unanimous, and from this day on, the group was referred to by all participants as Dalva and they started to sign the name Dalva in all their written homework and the gift cards they drew as illustrated in Chapter 10.

From my point of view, this moment represented not only the beginning of the group's identity but also proof that language issues were not a barrier between us anymore.

A common transitional object is established

From this point onwards, Dalva was ready to face new challenges. So, I started to show them full-length films, with the purpose of creating a potential space for processing their emotional world on specifics themes, i.e.: aggression, feelings/relationships, social competence, addiction, offences, and relapse, all of which were linked to the themes of the treatment. Through the introduction of full-length films, it was possible to follow the process of reflexive interrogations used previously with cartoons and short films. However, the reflections were now more detailed and referred to the dynamics of the characters' relationships during the course of the films, and these reflections were once more transferred to the group's dynamic in the *here and now*. At this point, the interpretations of the films turned into more introspective homework. All the films, without exception, were accompanied by a questionnaire, like the ones attached in the appendices to this chapter. By answering the questionnaire, the patients first had to reflect on the film by themselves and then in the group. Each block of films required approximately six group meetings. Table 4.4 illustrates several of the full-length films selected, with the focus point to be addressed as a theme in the group's discussion. The films were also ordered according to the sequence in which they were presented during the treatment.

I advise starting this work with films by selecting full-length motion pictures that draw attention to the topic of feelings/relationships and relating them to the group's dynamic and the treatment.

Table 4.4 List of films

Film	Plot summary	General themes connected to the treatment	Specific topics to be addressed in the group therapy
Bagdad Café (Percy Adlon 1987)	The film focuses on building relationships. It starts with a German couple's road trip, which is not how Jasmin (one of the main characters) had imagined her vacation in sunny California. Without speaking, the frustrated wife gets out of the car after an argument with her husband. She grabs one of the suitcases and from that point onwards makes her way through the scorching heat on her own. At the end of her tether, she finally comes across a motel run by Brenda called "Bagdad Café" and takes a room there. When Jasmin opens her suitcase, however, she experiences an unpleasant surprise: it is her husband's suitcase. The strange clothing further reinforces Brenda's suspicious attitude towards her. Brenda has to struggle with her own husband herself and has to take care of her family practically alone. Through honest communications, Jasmin and Brenda find out more and more about each other and also the café experiences an undreamt-of blossoming. But with Jasmin's visa soon to expire, the local sheriff appears on the scene and seems to put an abrupt end to the idyll.	Emotion, social competence, self-assurance, and quality of life	Building relationships: Jasmin's efforts to get to know all the residents of the motel whilst developing a new communication and developing deeper relationships with all of them, despite Brenda' suspicious (fears). In the end, Brenda becomes Jasmin's best friend. The scenes with the boomerang: a returning boomerang is designed to return to the thrower, and that was made very clear in the film. Metaphorically speaking, the boomerang can be perceived as a symbol of the bond what would develop between Jasmin and Brenda. At a certain point of the film, Jasmin needs to leave the United States as her visa has expired (the thrown boomerang). However, after some months, she comes back (the returning boomerang). Associations with the treatment: What does the term 'relationship' mean to you? Can you trust another person? Can you trust your therapist? In your treatment?

TICA in withdrawal therapy 67

Ladyhawke (Richard Donner 1985)	The film shows a couple in love struggling to keep their love alive, despite all adversities. By the spell of the jealous bishop of Aquila, the beautiful Isabeau d'Anjou and the noble knight Etienne Navarre are separated. During the day, Isabeau transforms into a hawk, while the night turns Navarre into a wolf. Only for a few minutes each at sunrise and sunset can the lovers meet in human form. They journey together day and night in solitude – by day a noble knight with his hawk, by night a beautiful woman with her wolf. Their love seems doomed to fail, but with the shrewd pickpocket Philippe, a form of rescue approaches: on his escape from the criminal bishop's henchmen, he meets the tragic couple and becomes the lone wolf's squire. Thanks to him, the two can at least exchange news again – and they gain new hope. Philippe and an old monk (who in the past had betrayed the couple and has now become a kind of witch) convince them to declare war on the bishop's black magic, as there is a remote chance of breaking the spell.	Emotion, social competence, self-assurance, aggression, and relapse	The couple completely relies on Philippe. They not only trust him with their secret spell, but also trust him as a person who will be able to protect them. For instance, Navarre gives Philippe the injured hawk to be saved, sure that Philippe will make it, even though Philippe does not know either the way to reach the old monk or to whom should he give the hawk to be cared for. Associations with the treatment: The meaning of trust How far should the therapist rely on their forensic patients as regards their genuine desire to be treated? How does one feel when no one trusts them due to their offence? Comparison with the Philippe role.
The Bucket List (Rob Reiner 2007)	The film focuses on relationship building whilst facing adversities. Billionaire Edward Cole and car mechanic Carter Chambers are complete strangers, until fate lands them in the same hospital room – two terminally ill men left with only six months to live. They make a bucket list comprising all the things they have never tried before. Against their doctor's advice, they leave the hospital and head off on a road trip to explore life before they die.	Emotion, social competence, self-assurance and quality of life	Recognition and respect for the boundaries in a relationship: Which personal boundaries do I set for myself? Which personal boundaries does one person set for themselves? How do I know when I have crossed another's boundaries? What does mutual respect mean?

(Continued)

68 TICA in forensic settings

Table 4.4 (Continued)

Film	Plot summary	General themes connected to the treatment	Specific topics to be addressed in the group therapy
			Different ways of dealing with negative issues in life, such as one's impotence against a terminal illness and further losses. Associations with the treatment: Do you feel impotent against your addiction? Can you recognize another's boundary? What about yours?
You, Me and Dupree (Anthony Russo and Joe Russo 2006)	The film portrays different levels of relationships involving conflict. Carl and Molly Peterson are newly married and are looking forward to a good time together in their new home. There's nothing that could disturb this harmony – except Randy Dupree, Carl's somewhat pushy best friend, who suddenly appears at the door. Dupree is unemployed, homeless and broke. Carl takes pity on him and temporarily offers him the living room couch as his sleeping place. But that doesn't last long, because soon the chaotic lodger turns the Petersons' peaceful house into an uninhabitable disaster area.	Emotion, social competence, self-assurance, anti-aggression, and quality of life	Recognition and respect of the boundaries in a relationship. Which personal boundaries do I set for myself? Which personal boundaries does one person set for themselves? How do I know when I have crossed another's boundaries? What does mutual respect mean? The negative consequences of avoiding conflict in a relationship, mainly when the avoidance is based on fears of limiting the other person's freedom Associations with the treatment: Have you ever had fears about setting your own boundaries? What about fears concerning crossing another's boundaries?

TICA in withdrawal therapy 69

| The Terminal (Steven Spielberg 2004) | The film is based on a true story. When Viktor Navorski, a visitor from the fictional Eastern European country of Krakosia, lands at New York's JFK airport, war breaks out in his country and he finds himself caught up in international politics. Since his passport is thus invalidated, the Department of Homeland Security won't let him enter or exit the United States. He is forced to settle down indefinitely in the terminal where he has arrived. It will be his second, if not first home. At the beginning, Victor can hardly speak a word of English. This leads him into many hopeless situations. Over time, he teaches himself the language and is able to communicate more and more with people. But even though Victor is always the outsider at the airport, he has a pure soul, which makes him popular among the airport employees. But the director of the facility is a thorn in the side of the uninvited guest, and he tries by all means possible to get rid of Victor. | Emotion, social competence, self-assurance, hidden aggression, and quality of life | Viktor's good nature is the central point of the plot. Every day, Viktor fights the obstacles of the airport authorities to get to his goal. His determination to understand what is going on around him and to communicate with those around him, his loyal patriotism; all this leads him to gain the trust and admiration of all the airport workers, thus building new reliable relationships. The film is a clear example of the development of a 'shared meaning communication' and its importance. Associations with the treatment: How have you been dealing with obstacles in your life? What about your drug consumption? Are you loyal to yourself like Viktor is to himself? |

(Continued)

Table 4.4 (Continued)

Film	Plot summary	General themes connected to the treatment	Specific topics to be addressed in the group therapy
Take the Lead (Liz Friedlander 2006)	The film is based on a true story. For dance teacher Pierre Dulaine, dancing is the most important thing in life. In his dance school, he teaches wealthy children and adults standard dances such as the waltz, foxtrot, and tango. One day, after a gala, when he sees teenager Jason Rockwell randomly vandalizing a car in the street, he confronts the boy and is shocked at how disrespectful and hopeless the boy is. This experience stimulates Dulaine to want to do something for these boys and girls from the problem districts of the Inner City. Dulaine wants to teach them inner poise, respect for the others, dignity, self-confidence, trust, and teamwork through classical dance. Dulaine's background at first without doubt clashes with that of his students. Far from being discouraged, Dulaine melds their hip-hop moves with his classical style, helping them to create a dance form and, in the process, becoming their mentor.	Emotion, social competence, self-assurance, anti-aggression.	Dulaine's determination to develop a shared meaning communication with his students via dance is a key issue of this film. In doing so, the diversities present among the students can be worked out. Associations with the treatment: How open minded are you? What does 'accept someone for who they are' mean? What does the word 'diversity' mean to me? How do I deal with diversities? Do I perceive diversities as dilemmas?

FURTHER FILM SUGGESTIONS

The Last of the Mohicans (Michael Mann 1992)
The Last Samurai (Edward Zwick 2003)
The King's Speech (Tom Hooper 2010)
The Devil's Advocate (Taylor Hackford 1997)

The Elephant Man (David Lynch 1980)
Inside Out (Pete Docter 2015)
The Intouchables (Oliver Nakache and Eric Toledano 2011)
Empire of the Sun (Steven Spielberg 1987)
Nell (Michael Mann 1992)
Interview with the Vampire (Neil Jordan 1994)
Rain Main (Barry Levinson 1988)

Film references

Bagdad Cafe, 1987. Directed by Percy Adlon: Bayerischer Rundfunk, Hessischer Rundfunk, Pelemele Film, Project Filmproduktion.

The Bucket List, 2007. Directed by Rob Reiner: Castle Rock Entertainment, Warner Bros. Pictures.

The Devil's Advocate, 1997. Directed by Taylor Hackford: Regency Enterprises, Warner Bros.

The Elephant Man, 1980. Directed by David Lynch: Brooksfilms, Columbia – EMI – Warner Distributors, Paramount Pictures.

Empire of the Sun, 1987. Directed by Steven Spielberg: Amblin Entertainment, Warner Bros.

Inside Out, 2015. Directed by Pete Docter: Walt Disney Pictures, Pixar Animation Studios.

Interview with the Vampire, 1994. Directed by Neil Jordan: The Geffen Film Company, Warner Bros.

The Intouchables, 2011. Directed by Oliver Nakache and Eric Toledano: Gaumont/TF1 Films Production, Quad Productions.

The King's Speech, 2010. Directed by Tom Hooper: UK Film Council, Momentum Pictures, Paramount Pictures.

Ladyhawke, 1985. Directed by Richard Donner: Warner Bros Pictures, and 20th Century Fox.

The Last of the Mohicans, 1992. Directed by Michael Mann: Morgan Creek Entertainment, 20th Century Fox, Warner Bros.

The Last Samurai, 2003. Directed by Edward Zwick: Radar Pictures, The Bedford Falls Company, Cruise, Wagner Productions, Warner Bros Pictures.

Rain Man, 1988. Directed by Barry Levinson: United Artists.

Take the Lead, 2006. Directed by Liz Friedlander: Tiara Blu Films, New Line Cinema.

The Terminal, 2004. Directed by Steven Spielberg: Amblin Entertainment, Parkes, MacDonald Productions, DreamWorks Pictures.

You, Me and Dupree, 2006. Directed by Anthony Russo and Joe Russo: Avis-Davis Productions, Stuber-Parent Productions, Universal Pictures.

I started with the film *Bagdad Café* (Percy Adlon 1987) since it has a useful plot for focusing on the meaning of being an 'Outsider', depicting the impact of this on developing and ending relationships – common issues among the members of the group. The topic of 'being an Outsider' should not be neglected; quite the opposite. From the beginning, it should be openly discussed in the group to better develop 'shared language/shared meaning'. Experiencing the diverse perspectives and feelings on this topic in the group is very thought-provoking. See the questionnaire in appendices.

Coincidently, the most significant impact of *Bagdad Café* on the Dalva group was surprisingly the unexpected creation of a common shared group symbol, which towards the end, turned into a common transitional object – namely 'the boomerang'.

Throughout the film, more precisely between takes, a young Australian man playing with his returning boomerang appears several times. In reality, the movement of a returning boomerang expresses the confidence of throwing and returning. Thus, one of the questions for their homework (in the questionnaire; see Appendix 4.1) was: "What did the boomerang mean? (The metaphor)". Most of the patients could not answer this question, as they thought that the question did not make any sense, since the scenes of the young man playing with the boomerang did not seem to be connected to the film's plot. A few, however, reflected on the influence of one's actions on one's own life, such as, what *one does, can return to one*. In the film, the returning boomerang metaphorically embodies the core feature of the relationship between the protagonists – the basis of confidence and trust in their relationship. When I told them that the boomerang represented the core feature of the protagonists' relationship, all of them asked me whether I might be 'high'. They were impressed with my interpretation, with the representation of my experience and fantasies. After a long discussion, they agreed that my fantasies were grounded. However, from that moment onwards, the word 'boomerang' turned into Dalva's common symbol, which meant *the ability to be high without drugs*. The 'boomerang' had become a common everyday term in our vocabulary, at least in their homework, when I introduced a thought-provoking question. I usually introduced this as though I were interacting with them, such as: "This is a small boomerang . . . are you happy with the boomerang?" or "Now comes BOOMERANG !". The *Ladyhawke* questionnaire (see Appendix 4.2) illustrates well what I mean. More than this, the representational meaning of the boomerang has been transferred from the therapeutic setting to a transitional object outside the therapy after a patient's release. Until this point, all the patients had received a stone on their release – a traditional transitional object that was supposed to symbolize strength and steadfastness against the drugs consumption. In Dalva's group, the stone was replaced by a boomerang key chain (see Figure 4.6) and also by the motto "The ability to be high without drugs. No matter what one does, one might always go back to them".

The *Bagdad Cafe* film may be perceived as a vivid illustration of the 'shared meaning communication' achieved – the acknowledgement of the Transient Interactive Communication Approach (TICA).

Figure 4.6 Boomerang key chain

The second film we worked through was *Ladyhawke* (Donner 1985), and although I was quite sure that it would be too romantic for all of them, my goal was not to drawn attention to the romance between the protagonists, rather to the reliable relationship with a criminal – a young pickpocket. The emphasis, as illustrated in the questionnaire (see Appendix 4.2), rested on connecting the topic's feelings/relationships to social competence whilst bringing the patients to reflect on the development of reliable relationships – an important issue for successful treatment.

Following this, we worked through *The Bucket List* (Reiner 2007); *You, Me and Dupree* (Anthony Russo and Joe Russo 2006); *Take the Lead* (Friedlander 2006); *The Terminal* (Steven Spielberg 2004) and other films. *The Terminal* was Dalva's favourite film, as it not only illustrates the protagonist's struggle as an 'Outsider', but also his need of achieving 'shared meaning communication' in order to survive. I kept using films until my last working day with the group. I also made effective use of the films when I was on holiday – interpreting the films was their homework. In this context, the films had the ability of replace the therapist's absence with the presence of a transitional object, and according to the staff, they had never before experienced a group of patients that was so willing to do their homework in the absence of their therapist as Dalva was.

Dalva faces a daunting challenge – a member of the group is a child sex offender

As previously mentioned, by the end of the admission phase, the patients should have dealt with the history of their addiction and delinquency. Therefore, they should have presented a written report of it first to the psychologist in their individual therapy and second to the group in group therapy. Up to this point, the members of the group did not know anything specific about each other's criminal records.

In the case of Mr. B., he had to face his offence and he knew that introducing himself to the group as a child sex offender would be similar to a death sentence.

In the individual sessions, the key discussion point concerned his grave doubts as to whether in the group presentation he should just talk about his previous offences while neglecting to mention the last one – the child sex abuse. At that point, we worked through the pros and cons of telling the truth or omitting it intensively. The latter, in fact, did not intend to lie, but rather to use a strategy of avoiding conflict or even to apply a survive strategy, as the rules for child sex offenders in prison were well defined. In addition, this situation also related to the significance of facing one's own reality, one's position in it and one's awareness about 'who am I?'.

Although it was an extremely delicate and dangerous matter, again I offered him the freedom to decide, even though I was aware that the trust of the group members under my supervision could be damaged. This damage was almost inevitable. If Mr. B. decided to keep his offence hidden, then I would be a traitor for harbouring a lie). If he decided to tell the truth, then I would be the one who had protected him until now. Surely my role would be placed into doubt. Whatever situation was likely to unfold, in the end, my position towards him was:

> It is your decision and not mine. As we saw, there are pros and cons. The only thing I am able to do is to make my position clear as a group conductor.
>
> So, if you decide to keep your offence hidden, Dalva's trust in me will be at risk because if by chance the truth comes out, they will know that I already knew; thus, this will mean that I, in a way, also betrayed them. Hence, I am going to face further difficulties in working out this delicate situation in the group, as their trust in me will be damaged. Things will not be different if by chance you decide to tell the truth to the group, as I might be perceived by the group as the one who protected you until now. Yet, I assure you that if this is the case, I will support you and will be with you along your journey in dealing with this taboo and the group.
>
> So please, just let me know your decision before the group starts.

I also made it clear to him that supporting him was related to one of the treatment's aims, which was to develop one's ability to understand each other's perspectives well enough to accept them, even if one may not agree with them. Therefore, in this sense, the truth about his offence might have posed a daunting challenge for the Dalva group.

As he was still insecure about his decision, he prepared two different presentations of his offences for the group. However, a day before the group meeting, he asked me for an extra individual session, as he wanted to inform me of his decision – he had decided to say the truth and cope with the group's reaction. Indeed, the assurance of my support as group leader had given him strength.

The group's reaction was divided. Despite the shared surprise at the Mr. B.'s disclosure, Mr. M. and Mr. R. showed their understanding, and from Mr. M.'s point of view, Mr. C.'s offence was worse than Mr. B.'s offence. Mr. C., in his turn, was silent and impartial. In contrast, Mr. T. and Mr. S. were completely against Mr. B. and urged the others to expel Mr. B. from the group.

I started posing them inquisitive questions, in the same way I had done in the past with the cartoons and films. My first question was:

"Let me understand please . . . why does Mr. B. need to be expelled from the group?"

The expected answer came from Mr. T. and Mr. S.:

"Because he is a sex offender; worse than this, he is a child sex offender!"

Then I replied:

"But I still cannot understand . . . up to now Mr. B. has been very welcomed in Dalva group, and everyone here has gotten along quite well with him, mainly you Mr. T. He is not a bad person, is he?"

MR. T.: "Yes you are right, Mrs. F., but up to now I did not know who he really was, nor what he had done . . . this changes everything . . . !"
ME: "So, let me see if I've got this right . . . for as long as you did not know about his offence, he was considered to be a good person, but from now on, since he is a sex offender, he becomes a bad person and does not deserve respect anymore . . . ?"
MR. T. AND MR. S.: "Yes, exactly! This is the prison rule; you should have known that!"
ME: "Yes, you are right . . . . actually, I did know . . . I just imagined that after such a long time working together in the group that perhaps you would have learnt more about how to understand each other's perspectives well enough to accept them, even if you did not agree with them . . . but I see that not all of you have learnt this . . . This is OK . . . . by the way, I still have a question . . ."
MR. T. AND MR. S.: "Yes, go ahead . . ."
ME: "Thinking about the moment from which the group gives itself the right to judge a person for his crime and not for who the person really is, could I use the same method of judgement with respect to each member of this group? I mean, from now on, I could start treating all of you according to your crimes and not as individuals anymore, as I have done until now . . . after all, this is the rule in prison, correct?"

Although this might have been dangerous, here, I was trying to trigger a mirroring effect, based on the 'affect attunement' idea (Stern 1995). In fact, I was trying to demonstrate the close ties within the group. Mr. S. was the first to respond to my statement.

MR. S.: "No, please, Mrs. F.; do not do that . . . hey everyone, I am not willing to be treated like a criminal!"

Mr. M., Mr. R., and Mr. C. agreed completely with Mr. S. Mr. T. was thoughtful at first, and then he replied.

MR. T.: "OK, I am not willing to be treated like a criminal either. So, Mrs. Franieck, I will accept Mr. B. in the group and will work together with him as long as I am receiving treatment . . . but don't ask me to greet him on the street after my release. I agree to having him in the group due to Dalva's principles".

ME: "Your decisions after your release are yours and yours alone. 'Here and now', we have a group, Dalva, and I need to know how I should progress with it!"

The group ended with a commitment – we would do our best to work together as a group, considering each other as a person and not as an offender, although I did need one more session to settle all the emotion still present, relating to this topic. In addition, I was quite careful in raising this topic in the first group session of the week, in order to ensure I could 'be with' the members of the group, rather than leaving them alone with this volatile situation over the weekend. This risky situation, for me, was one last piece of evidence for the interpretation training. Here, it was possible to assess the presence or absence of 'shared meaning communication', along with the flexibility and adaptability of thoughts, as well as the ability to grasp reality as it presents itself. It is true that the Dalva members were divided at the beginning due to their different levels of maturity. Still, in the end, Mr. T. and Mr. S. were able to understand my point of view about not expelling Mr. B. well enough to accept him in the group, even if they did not agree with his offence. Indeed, this risky situation also triggered a potential room (transitional space) for an open discussion about: levels of acceptance, bias, identity, and freedom of choice.

The last piece of homework

Two months before my departure, I took a three-week holiday during the Christmas season. At this point (after 14 months), the members of Dalva were mature enough to continue on their own. As usual, I had prepared a series of tasks and films to be performed and watched as homework during my holiday. However, as this would be the last piece of homework for the Dalva group, I decided to add in something different. So, among the papers I had used to prepare their homework, there was one item of homework with the following instructions:

> Now, you should organize a group presentation on the theme of social skills for Mrs. Franieck.
> The presentation can be a lecture, where you will be the teacher and Mrs. Franieck will be the student, and you can indeed set lots of homework for Mrs. Franieck!
> You can also prepare a play (theatre piece) . . . if you wish.
> Use your boomerang, please!!!! ☺
> The most important thing is that all patients should take part in the presentation.
> The presentation will take place in the first group session after Mrs. Franieck's holiday.
> Good Luck!!

In fact, I was intending to give them the freedom either of taking revenge on me due to all the annoying homework I had set, or of giving wings to their imagination whilst trusting in their creativity.

To sum up, they performed a true-to-life play. The play's plot was about the daunting challenge they might have to face after their release from prison. All emotions relating to their wishes, biases, and frustrations were addressed, as was – and above all – the loneliness of their struggle. It was an impressive illustration of their maturity, as well as their capacity to play with ideas.

I recall well that before they performed the play for me, they had given a preview of it to one of my colleagues in order to establish whether I would like it. My colleague was very impressed with Dalva's maturity and invited them to perform the play at the 'prison open day'. Surprisingly, they refused the invitation, as according to them, the play belonged to Dalva's closed community, and hence it was not a play to be made available to other people. In other words, the members of Dalva were not only aware of the existence of 'shared meaning communication' in the group, but also of its significance, as well as the value of a group identity.

I hope it is clear that all of the group's achievements over the course of the treatment are solely down to the patients' skills and that my role was just to propound a new form of communication – a Transient Interactive Communication Approach (TICA). The main characteristic of this approach to forensic withdrawal therapy is to suggest an external and concrete object – e.g., cartoons, films, etc. – as a channel of communication, whilst offering a playful free space to the patients, similar to a transitional area, where communication will happen. This approach is entirely suitable and also recommended for group settings in withdrawal therapy, though it demands the therapist's ability to perform the reverie function (Bion 1984, 1984/1970; Cassorla 2018) during the group sessions.

Follow up

Three years after my departure, of the six patients that underwent the 13 months of treatment in the Dalva group, three had still kept in touch with one of the nursing staff, whereas the other three only got in touch sporadically. At that time, the former were clean, working and in relationships. As regards the latter, they had at least not been rearrested.

About five years later, I accidently met Mr. S. on the street. He was together with a 'brother'. He was very pleased to meet me and introduced me to his 'brother' as his therapist and started to update me on his current living situation; for example, he told me about becoming a father, as well as about his current drug consumption – "Just marijuana, Mrs. F.; nothing else, I swear!" His 'brother' was embarrassed by the situation, and suddenly Mr. S. said to his 'brother': "You don't need to be afraid . . . she is my therapist . . . you could tell her everything . . . she was always behind me . . ." But since that setting was not a therapeutic one anymore, I just listened to him briefly and said I was in a hurry. He understood my position and we cordially said goodbye. However, it is worth realizing that he was able to understand a positive representation of his time in treatment.

Some personal observations

On group work

I think it is worth sharing that each group session was characterized by two short rituals – one at the beginning of the session – a warm-up conversation, initiated by the question: "How am I doing today?" – and a second one about ten minutes before the end of the group with the aim of summarizing the experiences triggered in the group. Hence, everyone had to comment on the question: "How was the group today?". In fact, in my view, the patients need a take away from each group session, as this might represent 'Hope' (Havel and Hvížďala 1991) of keeping their experiences inside.

I would also like to share some observations and advice as regards leading, or in Foulkes and Foulkes' words (1990, pp. 292–293) "conducting a group", which is mostly based on my personal experience and reflections on my role as a conductor, rather than on scholarly precision.

From my training as a psychodynamic psychotherapist, I have learned that the therapist should remain neutral whilst in contact with the patient, which requires giving as little information as possible about the therapist's private life, along with the therapist not raising any of their personal issues during the interaction with the patient. I completely agree with this, however, one needs to keep in mind that these general conditions can be easily met in a private analytical praxis context, where the therapist is more able to control external variables. However, in a prison or a big organization, the therapist comes into contact with a large number of colleagues/co-workers, and even though the therapist might try to keep a purely professional relationship with them, they nonetheless have access to some information about the therapist's private life (i.e., place of residence and some family details, such as marital status, number of dependents, etc.). Indeed, they probably have not completed psychotherapist training, and therefore commenting innocently about the therapist's private life with the patients would not be considered as disruptive by them. I remember once – in the second week of the cartoon work – that my group found out where I lived, as I had previously said that I lived in a city 75 km from my job and had to start my journey every day at 6 am in order to get at work at 7 am. Once, due to a heavy snowstorm, I got at work two hours late. On this day, my colleagues told the patients where I lived, so that they would understand why I was so late. Hence, keeping private matters private is something that one cannot have complete control over. Things like this just happen, and when they do, the therapist should be flexible enough to deal with this properly and convert this situation into something suitable for the treatment, instead of wasting time by trying to keep the neutral setting.

I recall well that on this day, the group's core topic was the distance that I had to travel daily to get to work, as well as my delay. The latter was discussed with reference to whether I had broken the group's rule – 'be punctual', which was quite true, and so their point had to be considered. The challenging point of this discussion was the strict attitude of some members of the group with regard to my tardiness – in fact, they could not forgive me.

According to them, I should have left home two hours before my normal departure time, in order to get to work on time, after all, there was a snowstorm – that is, I would have had to have started my journey at 4:00 am. This was a situation that opened up a range of possibilities for me as a therapist working in a group, at a moment when I was at the beginning of the 'interpretation training', i.e., idealization of the therapist, handling the therapist's failures, dealing with frustration, handling our lack of control in life (snowstorms, the control over the therapist's private life), and facing the consequences of our actions. In brief, I took advantage of this moment to link all these themes to their treatment through reflection.

Therefore, my message here is: it is worthwhile remaining neutral in the relationship with patients. However, sometimes working in organizations, we are unable to control all variables for this to be achieved. If this is the case, then I suggest the threatening situation of losing neutrality be converted into something constructive for the group. The therapist's inner security in threatening situations also has a positive effect on the treatment.

Still with regards to the theme of neutrality, another point is that when the therapist does not feel emotionally well enough to conduct the group due to problems in his or her private life, the therapist should notify the patients before starting the session that today, his or her contributions in the group might be not as significant, since he or she is not in a good mood due to issues relating to beyond the group. Indeed, it must be made clear that this will not be an issue for discussion in the group; rather, it is a useful piece of information that aims to avoid miscommunication in the group. That is to say, the patients have the right to know that the conductor is only human and therefore also susceptible to the influence of negative emotions, caused by personal issues, and not by the group per se. In my view, this distinction is crucial for the maintenance of the group setting, but it also requires awareness on the therapist's side. In my experience, in adopting this approach, the therapist is not failing in his or her role – in contrast, he or she is showing his or her ability to preserve the group and protect it from his or her external emotional variables, and up to now, the patients' responses have been extremely positive.

On holiday

Consistent with the withdrawal therapy framework, the group of patients received a list of homework to be completed while the therapist was on holiday. As mentioned before, while on holiday, I scheduled films with their respective questionnaires to be completed. The questionnaires were to be discussed on my return. In addition, I also used to give them a diary in a table format to be filled in such a way as if they were talking to me in an individual session (see Table 4.5).

The patients were supposed to leave all their homework in my pigeonhole one day before my return at the latest. In addition to the treatment's aims, my particularly therapeutic aims were: a) to propound a particular type of transitional object

Table 4.5 Self-assessment diary – social skills

Date	Goal of the day	Situation that happened and I did not like	Thoughts about them	Strategies to deal with them	Did I achieve my goal?
Monday					
Tuesday					
Wednesday					
Thursday					
Friday					
Saturday Free will					
Sunday Free will					

through the use of films and diaries; b) to spark their ability to reflection whilst on their own; and c) to trigger their sense of responsibility in a relationship.

The results were very impressive indeed. I read all the diaries and the questionnaires carefully on my first day back. By 'read carefully', I mean making notes (sometimes drawing smiles) on their homework, as though I were talking to them through their homework. I also discussed these notes with them in their individual sessions. However, I should advise that this involves a large amount of extra work for the therapist on his or her return to work, as he or she will find lots of homework in his or her pigeonhole. In my opinion, if I set homework, I at least need to read it and give feedback.

It was amazing to observe how pleased they were to receive the feedback on their work, even for those who seldom attended school. Once, during a group session, Mr. T. said: "I always hated doing homework; indeed, my mother never checked it. But since I've been here with Mrs. Franieck, I have seen how pleased she is to receive my homework and to read it, I have started to do it!"

To sum up, I think it is imperative for the therapist to be consistent in his or her behaviour towards his or her patients.

On individual sessions

As far as I was able to, I always scheduled individual sessions on the same day of the week, keeping the same time for each patient over the course of the treatment. This approach to proceedings also had a positive influence on the treatment, since from the patient's point of view; it offered a sense of security/certainty. Furthermore, I usually started my day with the more difficult patients.

References

Bagdad Cafe, 1987. Directed by Percy Adlon: Bayerischer Rundfunk, Hessischer Rundfunk, Pelemele Film, Project Filmproduktion.

Bion, W.R., 1959. Attacks on Linking. *The International Journal of Psycho-analysis*, 40, 308–315.
Bion, W.R., 1984/1970. *Attention and Interpretation*. London: Tavistock Publications.
Bion, W.R., 1984. *Learning from Experience*. London: Karnac Books.
The Bucket List, 2007. Directed by Rob Reiner: Castle Rock Entertainment, Warner Bros. Pictures.
Cassorla, R.M.S., 2018. *The Psychoanalyst, the Theatre of Dreams and the Clinic of Enactment*. Abingdon, Oxon and New York: Routledge.
Foulkes, S.H., and Foulkes, E., 1990. *Selected Papers of S.H. Foulkes: Psychoanalysis and Group Analysis, Edited and with a Brief Biography by Elizabeth Foulkes*. London: Karnac Books.
Havel, V., and Hvížďala, K., 1991. *Disturbing the Peace: A Conversation with Karel Hvížďala*. 1st ed. New York: Vintage Books.
Ladyhawke, 1985. Directed by Richard Donner: Warner Bros Pictures, and 20th Century Fox.
Perls, F.S., 1969. *Ego, Hunger and Aggression: The Beginning of Gestalt Therapy*. New York: Vintage.
Riesenberg-Malcolm, R., 1999. Interpretation: The Past in the Present. *In:* P.L. Roth, ed. *On Bearing Unbearable States of Mind*. London: Routledge, 38–52.
Sapolsky, R.M., 2017. *Behave: The Biology of Humans at Our Best and Worst*. London: Vintage Digital.
Stern, D.N., 1995. *The Motherhood Constellation: A Unified View of Parent-Infant Psychotherapy*. New York: Basic Books.
Take the Lead, 2006. Directed by Liz Friedlander: Tiara Blu Films, New Line Cinema.
The Terminal, 2004. Directed by Steven Spielberg: Amblin Entertainment, Parkes, MacDonald Productions, DreamWorks Pictures.
Winnicott, D.W., 1953. Transitional Objects and Transitional Phenomena: A Study of the First Not-Me Possession. *The International Journal of Psycho-analysis*, 34, 89–97.
Winnicot, D.W., 1955. Metapsychological and Clinical Aspects of Regression Within the Psychoanalytical Set-Up. *The International Journal of Psycho-analysis*, 36, 16–26.
Winnicot, D.W., ed., 1971. *Playing and Reality*. S.l.: Basic Books.
Winnicott, D.W., *et al*., 1984. *Deprivation and Delinquency*. London: Tavistock.
Winnicott, D.W., *et al*., 2012. *Deprivation and Delinquency*. Milton Park and Abingdon, Oxon: Routledge.
Worthman, Carol M., *et al*., eds., 2010. *Formative Experiences: The Interaction of Caregiving, Culture, and Developmental Psychobiology*. Cambridge: Cambridge University Press.
You, Me and Dupree, 2006. Directed by Anthony Russo and Joe Russo: Avis-Davis Productions, Stuber-Parent Productions, Universal Pictures.

Appendices

Appendix 4.1

Bagdad Cafe homework

1. Describe the relationship (main feelings) between Jasmine and her husband. Was it love?
2. What was Jasmin like? What was her husband like (as a character)?
3. Why did Jasmin hide from her husband? Was she scared? Was she courageous? Why?
4. Describe the relationship (main feelings) between Brenda and her husband. Was it love?
5. What was Brenda like? What was her husband like (as a character)?
6. Why did Brenda kick out her husband? Was she scared? Was she courageous? Why?
7. Describe the relationship (main feelings) between Brenda and her children. Why did the children not listen to her?
8. Was Jasmin welcome in Brenda's Motel? If so, for whom? If not, for whom? Was this also the case for the foreigner?
9. What's the significance of the foreigner? What kind of emotions does one experience towards a stranger?
10. How did Jasmin develop her relationship with the others? What was the emotional basis?
11. At what point did Brenda accept Jasmin?
12. What's the significance of the artist? What could he sense from Jasmin?
13. What did the 'magic' (the metaphor) mean?
14. What did the boomerang (the metaphor) mean?
15. Why did Jasmin have to ask Brenda if she could marry (the metaphor)?
16. Please identify and illustrate the following emotions and feelings in the film:
    a   Compassion
    b   Fear
    c   Shame
    d   Hope
    e   Satisfaction
    f   Dissatisfaction

- g Sadness
- h Trust
- i Distrust
- j Loneliness
- k Affiliation

17 Write your review of the film.

Appendix 4.2

Ladyhawke homework

1. Provide five examples of conflict resolution strategies when the outcomes were a success.
2. Give five examples of conflict resolution options when the results were not related to skills, and explain what problems occurred as a result.
3. In terms of social competence, how do you understand the scene when 'the Mouse' was injured by the wolf? What is the difference between the behaviours of the wolf and Navarre? (Don't forget: with regards to social skills) – this is a small boomerang. Are you happy with the boomerang?
4. Give two examples of the relationship between social competence, social awareness, and self-confidence.
5. Provide two examples of the link between frustration, identity, and social skills.
6. Give two examples of the relation between rejection, loneliness, and (non-) social skills.
7. Identify and give an example of the following emotions and feelings in the film:
   a   Compassion
   b   Fear
   c   Shame
   d   Hope
   e   Rejection
   f   Self-confidence
   g   Frustration
   h   Sadness
   i   Trust
   j   Distrust
   k   Loneliness
   l   Belonging
8. Now comes BOOMERANG 1: What is the connection between the scene when Isabeau and the wolf (Navarre) try to touch each other and your therapy?

9 And then BOOMERANG 2: Why was Navarre able to trust in 'the Mouse' from their very first meeting?
10 And finally, BOOMERANG 3: Why was Isabeau a hawk and Navarre a wolf?
11 Write your review of the film.

Chapter 5

TICA in pretrial detention

TICA: from 'interpretation training' to risk assessments and crisis interventions

Once, I got a phone call from the institution director of a prison for those awaiting trial. He reported that there had just been two cases of suicide in his prison, and he needed someone who had the ability not only to run accurate risk assessments but also to communicate with the prisoners. According to him, I was that person, as he had followed my work in the withdrawal therapy context illustrated in Chapter 10. He requested that I start working once a week in three pretrial detention centres, four hours in each. He made it clear that my tasks would be restricted to: a) assessing suicide risks; b) intervening in crises; c) giving psychological support to prisoners who were emotionally unstable; and finally d) giving psychological support to sex offenders, who could not share their trial worries with anyone else. Indeed, I should keep in mind that in pretrial detention, the prisoners have not yet been given any verdicts, which means the work should not be focused on the offence – rather an opposite goal to that of withdrawal treatment. Moreover, since the two suicides, a controversial procedure for new prisoners had been introduced that had to be taken seriously. For the institution director, the procedure was prevention; for the staff, it was an added stress, as it gave them more work to do. The procedure was that every new prisoner was not allowed to stay alone in any part of the prison for the first 15 days of incarceration, as the risk of suicide over the first days of incarceration was high. This procedure was called the 'observation period'. During the observation period, the newcomer should be assessed by the social worker and psychologist. Once the observation period was over, the newcomer's case was to be discussed in the weekly team meeting – a meeting with the service provider, officers, the social worker, the psychologist and sometimes the institution director. In this team meeting, every single case in the prison was discussed, including decisions about releasing prisoners from the observation periods. It was an important meeting for decision making and also for exchanging information across the team as regards prisoners' behaviour patterns.

To return to the previous point, yet again, I felt lost in my role as a psychologist, as though I were in limbo. On reflection I realized that being in limbo might also

DOI: 10.4324/9781003232087-7

have reflected how the prisoners felt – counter-transference issues (Alexandris and Vaslamatzis 1993) – since, until their verdict, they had to cope with transience and uncertainties in unison, mostly in respect of their distant future – apropos, a rather similar unstable and risky circumstance can been seen in children living in 'street situations'.

Once more, my mind was preoccupied by concomitant questions, such as the following. How could I provide an effective service in this milieu? How could I establish meaningful communication between both sides, myself as the psychotherapist and the prisoners as the patients? Thus, I had to start all over again, as well as needing to find a reasonable communication approach, which still remained a shared meaning one. Even now, I have never had so much freedom of choice in my work in which to develop something, nor have I so far ever had the time to run 'interpretation training'. The brief contact time with the prisoners, coupled with the risk of their sudden release or transfer, impedes the development of any regular intervention. I was faced with ephemeral encounters – a sense of nothing was going to last – a transient form of contact which could not be traced (Castrechini-Franieck 2014, pp. 45–46). Hence, the basis of a new communication approach had to be a correct one from my side – that is to say, in an ephemeral encounter, one needs to start and to end in the 'here and now', with all important issues being addressed at the same time. There is no room for 'unfinished businesses', as tomorrow, the prisoner might not be there anymore – the very same ephemeral setting, which I once encountered in my work with the children living in 'street situations'. Being aware of the fact that there were similarities between my circumstances at that time and the work I had developed with children living in 'street situations' brought me new perspectives with regards to these daunting challenges. In fact, I did indeed need to go back to the time when I worked with the children living in 'street situations' and recall situations I had experienced with them, as a form of 'Hope' (Havel and Hvížďala 1991) in finding my way in my work at the prison. In my search of memories of that time, I recalled the intense pleasure and full attention of the children whilst listening to the story stems I was telling them (Castrechini-Franieck *et al*. 2014; Castrechini-Franieck 2014; Castrechini-Franieck and Page 2017). There is certainly no sense in telling stories to prisoners, although I could transform their personal history into story stems. Instead of using Playmobil® characters to act out the story stems, I could draw the 'timeline' of their lives whilst providing them with a potential space (Winnicott 1953) for playing with new insights into their autobiographical history, intent on achieving an ephemeral or 'transient shared meaning communication'.

A 'timeline' is an effective method, and has been adopted both in clinical settings, such as within narrative exposure therapy (Schauer and Ruf-Leuschner 2014) and in human resources, such as in career assessments (Fritz and van Zyl 2015). For my ephemeral context in the prison, the application of the 'timeline' had to be adjusted, as is described below.

A further vivid memory of my work with the children living in 'street situations' was my encounter with John (see Chapter 3), principally when he merely defined himself as a 'record'. All these memories triggered clarity in my thoughts as regards how to adjust TICA to the prison milieu.

The first step was to avoid reading the prisoner's records beforehand. Despite the risk of being in contact with someone of high danger without knowing it, "*avoiding mental memory activity and desire*" (Bion 1970, p. 42, emphasis is in original) formed the basis of a successful ephemeral encounter. I did not want to have a picture of the person (the prisoner) in my mind before talking to them. Quite the opposite – I wanted to sense their presence, mood, fears, and maybe also the danger (Cassorla 2018, p. 8). In my understanding, the feelings that arose inside of me from the contact with this unknown person should lead me to the correct attitude, as the same had happened in my work with the children living in 'street situations'.

On this basis, I got used to introducing myself in the following way:

> Hello, I am Dr. Franieck, the psychologist here. We will talk a little bit, as one of my tasks is to interview everyone who is new here, to assess suicide risks. I guess you have already been informed about this. So, please tell me, why are you here? What did you do? What happened?

The prisoners' responses varied from case to case. With this type of approach, some were able to start talking without any problems; others, on the contrary, were more unwilling to talk. From the latter, I usually received responses such as: "I do not need a psychologist – I am not crazy, and I am not the guy that will commit suicide! So, why should I talk to you – just read my records!" (like John); "I will not tell you!"; or "I will not tell you because what I did is not very nice!"

With the more resistant person, I needed to go a little deeper like this:

> Hey, come on!! Talking to a psychologist does not mean you are crazy, or that you will commit suicide. I would just like to get to know you a little bit more. You don't know me, and I don't know you either. Would a short conversation hurt us? I don't think so, do you? However, I am not here to force you to do anything you don't want to – there is no sense in doing that! Actually, this might be the only time in this prison when you are free to do whatever you want . . . can you see . . . I give you some freedom . . . It is up to you!

This is quite a similar approach to the one I adopted in the past with John, although I adjusted it to suit an adult audience. Furthermore, it is very important indeed to highlight the patient's freedom to decide whether or not to enter into conversation – the central step towards successful communication. The feeling of being free to decide can minimize defences activated by the feeling of being subjugated. As a result, lots of people responded positively to this intervention.

However, there were cases where resistance was high, and in such cases, it was necessary to continue the intervention in this way:

> By the way, I would just like you to know that I do not hold any moral rules and it is not my business to judge what you have done, as this is not part of my job. In fact, I think that everyone here, at some point of their life initially acted without thinking properly . . . and so that is why they are here . . . I mean . . . at the moment of the offence, they lost their ability to think and were driven by deep emotions, mainly by anger and frustration.

Here the main purpose was to try to minimize possible fantasies on the part of the prisoner regarding the crime committed. The neutrality of the psychologist is important, so that the prisoner feels less threatened about the other person being quick to judge. In the same way, exemplifying one of the psychic processes which takes place during the act of the crime may promulgate reflection (and perhaps identification) on the part of the prisoner – the prisoner may feel understood by the other party. Following this, I went ahead with an intervention that might sound as a threat for some people. However, on the contrary, it is a way in which meaning is conveyed (Winnicott 1992/1987):

> And yes, you are completely right -, I could read your records; however, if I read them, I will have an impression of you from someone else who wrote about you, and this is not the real you. Would you like me to do this? I would prefer to create my own impression of you. By the way, if I sense you are trying to trick me, then I'll go and read your records, as you know I can do this anytime, though I will let you know before I do this. Actually, it is important to me to keep my work transparent with you. Up to now I have not read your records . . . so . . . it is up to you! Are you open to talking to me now?

This intervention contains a confrontation along with three significant and concomitant messages that set the communication framework:

1 Confrontation with reality – the psychologist holds free access to records.
2 First message: "I am initiating communication with you, and your word has more worth to me than what is written about you – I am simply trusting you".
3 Second message: "If you think I am foolish and will not reflect on what you say, blindly believing what you tell me, you are wrong. If in doubt, I will certainty go and consult your records".
4 Third message: "Although you tried to deceive me, my loyalty to you remains intact, so I will be honest with you, communicating that I am going to read your records".

Once the communication setting has been established, the 'timeline' is introduced.

If you are willing to talk to me now, then we can start . . . By the way, whilst we are talking, I will start drawing your 'timeline' on this paper and then I will show you it and we can talk about it later. Are you ready?

Based on my experience of interviewing over 3,000 prisoners, I have never received a further refusal after adopting this approach, which, once more, is a refined version of the approach I had adopted previously with the very resistant children living in 'street situations'.

I recall how a prisoner in his mid-50s once told me: "I will not tell you because what I did was not very nice!" I approached him in the same way as described above and his reaction was very positive.

He thought about my words a little bit and said:

OK, I will tell you even though it was not very nice! So . . . I murdered my wife with a hammer. We had a quarrel. I went to the basement. She followed behind me, talking, talking . . . then, I saw the hammer, took it and hammered her head seven times . . . then she fell down dead . . . . but she didn't talk anymore . . . it wasn't pretty . . . .

In addition, the prisoners frequently gave me more details of their offences than had been described in their records, as well as several confessions. All this information had to remain undisclosed due to compulsory confidentiality.

Drawings

The second step of the adaptation of TICA was to start posing random questions to prisoners in the interview whilst depicting their answers and real-life situations on a 'timeline' (Figure 5.1) as follows:

I took an A4 piece of paper and turned it horizontally and drew a horizontal line from left to right on the foot of the sheet (on the lower quarter of the sheet). Birth and death were the extreme points on the line. Birth was placed on the left with a date whilst death was on the right with a skull and a question mark. Then, I started narrating:

Look! Our life is like a line . . . it begins with our birth . . . here . . . and goes towards our death. Life moves from birth to death . . . in this direction . . . from left to right . . . no other way . . . from our birth we know that one day we will die . . . we can try to postpone our death, but we are unable to avoid it . . . at some point in the future. We will meet our death . . . when it will happen, no one knows [and I point to the question mark]. Birth and death are moments in our lives that we do not have control over – actually, we are completely powerless over them and deal with our lack of control at these moments, experiencing deep pain. On top of this, this line is made up

92 TICA in forensic settings

of points . . . each point represents the experiences we have gone through. Look, here is today . . . [Then I write the date on the line, usually in the middle of it] . . . and here are you [then I draw a stick figure on the line]. Now, we will start talking and based on our chat, I will fill your 'timeline' with your experiences . . . sometimes I will ask you some questions to understand your points more clearly. This way, I'm convinced I'll have a better picture of you, than I would if I were reading your records. Shall we start?

I would suggest keeping the conversation in the first-person plural, as the principle of the 'timeline' is the same for all of us – only the collinear points differ – on this level; we are all only human. In the emotional sphere, the use of the first-person plural has a positive effect on the process of identification in relation to the sense of equality. This approach aims to weaken the prisoner's defences, thus providing a more fluent and casual discussion between the two parties – a crucial point for starting communication in this ephemeral environment, especially when conducting an accurate assessment.

As to the interview, there was no set plan, as I always tried to keep an open mind when listening to the prisoners' answers and gave free reign to my thoughts when forming the next question. Thus, the interview was almost unstructured. The most important point during the interview was that while we were talking, I was both drawing and showing them their 'timeline'. I also made associations between situations on their 'timeline' and my remarks/thoughts about its content, based on what I had heard, as illustrated in Case 1, outlined in what follows, which was similar to a classical psychoanalytical interpretation, however less verbal and less

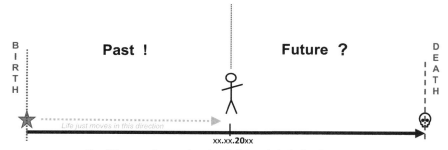

Figure 5.1 Timeline

TICA in pretrial detention 93

abstract in thinking, being based simply and concretely on drawings, such as those in Figure 5.2 and Figure 5.3.

When the interview ended, I always asked the prisoners if they would like to have a copy of their 'timeline'. Most of them asked me to keep it with me because it would be safer, which I did, bringing it with me to future meetings – remarkably, the prisoners were always pleased to have the chance to continue talking about their 'timelines' from the point we had got up to the last time. As regards my role

Figure 5.2 No words – sexual abuse

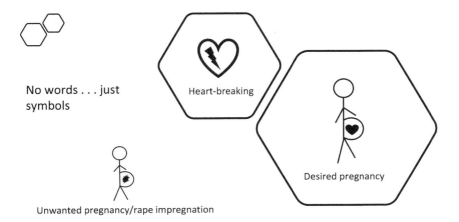

Figure 5.3 No words – pregnancy

as keeper of the prisoner's 'timeline', I can relate this to the similar role of the therapist as keeper of the child-patients' toy boxes in the psychoanalytical play therapy individual setting.

The method of drawing has two major benefits: first, it is per se a transitional object, and it thus also triggers a transitional space for playing with ideas and emotions, just as cartoons and films turned into transitional objects in the 'interpretation training' – hence, it is a chance to turn the ephemeral encounter into 'transient shared meaning communication'. Second, it is also per se an opportunity to represent the prisoner's personal life history via a unifying symbol and a form of representation – their 'timeline' – which provides them not only with a sense of wholeness through their "autobiographical review" (Fritz and Beekman 2011, p. 168), but also with an awareness of their coping strategies, as well as their resilience (Castrechini-Franieck 2014, pp. 45–48). In effect, drawing one's 'timeline' has, in addition, the purpose of containing one's sense of self.

In acute crisis (i.e., suicide risks), drawings have supremacy over words, as in such moments, patients act on impulse and lack focus on their capacity for abstract thoughts. Thus, a visual concrete approach is an appropriate form of communication in this type of situation as illustrated in the following Case 2.

Equally, drawing is very useful in cases where the prisoner is unable to speak the language and a challenge is posed by basic communication – cross-cultural issues. In these cases, an 'introductory drawing' on paper, like the one in Figure 5.4, is required before starting with the 'timeline'. The steps in creating the 'introductory drawing' are:

> I take a piece of A4 paper and turn it horizontally and draw a stick figure (me), on the left of the sheet (in the middle of the sheet). I point my index

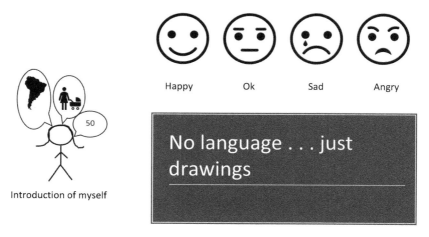

Figure 5.4 Introduction of myself

finger at the real me and then at the drawing on paper. Then, I draw another stick figure (the patient) in front of me on the right side of the paper and point my index finger at the real patient and then at the new drawing on the paper (pure body and visual language). With this gesture, the patient in front of me understands that I am inviting him or her to communicate.

The next step is to write down my fictitious age and the year I was born as if my figure on the paper were speaking . . . then I draw a speech bubble above the other person on the paper and draw a question mark. In general, the patient usually asks me for the pencil so that he or she can write down his or her age.

In the third step, I draw a map of Brazil (South America) and write 'Brazil' on it, as if the picture of me were speaking (again, I point my index finger at the real me and then at the drawing), then I draw a speech bubble above the patient's picture and a question mark; the patient usually writes the name of their country where he or she comes from.

In the fourth step, I draw a boy and a girl together with me, as though they were my children (the same procedure used previously is adopted, with body language), then the patient draws the number of children he or she has (or indicates that he or she does not have any).

In the fifth step, I take another piece of A4 paper and turn it horizontally and draw my short fictitious genogram and follow the same procedure in order to get the genogram of the person I am interviewing. At this point, communication has been established and the 'timeline' gestalt is not a daunting challenge anymore.

However, there are also cases in which the prisoner is unable to maintain communication on the representative level, even via drawings. I remember a case of a 30-year-old man from Ethiopia who had been homeless since the age of 7, travelling since then aimlessly until he finally arrived in Germany. Yet, he did not speak German, just Italian, as he had lived for a couple of years in Italy before reaching Germany. This is the brief information I was able to get from him by speaking Italian with him. When I started to try to draw his timeline on the paper, he started to bend down, lower his head and cover it with his arms, putting his feet up on the chair like a foetus in the womb whilst avoiding contact with me. His body language made evident the fact that he was not prepared to reflect or even symbolize his life in drawings. Also, his reactions showed me how traumatized he had been. The representation of my emotional experience with him, by seeing him as a foetus, indicates to me just how regressive his psychological state was and how careful I had to be. So, I interrupted the interview and he returned to his cell, together with another compatriot prisoner, but who could communicate in German. Minutes later, the prison alarm rang. They were fighting in the cell. I was called in to try to understand the situation and him. The prisoner who spoke German said that the other was crazy and that he hadn't done anything. The other one who spoke a little Italian was shouting with his finger "Christian! Christian!" I asked him then if he was a Muslim and he nodded. I explained to the officials that it was a religious conflict and also that this was a big contentious issue in their culture. The officials decided that it was better to separate them then. As the prison was crowded, the only solution they had was to put one of them in the cell used for solitary confinement. Since the Italian-speaking prisoner was the problem, due to his language barriers, he had to be sent to solitary. The officials asked me to explain to him the change of cell and its function. As a result of this conflict, this prisoner regressed emotionally and positioned himself on the floor, in the corner, again like a foetus in the womb, hiding his head between his arms and running away from any visual contact. Observing this, I decided to approach him using body language. So, I did exactly what he did – I sat on the floor and mirrored him physically. Not surprisingly, the officials did not understand what was happening and were scared that he might attack me. After a few minutes with him in this position, I called his name, and he raised his head and looked me in the eyes. I then explained in Italian what needed to be explained. He agreed to change cells without any resistance. This case reminded me of my approaches with abused children and children living in 'street situations'. Here, I would like to emphasize the importance of being sensitive towards the needs of the other person, whilst appreciating their communication abilities.

Returning to the previous point, besides drawing, another method of approach is to swap the patient's vivid life situations with seemingly harmless tales portrayed by apparently inoffensive characters/symbols, as I did in Case 3, outlined in what follows. Having said that, the tales should always be connected to the personal history of the person being interviewed.

For severe personality disorders cases, I adopted two different approach techniques, in addition to drawings, which I called: a) ironic mirror images; and b) guide pedants. The former was acted out as a communication approach in cases where the patient did not express any kind of remorse for their crime and even felt proud of it, like in the Case 4. The latter was implemented in the communication approaches in cases of paranoid personality disorders where patients had a clear lack of control over their range and demonstrated destructive fantasies as illustrated in Case 5.

The 'timelines' presented in what follows are not the original ones.

Case 1: blurred distinctions – "By hitting others . . . I'm with you, Mom!"

Mr. B. is a 30-year-old bossy man with numerous criminal records for violent assault and drug trafficking. His motto is: "There is no 'mercy' in life". Furthermore, people and relationships are all ephemeral for him. He did not feel attached to anyone apart from his grandparents on his mother's side, who had raised him since he was 8 years old. From his early childhood, he had described his mother as being a detached, frivolous woman who had several partners. Being assaulted by her and/or by her partners was quite a daily occurrence.

In the prison, due to his latent aggressiveness, as well as his bossy personality (a potential danger), I frequently had to talk to him – assuming he wanted to, and he did most of the time.

The main topic of our conversations was about his temperament. He frequently tried to impress on me his need to remain detached from people. Once he told me that he had beaten someone, leaving them in a coma. Although he was aware of what he was doing, he did not want to stop beating them until they fell into a coma. Suddenly, he started to narrate memories of when he was a little boy, explaining that he had experienced many physical assaults himself from his mother and her partners. The violence was so intense that often the police were called by the neighbours. At that time, the presence of the police evoked a deep feeling of security inside of him. Then, unexpectedly, he interrupted his speech and said that he did not understand what was happening with his mind and why he was telling me all these stories.

Through his narration, it became clear to me that for this person the definition of love and hate was totally mixed and blurred. Probably when he beat someone, he felt pleasure, and this pleasure directly related to his childhood memories with his mother. In this case, violence would be equivalent to expressing the love of this mother. Acting out violently would be akin to being constantly connected to his mother.

At this point, I decided to draw my thoughts on his 'timeline' (Figure 5.5) and presented it very simply to him despite my uncertainty about his possible reaction to my thoughts. However, first I told him:

> I would like to share some thoughts with you about what you have just told me, by showing you them on your 'timeline'. You might get angry at me and you might not want to keep talking to me either, please do not be offended by them. Keep in mind that I am being honest with you. Would you like to hear them, anyway?

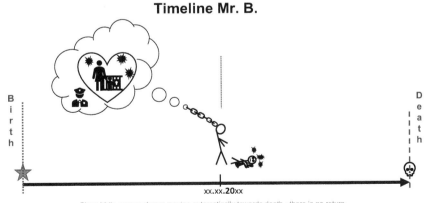

Figure 5.5 Timeline Mr. B.

This is an intervention I adopt every time I realize that what I am going to say may not be in harmony with the patient's 'timing' and therefore quickly activate psychological defences, such as denial, or even be understood as a form of aggression (offence) on my part. That is to say, the patients might perceive the representations of my experience with them as an example of failure in our communication, failure in the mutuality course (Winnicott 2018, 1992, p. 19), and failure in the 'reverie' progression (Bion 1984). Hence, my intention is to provide patients with a representation of this potential miscommunication in advance. In doing so, I am somewhat diminishing the impact of the likely miscommunication, whilst remaining honest with them and expressing my ability to cope with possible aggression from their side at the same time. In other words, I am communicating that despite possible miscommunication, I will remain with them anyway.

He listened to me very attentively and was thoughtful afterwards. He seemed to be relieved for a few seconds, but then he talked to me in his bossy tone of voice, although not an aggressive one:

I will not come here to talk to you anymore . . .

And I asked him:

You are angry with me, aren't you? You didn't like my thoughts, did you? Yes, you have the right to be angry. Should I fear your anger towards me from now on?

When I highlighted his right to be angry with me, I was in fact stating that I had expected my words might disturb him, and that I was expecting to have to deal with his frustration and potential aggression, but I was also showing that I did not fear them – at this point, I had the same role as the police did in the very violent situations with his mother in the past. Furthermore, when I asked him whether I should fear his potential aggression towards me, I was confronting him with his own fear of his aggression, which was connected to the aggression experienced by him in childhood.

He answered me:

No, you do not need to be afraid of me . . . I will not do anything against you . . . I will just not come here anymore because it doesn't help me!

I replied:

That is OK! I fully appreciate that! By the way, thanks!

When I expressed my appreciation and then thanked him further, I made it clear that I had acknowledged his controlled behaviour as a sign of respect towards me (Gilligan 2001, pp. 120–121).

He left the room and did not come back anymore, although every time we occasionally met in the prison corridor, he was very polite and respectful towards me.

Mr. B. has not only broadened my knowledge of symbolization and its multiple layers of meaning in the primitive communication level, but he has also improved my skills in communication at both levels: the verbal and the primitive one. Although this case could be defined as a typical 'lost case', I see it quite differently. In view of his criminal record, I must confess that I was quite impressed with his control over his rage during our last meeting. In my opinion, despite our ephemeral encounter, restricted 'transient shared meaning communication' had been achieved with him.

Case 2: an abused little boy

Mr. I. was a married man in his mid-30s and a father of four children, without a professional education and without any previous criminal record. He was incarcerated due to causing severe damage to and stealing from a public organization. As shown in his brief family history, his parents were immigrants and his mother had separated from his father when he was only 7 years old, due to family violence. She married again to another immigrant man, and from then, Mr. I. was constantly sexually abused by his stepfather until the age of 16. He was the second child of a family with three children from the first marriage. There were no children from the second marriage. His eldest sister was single and had psychological problems, and his youngest brother was a transsexual. He had always imagined that his siblings had also been abused by his stepfather just as he was, although this was a taboo subject. Until we met, his sexual abuse had been kept in secret, but by doing his 'timeline', he was able to talk about it for the first time. Despite the continuous support from his siblings and, in particular, from his wife, regarding his imprisonment, he was emotionally very emotional unstable, like a little boy. In addition to his low self-esteem and his insecurities related to his role as a man and a father, the conflicting relationship with his mother was also an issue that took up considerable space in his emotional world. His mother had two opposing roles in his mind: she was a victim of the maltreatment in her first marriage, and at the same time, she was someone who was negligent and tortfeasor, someone who failed in protecting her children from the second sexually abusive husband. In fact, she had transferred the violence to her children. His father representations were completely destroyed, and for him, men were either violent or sexual offenders, unable to be good fathers. He was mostly depressed as he spent a lot of time thinking about his past. In the present, he was scared of getting a long sentence, and thus becoming a failure in the eyes of his children. The risk of a long sentence was real and not imaginary. One day, he got a letter from the prosecutor, in which the prosecutor was demanding a five-year sentence for his offence. On that day, he became very emotionally disturbed and tried to commit suicide by hanging himself in his cell; however, he was interrupted by his cellmate. At that point, I was called by the guards to talk to him, and I decided to approach him

100 TICA in forensic settings

by drawing my thoughts, rather than by trying to maintain a logical and verbally discussion with him. Hence, I told him:

> You don't need to talk to me if you don't want to, but please, give me just a little bit of your attention as regards what I will draw for you now.

Once again, I would like to draw attention to the great importance of giving the patient the freedom not to talk, which also implies giving back to them a sense of confidence that had recently been lost.

Hence, I started to draw his 'timeline' (Figure 5.6) once again; however, this time, I drew the line from birth to the current date, as he had wanted to end his life. Then, I wrote the current date on the line, besides which I also included a skull. After this, I drew a stick figure (him) on the line thinking about his past when he was abused by his stepfather, as well as his anger towards his mother and his natural father, represented by a violent assault. Next, I drew him in the present, thinking about being in prison. Finally, I suddenly drew a vertical line, cutting through the 'timeline'. Whilst I was drawing, I talked to him like this:

> Look here please! Here is your 'timeline'... do you remember it? This point here is when you were born... and this point is today's date... the skull is your wish to end your life right now. You are here... but your mind is not here, but rather in your past... your mind is full of things that happened in your past [and I showed him the picture of the sex offender], also the

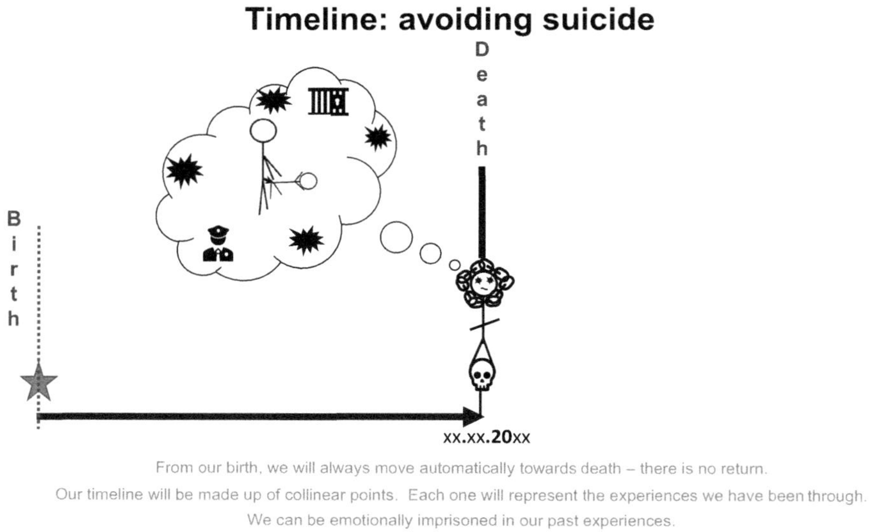

Timeline: avoiding suicide

From our birth, we will always move automatically towards death – there is no return.
Our timeline will be made up of collinear points. Each one will represent the experiences we have been through.
We can be emotionally imprisoned in our past experiences.

Figure 5.6 Timeline Mr. I.

emotions you have felt due to your past [I show his anger towards his mother and father in a violent assault in the form of small explosions] . . . the only thought you have that is connected to here and now is your wish to end your life. You are scared of the idea of getting a long sentence and being in the prison for a long time and therefore not being able to be a respectable father anymore [then, I show the cell and draw the vertical line].

The next step involved going further, showing him the foreseen future (Figure 5.7). I started drawing a dotted line from the current date, as if his 'timeline' were continuing. Then, I put a small stick figure (representing his children) altogether on this dotted line, thinking of their father, and said:

However, whilst you are thinking about your past and also about taking your life, your children are here [and I pointed to the hypothetical future] . . . you are unable to think that your children are expecting to have their father in the future . . . expecting to be together with him . . . actually to be together with you! Your children don't know about your past . . . the only thing they know is how they love their father and how they are longing to be with him . . . with you . . . . So, you can take your life if you really want to . . . actually, it is your life, not mine; however, I would say it is almost selfish of you to end your life without considering your children. Your children are not to blame for what happened to you in the past, and above all, they love you for

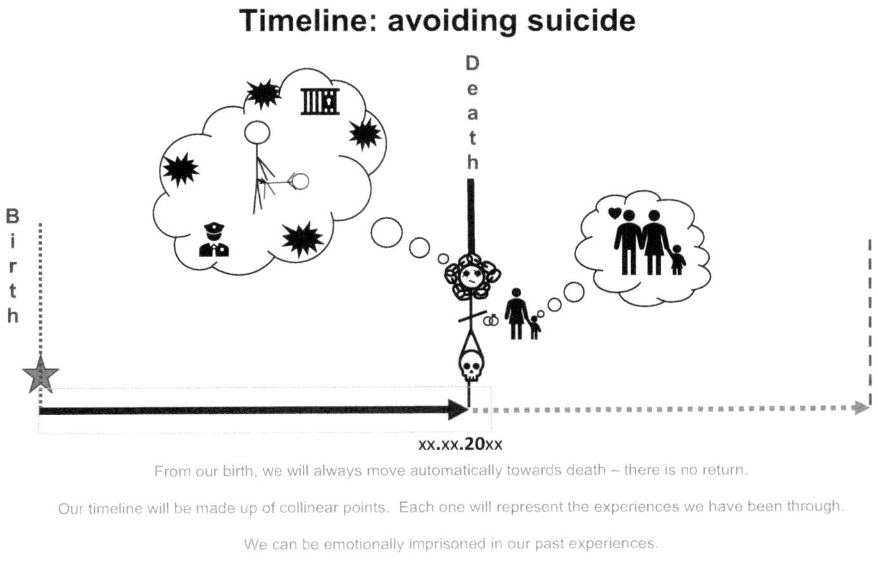

Timeline: avoiding suicide

xx.xx.20xx

From our birth, we will always move automatically towards death – there is no return.

Our timeline will be made up of collinear points. Each one will represent the experiences we have been through.

We can be emotionally imprisoned in our past experiences.

Figure 5.7 Timeline Mr. I. [2]

who you are, regardless of your past. Think about it! In any case, your life is yours!

Once again, I would like to draw attention to the importance of appreciating and highlighting the freedom of the other person's choice in communication, despite all the potential harm their choice could bring. In fact, I would define this attitude as a vivid expression (acting-out) of the 'shared meaning communication' principle – one's ability to understand the other's perspectives well enough to accept them, even though one may not agree with them. From my experience, this kind of attitude in communication has a major impact on the patient. In this attempted suicide case, after this approach, Mr. I. started crying and was able to realize how selfish and unfair he was being towards his children. He understood that he could be a better father in prison than in death. The drawing had an impressive resonance on his impulsive thoughts. As a result, he asked me for a copy of the drawing, as he did not want to forget our 'chat'. From this point onwards, Mr. I. became a more sociable person in the prison and less depressed. In the end, Mr. I. got a long sentence; however, he was convinced that he could make better use of his time in prison, for example by doing a professional training course during his imprisonment – and so, he did.

It is worth emphasizing that I did not draw his wife thinking about him on the dotted line because no one knows the details of their relationship, nor if the relationship will last until the end of his sentence and beyond. On the other hand, children will always remain children. Indeed, the key issue of his emotional lability (caused by the traumatic experiences with his father and stepfather) was about his ability to perform the role of a loveable father for his children, as to him, father representations were always connected to feelings of rage. In this case, being arrested, had for him been a statement that he was unfit – 'a bad guy' – in the same way as his father and stepfather had been 'bad guys'.

Case 3: the irony of fate – "Who am I? What have I done? I cannot recognize myself!"

This case was presented in the 25th Annual Conference of the International Association for Forensic Psychotherapy in spring 2016 in Ghent, Belgium, under the title: "How far can we go with our work with offenders?"

Mr. R. was a middle-aged single man with a history of repeat offending related to drug trafficking and severe alcohol and drug consumption. On a typical holiday, after consuming some alcohol, he had a quarrel with his girlfriend and a near relative in a bar. In order to avoid any escalation, he left both of them behind and went back home alone. Later, the near relative and his girlfriend came together to his home. The argument between the two men started again and a brutal assault took place. The brutal assault ended in a tragic homicide.

By drawing Mr. R.'s 'timeline', it was possible to get some information about his personal history, such as the fact he came from an ordinary German family – he had old parents who had seven middle-aged children. He had undoubtedly defined himself well as the family's 'black sheep', due to his history of offences – he was the only problematic child in the family – an 'Outsider'. The victim, conversely, had been married and had children. He had had his own business and was very successful in it.

When I met Mr. R. for the first time, he was able to take responsibility for the offence committed, although he could not understand why he had committed it. He was unable to recognize himself as a person, only as 'a monster' – "How could I have done that? How had I been able to kill my own relative? Who am I? What have I done? I cannot recognize myself!" He was very confused and at risk of committing suicide. Therefore, the focus of our ephemeral encounters was on rediscovering his sense of 'self'. This could only be achieved by getting a deep understanding of the offence committed. Aware of his conflicting feelings towards his near relative, in addition to his blurred memories of the offence committed, coupled with his intense fear of speaking about it, I swapped the offence for a harmless story about a cat-and-mouse fight, as illustrated in what follows. The aim was primarily to implement storytelling and story-listening as a new communication approach, while intending to create a potential space for more free communication (Stein 2017). Thus, our second encounter started with me telling him:

> You know, last time, when you described the fight between you and your near relative on that day to me, my mind associated that with a cat-and-mouse fight. Actually, it seems like one, don't you think? So then, tell me . . . in this cat-and-mouse fight, were you the cat? Or were you the mouse?

Mr. R. answered:

> At the beginning, I was the mouse . . . the cat jumped on the mouse . . . the mouse was helpless . . . the mouse would die if he didn't do anything . . .

I asked him further:

> Then the mouse turns into a cat, am I right?

He answered me:

> Yes!

From that moment on, talking about what had happened became easier. In the end, he was also faced with his own fears, as well as with his potential aggressive defences against these fears. We had two or three more sessions after this day, as my task was just to stabilize the prisoners. Six months later, shortly before his trial, he asked to talk to me again – in fact, he wanted to thank me for our meetings. At the end of our chat, he said:

> Whatever the sentence is, nothing will change what I have done; I won't have this person with me anymore. Not to mention how difficult it will be to face my whole family in the trial and after my release . . . actually, I can't predict what would be the best sentence for me.

He went to the trial expecting (and also hoping) to get a reasonable sentence. However, surprisingly, he was judged as not guilty and was immediately released. The offence was interpreted as an act of self-defence by the judge. Everyone was astonished by the outcome of his trial, including himself.

Two years later, I met him again in the same prison. The prosecutor appealed for a review of the case, which was followed by his imprisonment. Talking to me was one of the first things he wanted to do in prison. He told me how difficult it had been to return to his village and face the whole neighbourhood and his family after the trial. Until the moment of his current imprisonment, he had led a private life, dedicated exclusively to his work and home. He had also stopped consuming drugs and was only drinking occasionally. He was a different man, more reflective and more reserved. His change of attitude was perceived by all and especially by the guards who had known him for years. According to them, Mr. R. had become more centred, quieter, and more isolated. A good example of this is the fact he was no longer able to get on with the other prisoners, nor work in the production of electronics in the prison, as the other prisoners' jokes whilst working were – from his point of view – extremely immature and childish.

When I had finished my work at this prison, the date for his second trial had not yet been set. So, I would like to close this case by raising the following two questions for reflection.

1   Since our aim is to help the offenders understand why they committed the offence and take responsibility for it (Welldon and van Velsen 1997), how could our work still be helpful in this case?
2   Where might the boundary between ideal and real future for Mr. R. lie?

Case 4: "Please don't let me fall into depression!"

Mr. T. was a young man of 18, with solid cultural convictions, yet without a previous criminal record. He was incarcerated due to once committing a high level of physical assault: punching someone's face until that person fell into a coma. Communicating with him was a demanding job, as he was almost always unfriendly. Still, by drawing his 'timeline', it was possible to run a short personal history with him. Mr. T. came from an immigrant family and was the only boy, the youngest of three children. Although in his family's culture, marriages were arranged and had to last a lifetime (divorce brings shame on the family), his parents split up when he was just 11. His father raised a new family, while his mother remained alone in the name of the family's honour. His parents' divorce had always been an issue that disturbed in his life, since it threatened his solid cultural convictions by posing doubts about his feelings towards his own parents.

In our first ephemeral session, he tried to scare me with a threatening, cold, and remorseless rendition of his offence, as though trying to convince me of his powerful aggressiveness. However, via primitive communication, I was only able to perceive him as a scared, lost and lonely young boy, struggling to avoid and in denial of his depression. In this setting, I decided to adopt what I call an 'ironic mirror image approach' and replied to him:

> Really? You do not feel any remorse for what you have done? Tell me how you can do that? I need to learn with you, how one can do that. Actually, if I were in your shoes, I would feel so guilty – I would experience great remorse. You know, I usually feel so guilty about even small matters because I usually try to put myself in the other's position. So, now I can learn with you how not to feel any remorse! Tell me how you do this? What is your secret?

The core point of this approach involves neither going into the details about the offence, nor being affected by the degree of aggressiveness shown, nor letting oneself be dominated at the verbal level of communication; but rather trying to understand the discussion 'here and now' whilst asking oneself "Why is this person telling me this? Which kind of feelings is this person trying to trigger inside of me?" Although, this attitude can only be achieved if the therapist remains neutral towards barbaric attacks (McDougall 1993), as well as being able to keep his or her role as an observer of the relationship (Caper 1997).

In this case, when we focus on these questions, it is possible to understand what underlines his comments. As long as a person is able to articulate "I do not feel any remorse about what I have done and I would do it again", in some way this person is showing us that they are aware not only of what remorse means, but also, of the social expectations on them. However, this person experiences a desperate struggle in denying these facts by projecting their fears and weaknesses onto the therapist through their remorseless statements. Hence, any attempt to convince them to take responsibility for the offence committed will fail. From my point of view, the therapist's task in this setting should be to face the other with awkward questions as an approach that intends to disturb their struggle. In this case, Mr. T. was unable to give me an answer to my question; however, he started coming every week to talk to me. Our sessions were characterized by a ritual, always maintaining the same dynamic. He had insistently tried to scare me with his remorseless comments whilst via an 'ironic mirror image approach'; I had tried to leave him with questions in his mind. After several meetings, he came to me one day and told me:

> Mrs. Franieck, I have been dreaming of the victim almost every night . . . what does [this] mean?

My answer was a further question to him, as any possible association or insight should come from him and not from me:

> I don't know . . . I have no idea . . . would you have any idea? Have you already thought about this?

After a short reflection, he answered:

> Maybe I feel guilty about him?!

And suddenly he started yelling:

> No! no! I will stop coming here . . . I do not feel any guilt or remorse! I will stop coming here! I'm going now".

And he went away. Although he never came back after this day, I was sure that even for a few seconds he capable of being in touch with his remorse. It was a powerful transient experience.

Three years later, I met him again in another pretrial detention centre. At that point in time, he had already served two years of his sentence in a juvenile prison. However, due to a family hearing connected to his mother's issues, he had been transferred for a couple of days to this prison, where I was working, as the court was nearby. I can well recall how the guards were disturbed by him when I got in the prison. At that time, the prison was crowded and there was no way of offering individual cells. According to the guards, this new, dangerous, and violent prisoner was refusing to share a cell with other prisoners. Indeed, he had threatened to destroy the whole cell if he did not get an individual cell by the next day. The tension between the new prisoner and the others (prisoners and staff) was high in the prison. The guards then asked me to talk to him. When the guards told me the name of this dangerous prisoner, I had already known that this person was Mr. T.

I must confess that I was doubtful about meeting him again after so long, besides I had no idea how he would react to meeting me again. So, I went to his cell, opened it and just called his name when suddenly I heard:

> Hey, I can recognize this voice . . . Mrs. Franieck is that you?

Indeed, I have a quite unique voice, but I was still surprised by his reaction, and I said:

> Yes, Mr. T. it's me!

Then he walked to the cell door and said:

> Mrs. Franieck, I am so pleased to meet you again! How are you doing?

I then invited him to a chat in the office, and he came quite happily.

The dynamic of our discussion had not changed. Once again, he tried to impress me with all his stories about the prison, in which he was able to show how powerful his aggressiveness was. Then, he started to share his future plans with me. Based on his cultural values, he dreamed of getting justice, and hence, he was convinced that he should go to his parents' fatherland and fight against the Taliban. Then, based on his reaction when he had met me again, I decided for the first time to draw attention to his depression, and told him:

> You know I think that fighting against the Taliban would be very appropriate for you, after all, in your fight with them, you could express all your anger whilst placing yourself at the risk to be killed . . . and if you were killed, you would be able to stop your depression. Indeed, it would be a kind suicide.

I was afraid of his reaction at my words, but he laughed and said:

> You are pretty good! Not as good as another psychologist I know, but I must confess that you are good!

I replied: "Of course, I am not as good!" and we kept talking for almost an hour.

At the end of our ephemeral meeting, I was able to gain his understanding of the prison's administrative inability to offer him an individual cell and he agreed to share a cell with someone else. He stayed in this prison for five more days – and according to the guards, after our discussion, he became calmer und more friendly.

Like the case of Mr. B., in my view, restricted 'transient shared meaning communication' had also been achieved with Mr. T.; if it had not been achieved, then I would not have been able to gain his understanding of the controversial issue about individual cells, nor would I have received his warm welcome after three years.

Case 5: the wolf in sheep's clothing

This case was presented in the 28th Annual Conference of the International Association for Forensic Psychotherapy in spring 2019 in Constance, Germany, under the title: "Just talking to a Terrorist: the wolf in sheep's clothing".

First step: the case of the chase

In October 2018, one Sunday morning, I received a message from the institution director of one of the biggest prisons in Germany (the same person who had once invited me to work at their pretrial detention centre) – he said "an incarcerated traumatized refugee needs help". According to him, the young man demonstrated very unusual behaviour, e.g., he panicked every time he heard planes flying overhead and he avoided contact with other people. The idea that I should talk to him came from the institution director, together with a social worker at the prison who had also worked with me in the past. At that time, I was committed to a full-time job with another employer, but then I decided to take the case on a volunteer basis due to German work policies. The young man's trial had been set for four months' time, so I did not have much time to work with him properly. Hence, I needed to pursue primary goals in my work, such as: reducing traumatic symptoms, adapting and accepting imprisonment, decreasing the risk of aggression (towards others as well as self-harm/suicide), and accepting the future trial and sentence.

Second step: looking beyond the sheep's clothing

Mr. J. was a young male refugee (22 years old) from East Asia, who seemed to be very kind, educated, and completely integrated into his new country. In one and half years, he was able to learn the German language, get a job, and start a relationship with a European girlfriend – he was a clever young man. He held a touching life story, in which he had been arrested by the Islamic State (IS) for several months, and during his imprisonment, he had been psychologically, sexually, and physically abused. Due to these traumatic experiences, he had developed some paranoid symptoms. In particular, whilst we were talking, he compulsively looked over his shoulder to double check if someone might be behind him. He had only agreed to talk to me because the psychologist at the prison, responsible for his case, had told him to do so. He described the psychologist like an angel in his life – a massive projection with clear idealization. Indeed, the psychologist was present at all times during our meetings.

Third step: figuring him out

In drawing his 'timeline', I was confronted by incongruent and contradictory information in his discourse, which led me to suspect that he was actually a member of IS. As usual, I had not read his records beforehand. After drawing his 'timeline', I asked the psychologist about his records in order to get answers to my suspicions. She not only confirmed my suspicions but also informed me that the reason for his incarceration was child sex abuse.

Fourth step: facing the wolf

Gradually, Mr. J. showed himself to be a vengeful person who was unable to forgive; nor did he have any control over his hate or his cold, violent revenge. He mostly hates the other person in silence while planning, in a Machiavellian-like fashion, the death of this person. Killing (eliminating) others was the way he had found to cathartically relieve his evil feelings with confidence that justice would be done. He showed no trace of remorse. Despite his intelligence, emotionally he behaved very regressively, and he was unable to cope with his own feelings. Instead, he rescued himself in an inner emotional war while drastically splitting up reality.

Once, during a talk, he reported to me that every night before lying in bed, he could clearly see the faces of all the people he hated, just like in a film. So, every night, he was able to recall who needed to be killed. Naïvely, I asked him whether he had already seen my face in this evening film. He answered:

MR. J.: "Yes!"

Despite a sense of threat, I tried to preserve my ability to daydream (Cassorla 2018) and asked him:

ME: "OK! Since when have you seen my face in this film before lying in bed?"
MR. J.: "Since the day you asked me about my mother!"

I could not recall anything wrong or hurtful from our chat that day. I was quite puzzled. On reflection, I realized that he was unable to distinguish his inner world and himself from reality – an internal miscommunication. On the language communication level, he was unable to express his feelings of anger or frustration towards the other. On the contrary, he kept those feelings inside him while blaming the other as the source of his evil feelings. Thus, killing the other person is quite a comprehensive way out of this emotional mess (Segal 1957).

Facing this situation and keeping in mind my goals, as well as the short timeframe I had with the prisoner, I had to pursue a simple and effective remedy for communication, so I started thinking about how I could help him express his frustration and rage in a more secure manner. Since he could not express those evil feelings in verbal communication, or by looking into my eyes, I provided him with something like a transitional object that could symbolize a bridge in our communication, as well as in his own communication (the interaction between his primitive and language communication). This object was meant to both contain and express his feelings. Without a doubt, it should be something little, easy to carry, and above all, inoffensive in order to match the security rules of the prison. Hence, I used wooden pendants with the symbol for peace in different colours (red, green, white, and black), bought at a hippie fair, to help us communicate (Figure 5.8).

The red and green pendants were used throughout the communication process in this way: during our conversation, Mr. J. was to keep his eyes fixed on the pendants put on the table and not on me. That is to say, he should just listen to my voice and not look at me. The red pendant symbolized the expression: "I am getting angry/I am angry, please stop!" The green pendant symbolized the expression: "I am OK, please let's keep talking!" We started talking, but if throughout our chat evil feelings should arise inside of Mr. J., then he should move the red

Figure 5.8 Pendants

pendant towards me as a signal of his rage and I should stop talking. Controversially, if he was happy with the topic of the conversation, he should move the green pendant towards me. If someone were to ask me about why he was not to look at me, I cannot give a proper answer. This was just a feeling I had that he needed to be protected, like a baby still in the womb that can listen to the sounds of his mother's heartbeat and perhaps her voice – I perceived this as a very primitive form of communication between us, and I simply tried to give representation to it.

As regards the black and white pendants, they were used to evaluate our session at the end. Thus, the black pendant symbolized the expressions: "I didn't like our discussion today!" or "Our chat was really hard for me today!" Here it is useful to make it clear to the client which of the sentences the black pendant represents – the former, the latter, or both at the same time. The white pendant symbolized the expressions: "I feel pleased with our chat!" or "I feel relieved after our chat!" – The same procedure was followed as with the black pendant. It was also possible to use both pendants at the same time, which meant: "It was OK!" In this case, it is important to clarify which parts of the conversation were more black or white.

Fifth step: 'dancing with the wolf'

With the use of the pendants, he was able to show me in a more secure space (and without fear) at which point/moment he had started hating me, and I was able to assist him in dealing with his evil feelings. Over time, he was able to listen to me without feeling threatened. In particular, he stopped looking over his shoulder, since I had told him that what he feared was his own hate and not someone else. In addition, he became more sociable with the others in the prison. Furthermore, using the pedants, he was able to learn how to detect his own feelings, at least when in contact with me. Without doubt, our encounters became less tense. I kept talking to him until a week before his trial. From the psychologist, I received news that he had been transferred to a sentencing prison, and that he had been able to face his trial, as well as his sentence, and that he had accepted the idea of future psychological treatment.

So far, this was my last case in the forensic setting. Getting my emotions in balance, in such a dangerous and threatening moment of communication, while also assessing a mentally ill person properly, was a daunting challenge. Many times, during our discussions, I had had to put my fears to one side while dealing with his assessment. But then again, I was also required to confront them; otherwise, I would not have been able to go further and initiate our conversation, or the 'analytic third', as referred to by Ogden (2004/1994).

Some personal observations

It is true that the work in an ephemeral milieu is to a certain extent frustrating, as one is unable to track any progress. Indeed, the sense of anything lasting should be continually dealt with, in order to avoid a negative influence on the development of communication. Nevertheless, it can be perceived as a unique form of training in which the therapist has to cope with frustration, uncertainties, and transience. Not to mention the variety of offences one learns about – from simple theft or possession of marijuana to barbaric murders or unimaginable sexual abuse. This ephemeral milieu is really another world, in which one gets to know about what I call *the dark side* of humanity (italics are mine). It is true that my experience in this milieu helped me to quickly recognize patients' aggressive potential and not to fear them as well. Nevertheless, in my work, I became less idealistic, more realistic, and probably colder as I started perceiving *the dark side* of all patients, including the most traumatized one. Case 3 in Chapter 6 illustrates well what I mean. As to whether this may be considered as a positive or negative feature, this will be addressed in Chapter 10.

References

Alexandris, A., and Vaslamatzis, G., eds., 1993. *Countertransference: Theory, Technique, Teaching*. London: Karnac Books.

Bion, W.R., 1970. *Attention and Interpretation*. London: Tavistock Publications.
Bion, W.R., 1984. *Learning from Experience*. London: Maresfield Reprints.
Caper, R., 1997. Symbol Formation and Creativity: Hannas Segal's Theoretical Contributions. *In:* D. Bell, ed. *Reason and Passion: A Celebration of the Work of Hanna Segal*. London: Routledge, 37–56.
Cassorla, R.M.S., 2018. *The Psychoanalyst, the Theatre of Dreams and the Clinic of Enactment*. Abingdon, Oxon and New York: Routledge.
Castrechini-Franieck, M.L., 2014. We Were Born on the Street, How Do Experiences of Transience and Permanence Affect Us? *Other/Wise Uncut*, 3 (Winter), 43–67.
Castrechini-Franieck, M.L., Günter, M., and Page, T., 2014. Engaging Brazilian Street Children in Play: Observations of Their Family Narratives. *Child Development Research*, 861703.
Castrechini-Franieck, M.L., and Page, T., 2017. The Family Narratives of Three Siblings Living in a 'Street Situation' Since Birth. *Early Child Development and Care*, 189 (10), 1575–1587.
Fritz, E., and Beekman, L., 2011. *Engaging Clients Actively in Telling Stories and Actualising Dreams*. Leiden, The Netherlands: Brill, Sense, 163–175.
Fritz, E., and van Zyl, G., 2015. Lifelines. *In:* M. McMahon and M. Watson, eds. *Career Assessment: Qualitative Approaches*. Rotterdam: Sense Publishers, 89–96.
Gilligan, J., 2001. *Preventing Violence*. London: Thames & Hudson.
Havel, V., and Hvížďala, K., 1991. *Disturbing the Peace: A Conversation with Karel Hvížďala*. 1st ed. New York: Vintage Books.
McDougall, J., 1993. Countertransference and Primitive Communication. *In:* A. Alexandris and G. Vaslamatzis, eds. *Countertransference: Theory, Technique, Teaching*. London: Karnac, 95–134.
Ogden, T.H., 2004/1994. *Subjects of Analysis*. 1st ed. Lanham, MD: Rowman & Littlefield.
Schauer, M., and Ruf-Leuschner, M., 2014. Lifeline in Narrative Exposure Therapy. *Psychotherapeut*, 59, 226–238.
Segal, H., 1957. Notes on Symbol Formation. *The International Journal of Psychoanalysis*, 38 (6), 391–397.
Stein, H.F., 2017. *Listening Deeply: An Approach to Understanding and Consulting in Organizational Culture*. Columbia: University of Missouri Press.
Welldon, E.V., and van Velsen, C., 1997. *A Practical Guide to Forensic Psychotherapy*. London: Jessica Kingsley.
Winnicott, D.W., 1953. Transitional Objects and Transitional Phenomena: A Study of the First Not-Me Possession. *The International Journal of Psycho-analysis*, 34, 89–97.
Winnicott, D.W., 1992/1987. Communication Between Infant and Mother, Mother and Infant, Compared and Contrasted. *In:* D.W. Winnicott, *et al.*, eds. *Babies and Their Mothers*. Reading, MA and Wokingham: Addison-Wesley, 89–104.
Winnicott, D.W., 2018. The Mother-Infant Experience of Mutuality. *In: Psycho-Analytic Explorations*. London: Routledge, 251–260.

Part three

TICA in intercultural settings

Chapter 6

TICA in short-term therapy with traumatized refugees

A substantial part of this chapter is based on the article "Giving deeply traumatised refugees the space they need in which to reconstruct the boundary they have lost between reality and fantasy, while they face language and cultural barriers" which was presented in the 26th Annual Interdisciplinary Conference of the International Forum for Psychoanalytic Education in autumn 2015, in Philadelphia, United States and originally published in *Other/Wise: The Online Journal of the International Forum for Psychoanalytic Education* (Castrechini-Franieck 2017a).

Working simultaneously with tormentor and prey

I started working clinically with traumatized refugees already when I was working in the pretrial detention centre. As referred to in Chapter 3, despite the drastic change in the patients' profiles, the focus on the psychological work was kept unaltered, although the methods were quite distinct from one another. While transience (Castrechini-Franieck 2014) was a core feature of the sessions with the patients in pretrial detention, permanence and 'holding' (Winnicott 1990/1984) were the key characteristics in the work with traumatized patients. It is true that language issues can be overcome through interview drawings in ephemeral meetings, as was illustrated in Chapter 5. However, it is not sufficient enough to support lasting contact with the patients. In this new milieu, an interpreter had to be involved in order to handle major verbal communication barriers – this daunting challenge had a major effect in advancing TICA.

Brief understanding of refugees' issues

Social situation

The refugee crisis in Europe has drawn attention to those who have been struggling to feel safe and to rebuild their lives in a 'dream country'. Migration always embodies three phases: pre-migration, migration, and post-migration, which together may result in a series of adverse experiences. Prior to migration and during the migration process, refugees may experience traumatic events such as

DOI: 10.4324/9781003232087-9

war and violence, followed by torture and persecution. Following migration, refugees are confronted with other challenges. Issues playing a key role in contributing to other levels of distress include the length of the relocation, the degree of similarity between the home country and the country to which they are fleeing, language differences, and access to social support systems, employment, and educational opportunities, as well as acceptance by the new culture. From the need to leave home to the perils of migration, refugees and asylum seekers experience an extremely high prevalence of psychiatric disorders, usually depression and/ or post-traumatic stress disorder (PTSD) (Castrechini-Franieck 2017a; Slobodin and Jong 2014). Nearly 40% of refugees are deeply traumatized (Jensen 2013; Burnett and Peel 2001) and are thus in need of urgent psychological support. Nevertheless, the psychological centres in Europe are overcrowded and are unable to assist all the refugees. Given the length of time and the expense of psychoanalytic treatment, it would not be feasible to apply psychoanalysis to so many vulnerable people, despite its valuable contribution to the treatment of trauma. Studies report positive outcomes for short-term interventions, like narrative exposure therapy (NET) and cognitive behavioural therapy (CBT), when it comes to reducing trauma-related symptoms. Nevertheless, hardly any patients are in fact free from PTSD at the end of such interventions. An intervention cannot merely focus on isolated symptoms, since other dimensions of personality – such as improvements in relationships, and social/cultural identity – should equally be included as indicators of intervention (Slobodin and Jong 2014). From my understanding, the intervention should predominantly focus on reconstructing the boundary between reality and fantasy, lost during the experience of a traumatic event, by rescuing symbolizations and representations – a way to help them to rediscover their sense of self.

Psychological situation

The features of an individual's reaction to the traumatic experience are grounded in feelings of helplessness, which in turn are rooted in the trauma experienced at birth, alongside the loss of the "containing object" (Grinberg and Grinberg 1989, pp. 81–82). Unquestionably, immigration consists of leaving behind one's roots and moving in search of something still unknown and unclear. For this reason, a deprived refugee, metaphorically speaking, may be compared to what Winnicott *et al.* (2012, p. 106) referred to as the "deprived child". Without doubt, any form of immigration not only involves a withdrawal from the 'mother country' for the individual, but also a loss of something good that has been positive in one's life up to a certain point in time (Winnicott *et al.* 2012, p. 106). In most cases, the withdrawal might last for a period of time which is longer than the containment feeling can be kept alive. When that occurs, the transitional space needed for 'interplay' between the culture of origin and the new culture (between the past and the future) remains restricted (Winnicott 2005). Indeed, the new country obviously will be unable to fulfil all idealized expectations built on the losses left behind. Hence, the feeling of not being contained is – to a certain extent – real and not just phantasy. Due to different circumstances and depending on each individual's personal experience, this can also trigger the feeling of not belonging anywhere – the feeling of being an 'Outsider' – which in turn challenges ego cohesion (Castrechini-Franieck 2017b). Undoubtedly, by undergoing adverse situations, refugees and asylum seekers will probably experience their phantasies in a concrete, non-symbolic way that will inhibit abstract thoughts and symbol formations, while sparking fears of ego disintegration and disillusion. Consequently, the boundaries between the inner world and the external world (phantasies and external/real objects) become blurred, and the ego feels threatened (Caper 1997; Grinberg and Grinberg 1989). Moreover, language issues present a challenge for refugees and asylum seekers. Often compelled to cope with mourning processes without experiencing a container object, their ability to use symbolization might be severely diminished, bringing about a lack of communication – one of the key issues in the onset of psychosis. Needless to say, in any form of migration, a pattern of factors emerges which triggers anxiety and sorrow: individuals are forced to cope with mourning processes over and over again while facing future uncertainties. Immigration seems, therefore, to put an individual's whole identity at risk (Grinberg and Grinberg 1989), since some values from the previously introjected cultural ideal have to be sacrificed and/or altered (Franieck and Günter 2010). Metaphorically speaking, this experience is almost an act of regression towards a primitive state where self-symbolization and language skills still need to be developed (Castrechini-Franieck 2017b).

Triangular constellations

Metaphorically speaking, every immigration process evokes quite similar psychological responses to those found in the Oedipus complex, since when immigrating, one has to abandon one's 'mother country' in favour of a 'new object' (it is no wonder that the Oedipus tragedy begins with Oedipus' immigration).

The work with traumatized refugees is characterized by dealing with triangular constellations at several levels, as will be described further. Being aware of the existing triangular constellations and understanding their mechanisms is fundamental for establishing meaningful communication (Castrechini-Franieck 2017b).

The role of the interpreter in the therapeutic setting

The collected works on interpreters shows several differences between interpreting in mental health settings and in other settings. Mental health is a specialized area; interpreters may be affected by the emotional waves of interpreting in mental health services (Green *et al.* 2012), requiring advanced interpreter knowledge and skills (Leanza *et al.* 2014; Searight and Searight 2009). In addition, the literature has mostly drawn attention to the fact that psychotherapy with interpreters means having the dyad setting changed into a triad. Against this backdrop, the interpreters are usually placed in the third position, which must only serve to provide clear communication between the other two, in a neutral way – an interpreter is there to translate what the therapist and the patient say; the focus is not on a form of cultural mediation (Bot and Wadensjö 2004; Becker and Bowles 2001). To some extent, in this perspective, the interpreter remains as a non-person (Prosser and Bawaneh 2010). Controversially, some authors defend the complexity of working with interpreters by emphasizing several variables that should not be neglected in this framework, such as interpersonal and intrapsychic experiences in the setting, equivalence of words in the patient's language while expressing various psychological concepts, and cultural identity (Resera *et al*. 2015; Engstrom *et al*. 2010; Mahtani 2003; Tribe and Morrissey 2003).

From my experience, the interpreter needs to be integrated as a central element belonging to the setting; after all, both therapist and patient depend on him or her for a basic verbal communication process to take place. It is also true that generally the interpreter may often embody the symbol of container for the refugee-patient, as the mother tongue triggers all childhood experiences, memories, and feelings about early object relations (Grinberg and Grinberg 1989, p. 90). Even so, the interpreter is a stranger to the patient's internal world and very likely does not correspond to the archaic internal objects of the patient (Riesenberg-Malcolm 1999, p. 39).

The therapist's role in the triangular constellation

In this setting, the therapist should have the ability to turn this triangular setting into a scenario in which the therapist is the leader (group psychology is being referred to here and not group psychotherapy) – with similar flexibility as to leadership in a multicultural team (Maude 2016, p. 128). There are two things that need to be dealt with in this regard.

The first is related to the triangular setting referred to as therapist, patient, and interpreter. In this setting, the therapist should remain aware of the fact that the patient and the interpreter share the same language, as well as a similar cultural background, and the therapist should respect this – in most cases, they share the same cultural ideal (Franieck and Günter 2010). In other words, the therapist needs to not only be able to perceive himself or herself as the third person in a triangular relationship (and not transfer/or project the third position onto the interpreter), but also to master his or her regressive ambivalence (hatred/jealousy) while rediscovering his or her personal impulse. In doing so, the therapist displays his or her ability to cope with exclusion, and therefore the patient can identify himself or herself with the therapist through feelings of exclusion and/or loneliness (Grinberg and Grinberg 1989; Winnicott 1958) – a therapeutic bond can be established.

The second aspect that needs to be addressed refers to the triangular relationship established between patient and therapist exclusively, whereby the interpreter is left out. This autonomous scenario occurs in parallel to the previous one and should become the centre of communication with the patient – with its verbal, non-verbal and pre-verbal forms of communication. In other words:

> This means that the recognition of projective identification is central to the understanding of the psychoanalytical material . . . The patient does not only express himself through words. He also uses actions, and sometimes words and actions. The analyst listens, observes and feels the patient's communications. He scrutinises his own responses to the patient, trying to understand the effect the patient's behaviour has on himself, and he understands this as a communication from the patient.
> (Riesenberg-Malcolm 1999, pp. 39–40]

> [T]he analyst must have the capacity to be affected by the patient's projection- to form countertransference- in order to be sensitive to the patient. But he must also be able to distance himself from the projection, so he may observe the countertransference . . . . The analyst is indeed in a triangular relationship with the patient, on the one hand, and his internal object, on the other.
> (Caper 1997, p. 48)

To put in another way, pre-verbal and non-verbal communication in this setting should have supremacy over a verbal one; hence, the dependence on the interpreter can be diminished. Pre-verbal and non-verbal communication can be grasped by the way in which the patient brought his or her communication (Joseph *et al*. 1989), above all through a counter-transference reaction (Alexandris and Vaslamatzis 1993). That is why the therapist should concomitantly display the role as observer of the communication field created between him or her and the patient (Caper 1997, pp. 48–49) – coping with this triangular relationship is a key part of the communication process.

TICA – building 'shared meaning communication' while rescuing symbolization

When I started working with traumatized refugees, my mind was once again preoccupied by lots of questions. As with the withdrawal therapy setting, my main concern was how I would be able to communicate with the patients, considering all the verbal linguistic challenges. In the past, in withdrawal therapy, I was the only immigrant and 'shared meaning communication' was able to be developed with the patients through 'interpretation training' in the German language. Although German is not my mother tongue, at least it represented a common bond between us. Now, my traumatized patient was also an immigrant like me, from quite a different culture than mine; however, we both came from a collectivist dimension (House 2004; Trompenaars and Hampden-Turner 1997; Hofstede and Bond 1984). Since the German language was a foreign language for both of us, there was a reversed common bond in this setting when compared to a withdrawal therapy setting. How was I going to achieve 'shared meaning communication' in this new milieu? What could be the basis of our communication? On reflection, I realized that the communication should start from our shared experience of being 'Outsiders', from our feelings of relearning to express ourselves again – this was the seed of our 'shared meaning communication'. Instead of 'interpretation training', we could "invent a third language' with the purpose of developing our 'shared meaning communication" (Grinberg and Grinberg 1989, pp. 99–112), or the 'analytic third' as perceived by Ogden (2004/1994).

So, my role in this setting was to offer a neutral space for communication between me and the patient – an intermediate area of experience (Winnicot 1971), to facilitate the communication through the experience of 'mutuality' (Winnicott 2018) or 'affect attunement' (Stern 1995) as well as the 'reverie' ability (Bion 1984a, 1984b). To this end, most of the communication between me and the patient was to be encouraged via an external object, such as a picture/cartoon with very specific themes, like the ones adopted in the withdrawal therapy described in Chapter 4 and/or the drawings as described in Chapter 5. For instance, the 'duck and rabbit' cartoon presented in Chapter 3 and Chapter 4 is more than an accurate way of communicating in this intercultural milieu. With regards to the interpreter's role in this context, this kind of approach gives more freedom to the therapist, since the basis for communication between patient and therapist takes place using the external object. The communication needs to be less verbal, short and more concrete, which could, for example, be achieved by drawing the 'fairy-tale' picture as in Case 1, which represents what the therapist understands from the patient. The steps in the 'fairy-tale' drawing (Figure 6.1) are as follows.

> I take an A4 piece of paper and turn it horizontally and draw (or do not draw) something on it. To illustrate: if the patient is silent for a long time and the therapist notices that he or she is locked in his or her inner world and does not speak due to the language barrier, then I ask the interpreter to ask the patient what he or she has in mind at that precise moment, what is he or she thinking about? In most cases, the patients answer "Nothing!", which is to be expected considering their difficulties in transferring their feelings into thoughts, due not only to the trauma experienced but also due to the language issues as was emphasized previously. It is true that this answer could also indicate a defensive reaction or an attack on the bond developed between therapist and patient. Nonetheless, I would emphasize that my goal is focused on communication, accompanied by interaction and not simply interpretation. Then, I usually take a white A4 piece of paper and point my index finger towards the patient's head and then towards the white paper and say: "So are you telling me that your mind is like this white paper? There is nothing in your mind?!"

The patients usually understand my '*verbal communication*' before the interpreter is able to translate it, as they smile and shake their head just after I have

Figure 6.1 Blank paper

spoken. Even so, the interpreter translates. Usually, I receive this as an answer: "He or she had already understood what you meant and says that no, his or her mind is not like this white paper. There are lots of confused thoughts!" After this approach, the process of interaction between the patient and myself is simplified and the patient feels more secure about talking, especially with the help of the interpreter as it is illustrated in Case 1. Here, any interpretation should rely more on the object relations aspect or corrective attachment experiences (Stern 1995) and less on the past. In addition, the transference needs to be understood as an emotional relationship experienced in the present – that is, the "here-and-now" (Riesenberg-Malcolm 1999, p. 52).

As mentioned in Chapter 5, drawing has two major benefits, and it is also a simple and attractive approach that has an immense impact on communication with the patient. In work with traumatized refugees, drawing is a very beneficial method, since it allows the spontaneous creation of an exchange between therapist and patient, despite the interpreter's presence. It is quite common for the patient to ask for a pen or a pencil to be able to add something to their 'fairytale' story. Indeed, drawings may also embody metaphors that belong to language and culture in a setting in which the therapist's and the patient's mother tongues are so diverse – a vivid pathway on building 'shared meaning communication'. The 'timeline' described in Chapter 5, for instance, has an extremely supportive emotional effect on the traumatized patients. Through the development of this timeline, the patients can spontaneously talk about their traumatic event without fearing their ego disintegration. On the contrary, the patients feel their traumatic and awful phantasies as becoming more manageable as well as contained, whilst they also undergo a process of representation, as illustrated in Case 3.

The 'feelings wheel' (Figure 6.2) is another useful drawing approach that can be replicated from time to time to assess the possible progression of the therapy, as it was in Cases 1 and 2.

The 'feelings wheel', which I adopted, is an adaptation of Plutchik's wheel of emotions (Plutchik and Kellerman 2014), combined with four of the five basic feelings of Casriel (1972). The two steps of performing the 'feelings wheel' are as follows.

Step 1: The introduction of the task

> I usually have an A4 piece of paper with the 'feelings wheel' printed on it, as in Figure 6.2, and I have coloured pencils with me. However, one can simply take an A4 piece of paper and spontaneously draw the 'feelings wheel' on it, writing the five feelings and working without coloured pencils, as Figure 6.3 illustrates.

Then, I ask the interpreter to start translating my speech:

> Look at this paper, please! This is the feelings wheel. This circle here represents your emotional world, or I would say your heart.

Feelings wheel

- Joy/pleasure
- Love
- Anger/hate
- Sadness
- Fear
- Any other?

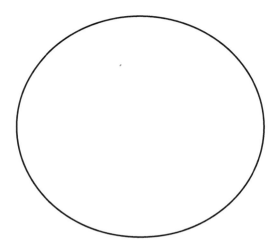

Figure 6.2 Printed feelings wheel

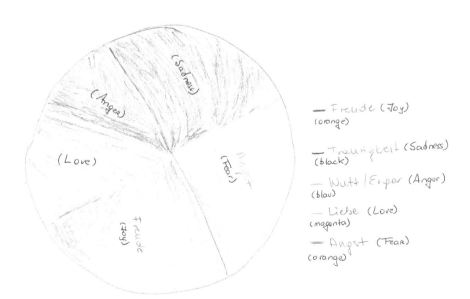

Figure 6.3 Feelings wheel

[Pause for translation.]

> Here there are five feelings: joy/pleasure, love, anger/hate, sadness and fear.

[Pause for translation. If the patient is literate, the interpreter writes the names of the feelings in their mother tongue.]

> Please give a colour for each feeling. One colour may mean more than one feeling, if you want.

[Pause for translation and wait for the colours to be chosen.]

> OK! Please mark each feeling with its respective colour!

[Pause for translation and then wait for the patient to mark the feelings.]

> Now, look at this wheel please . . . your heart . . . try to share all the feelings in your heart . . . how do you sense these feelings inside you now? . . . I mean, how big is the feeling of pleasure in your heart now? And love? And anger/hate? (Pause for translation). Sometimes the patient does not understand the task. In which case, a further explanation is necessary, such as: 'Here you have five feelings and all of them are inside your heart (show the wheel and point towards his or her heart), but each one takes up a certain amount of space inside your heart . . . show me here in your heart how big the felling of sadness is. Take your time and think about it . . . I'm not in a hurry!

This explanation usually triggers a positive response.

Step 2: Interpretation of the drawing

> Once the patient has chosen the colours for the feelings and has shared and drawn them in the wheel with their respective colours, it is time to talk about the wheel – to give representation to it. There is no structured analysis of it; each patient can provide different representations of their feelings. After all, they are representations of one's emotional experience in the 'here and now' with the patient (Bion 1965).
> I usually first try to observe which colours were chosen, whether they are primary or secondary ones, as well as if a colour was chosen twice or more than twice. The latter is very important, as a colour defining more than one feeling could mean that these feelings may be experienced in a blurred emotional way and are related to one another. Second, I observe the feelings wheel gestalt. That is, the size of each feeling (similar, different, bigger, smaller), which feelings are near to each other (in my chat with the patient, I usually use the word 'neighbour'), and the general position of the feelings in the wheel (whether or not there is any supremacy). Then, I start to

verbalize my first impressions and the feelings triggered inside of me by their 'feelings wheel', as illustrated in Cases 1 and 2. To do this, the therapist needs to be open to experiencing his or her 'daydreaming' (Cassorla 2018).

To illustrate the therapeutic benefit of drawings during communication, some cases will be presented in what follows. Here the treatment of trauma is not in question, but the achievement of 'shared meaning communication'.

Case 1: love burns

Mrs. A. was a woman from Asia in her mid-30s. She was five months pregnant and the mother of three male children. When I took on her case, the indication for therapy was based on fortnightly sessions and the diagnosis was depression caused by trauma. During our first encounter, she came accompanied by a man, who needed to wait for her in the waiting room. She was wearing a black dress and a black headscarf. The dress was long, with long sleeves, and it covered her entire neck. From what little one could see of her face and her hands, it was clear that she had burn scars. Her facial expressions were plastic if not paralyzed, without any signs of emotion. We introduced ourselves with the help of the interpreter. Then, she was far away with her thoughts, a long silence fell in the room, and I approached her by drawing the 'fairy tales' described previously (the white A4 sheet of paper). After this approach, our bond was better, and we were able to draw her 'timeline'.

Her 'timeline' in short covered the following points: she got married very young (at 13 years old) to an older man – a forced marriage, which is a tradition in her culture. It is also a cultural tradition for a woman to be beaten by her husband if he thinks his wife needs to learn a lesson. In her marriage, this was a common occurrence. One day, during a visit to a relative, she met a single man of the same age (the man who was in the waiting room), who was also a relative. The connection between them was so intense that they fell in love immediately. They kept meeting in secret for a while in this relative's house, though they were afraid their love might be revealed. A wife betraying her husband in their culture could mean a death sentence for the wife by stoning, so they planned to flee together; however, as she wanted to bring her children with her, it was not possible to flee quickly. In the meantime, her husband found out about the betrayal and threw her out of the house and imprisoned her children.

It is important to understand that in her culture, in the case of a wife who is cheating on her husband, the woman will lose the right to see her children forever, as the children belong to the father. Similarly, in the case of widowhood, the husband's stepbrothers have the right over the children if the widow decides to remarry to a non-family member. A widow must usually marry one of her brothers-in-law in order to keep her children.

Mrs. A. became desperate without her children; however, she had to flee quickly before receiving her death sentence. She tried to see her children one more time before leaving and was then set on fire – her husband threw petrol over her body and set her on alight – 80% of her body was burnt. After a long time in hospital, both Mrs. A. and her lover fled to Europe without her children.

After drawing her 'timeline', I was able to create some first impressions of her by considering the features of her clothes, her plastic facial expressions, and her mental absence. In our second session, we worked with the 'feelings wheel'. For her, joy/pleasure was moss green, sadness was black, fear was yellow, love was red, and anger/hate was purple (Figure 6.4).

What attracted my attention first was that anger/hate was a secondary colour based on red, a primary one. So, in my free association, I asked myself whether the meaning of love and anger/hate could be blurred symbolically inside her due to her personal history (marriage = violence; to be in love = loss, pain). Then, she divided the wheel into six parts, one of which had no colour.

When I asked her "What does this uncoloured part mean?" She answered me: "Emptiness!"

Then, I simply said: "Yes, I understand. Thanks! So, I see that two-thirds of your heart is full of sadness and emptiness! [Pause for translation.] Emptiness separates love from the other feelings and love can only be in touch with sadness! [Pause for translation.] On the contrary, sadness is the only feeling that is in touch with all the other feelings, including the feeling of emptiness! [Pause for translation.] It seems very confusing . . . and very painful indeed!" [Pause for translation.] She listened to the interpreter very attentively while nodding. Then, I asked her whether my thoughts made any sense to her and she answered: "I feel relieved now!"

Feelings wheel

- Joy/pleasure
- Love
- Anger/hate
- Sadness
- Fear
- Any other?

Second meeting

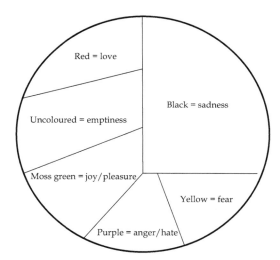

Figure 6.4 Feelings wheel – Case 1 – second meeting

From my experience, I have learnt that simply talking about possible strange fantasies (or, like in that moment, about the 'feelings wheel') without fear, without prejudice, and above all, by accepting them as they are, may be analogous to the process of transforming β-elements into α-elements – 'maternal reverie' (Bion 1984a) – thus the patient feels relieved.

Given that she was pregnant, I decided to focus the work on improving her depressive psychological state by the time she gave birth. Thus, the 'feelings wheel' was our thematic treatment for a couple of meetings and our chat focused on whether the emptiness and sadness might be an expression of the blurred connection between love and anger/hate. Once, when talking about her emotional situation, I approached her with the 'fairy-tale' drawing, as follows: "Look at the picture I had in my mind during our discussion". Then, I started to draw (see Figure 6.5).

> I see a flame burning . . . however, there are two arcs that limit the growth of this flame . . . [Pause for translation.] It is like the flame should not grow . . . but just be maintained . . . Would you fear it? [Pause for translation.] What about what the flame means? I am still not sure whether it means the warm and power of your love . . . or whether it means sadness and the power of your anger . . . [Pause for translation.] Love and anger are two different feelings . . . but here in a single picture . . . a flame . . . with the same power . . . .

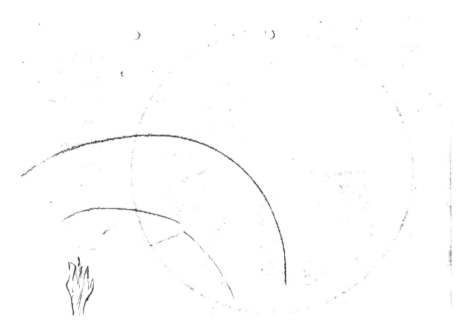

Figure 6.5 Flame

128 TICA in intercultural settings

leaving you in fear. [Pause for translation.] Does my picture make any sense to you? [Pause for translation.]

Then, she answered: "*Yes!*", and despite her tears, we were able to talk in more depth about her conflicting feelings towards her choice of love, which had also cost her the loss of her children, as well as the loss/damage of her own body – this was the seed of Mrs. A.'s case.

In my experience, I have perceived that during the traumatic moment, one immediately experiences antagonistic feelings, and their psychological apparat is unable to give them representations. Then, I would say, it becomes an ongoing psychic wound. Talking about these antagonistic feelings without moral values and without any fear is extremely helpful for the patients.

To return to Mrs. A.'s case, in the course of time, I noticed that she was coming to the session wearing more colourful clothing and was not so worried about hiding her burn scars. In our last meeting before Mrs. A. gave birth, four months after the start of her treatment, I replicated the 'feelings wheel' for the purpose of assessing possible changes. This time, her feelings of joy/pleasure were violet-red, sadness was brown, fear was still yellow, love was still red, and anger/hate had turned into green (see Figure 6.6).

What attracted my attention in particular this time was that joy/pleasure represented a secondary colour based on the primary colour red, and anger/hate had changed to green, still a secondary colour although not based on red, but based on yellow. That is to say, four months into the treatment, she had connected love to joy/pleasure and anger/hate to fear. She had divided the wheel into six parts again – and again, one part had no colour. When I asked her "What does this uncoloured

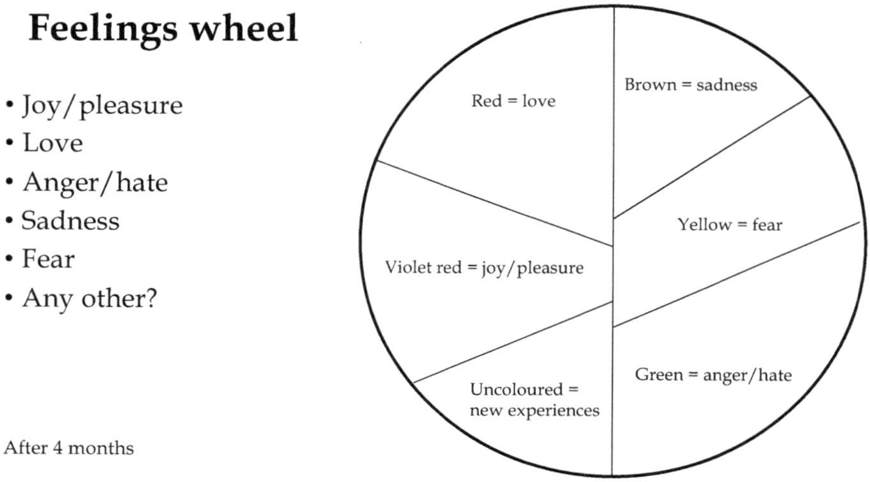

Feelings wheel

- Joy/pleasure
- Love
- Anger/hate
- Sadness
- Fear
- Any other?

After 4 months

Figure 6.6 Feelings wheel – Case 1 – after four months

part mean?", she answered me: "The unknown and new experiences that will still happen in my life!"

At this point, I felt it necessary to connect the changes with the upcoming birth of her child; thus, I replied: "So emptiness has become expectation, a beautiful metamorphosis, and I think this is related to the approaching time of birth".

She replied: "Definitely!"

Then, I added: "What I can see now is that half of your heart is full of joy/pleasure, love and expectations. [Pause for translation] . . . and joy/pleasure and love are touching and have quite similar colours. [Pause for translation] . . . the other half of your heart is full of sadness, fear and anger/hate. [Pause for translation] . . . fear stays between sadness and anger/hate and also is connected more to the latter. [Pause for translation.] . . . But then when I look at your heart as a whole, I notice that all six parts of it (or six feelings) are also equally divided. [Pause for translation]". After the end of the translation, she smiled and said: "I feel lighter. Thank you!" I followed this case for nine more months. Her development can be metaphorically compared to the metamorphosis of a butterfly.

Once again, I would like to draw the reader's attention to the fact that my focus was always to offer her a neutral and protected space for communication between us, where she would feel embraced, whilst rescuing symbolizations. By the achievement of 'shared meaning communication', it was possible to recreate a new and corrective experience in the interpersonal relationship with me, the therapist (Stern 1995). As a result, she was able to be more attentive and open to a new and important form of communication with her little baby, instead of remaining closed in her internal world.

Case 2: overcoming a taboo

Mrs. B. was a woman in her early 20s, married, without children, with a diagnosis of depression caused by trauma, and an indication for therapy on a fortnightly sessional basis. During our first encounter, we were able to draw her 'timeline' and the 'feelings wheel'.

A summary of her 'timeline' is as follows: she belonged to a religious group that was not welcome in her country and made up approximately 11% of the population. From an early age, she was faced with prejudice and bullying due to her religion. Bulling in particular was a constant trial for her at school, especially in her teens, which she describes as very painful indeed. She got engaged very young to a boy of the same religion, which according to her, relieved the pain of exclusion experienced at school. Just after their marriage, her husband started being persecuted by soldiers opposed to the couple's religion. In fact, he was a political activist and had to flee and stay in hiding for a long time. Meanwhile, her house was raided by the soldiers looking for her husband. They held her prisoner. At this point, she reports having been mistreated, having been beaten, but not having been raped. After some time, her husband returned, and they fled to Europe.

130 TICA in intercultural settings

Based on my intercultural experience and being aware of the religious conflicts that took place in her country, I was almost convinced that she would have suffered multiple and concomitant instances of rape, although I was facing a taboo. My hypothesis was also reinforced by the fact that she had not yet become pregnant (an exception in her culture), considering that she had fled with her husband more than two years ago. In an effort to widen the neutral space and improve communication to overcome the taboo, I proposed the drawing of the 'feelings wheel' (Figure 6.7).

Her 'feelings wheel' was deeply expressive. Absence, emptiness, non-existence, low self-esteem, loss and death were feeling representations that preoccupied my thoughts as I saw her 'feelings wheel'. Joy/pleasure and fear shared the same colour – dark grey, sadness and anger/hate also shared the same colour – orange-brown, and love was orange. So, all the colours (and feelings) were in connection to one another, and the boundaries between them were very fine, hence the feelings might have remained without any distinction, without any clear representation. Indeed, they were just little empty points. This gave me the idea of telling her:

> When I look at your 'feelings wheel', I sense feelings of loneliness, puzzlement, emptiness, non-existence, as though everything were broken inside and there were no differences between your emotions. [Pause for translation.] I do not think that all these feelings have been roused because you were just beaten . . . [Pause for translation] . . . you know, I think that the soldiers did more to you . . . I think that they raped you . . . but maybe you might be ashamed to talk about this or maybe you even feel that you should not talk

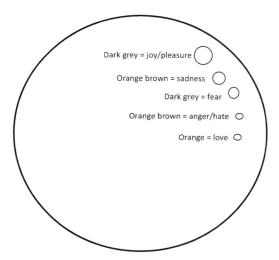

Feelings wheel

- Joy/pleasure
- Love
- Anger/hate
- Sadness
- Fear
- Any other?

First meeting

Figure 6.7 Feeling's wheel – Case 2 – first meeting

about this [Pause for translation] . . . I understand . . . and I am not expecting you to tell me anything if you don't want to . . . however, I do think that I need to tell you what I have in mind . . . and to be honest with you. [Pause for translation].

My last sentence to her was a similar approach adopted in Case 1 in Chapter 5 – by offering her the freedom of not telling me, I am actually giving her back her ability to have some control over herself – control that was lost when she was raped. Simultaneously, my openness in sharing the fantasies raised in my mind by her drawing, expresses my willingness to understand her mutually, my attempts to transform β-elements into α-elements, and finally my tolerance with regards to taboo issues. During the translation, she had tears in her eyes whilst nodding affirmatively with a slight smile. Then, I asked her:

Tell me please, how do you feel now? Do you think I was too intrusive? I am worried that you might interpret my words as another violation!

Her answer to my question was:

No, I feel embraced! I feel myself relieved, as if a burden has been taken off my shoulders!

The sessions with her which followed were focused on bringing back her sense of self. Our discussion was characterized by 'fairy-tale' drawings, which had a positive resonance for her. Two months later, I replicated the 'feelings wheel' to assess possible changes. The second 'feelings wheel' surprised me again (see Figure 6.8).

This time, joy/pleasure was light blue, sadness was moss green, fear had turned into brown, anger/hate had become orange now, and love had turned into red. Indeed, each feeling had been given a new colour. Love was a primary colour, connected to anger/hate as well as fear (secondary colours); and joy/pleasure, also a primary colour, was connected to sadness (a secondary one). The little empty points were transformed into small circles. Some circles were completely filled with colour (fear and anger/hate), others were only half filled with colour (pleasure/happiness and sadness) and finally, only one was empty (love). I verbalized all of this to her, which had a positive effect. Unfortunately, the short-term therapy had to be interrupted after two weeks as she moved with her husband to another city, where he had got a job. The abrupt end to our therapy became a theme for our last encounters, which was approached as a normal development in life. I also focused our final discussions (with the help of the drawings) on rediscovering her potential and highlighting her strengths. After all, since she had survived an awful experience, she must certainly have some unique psychological resources.

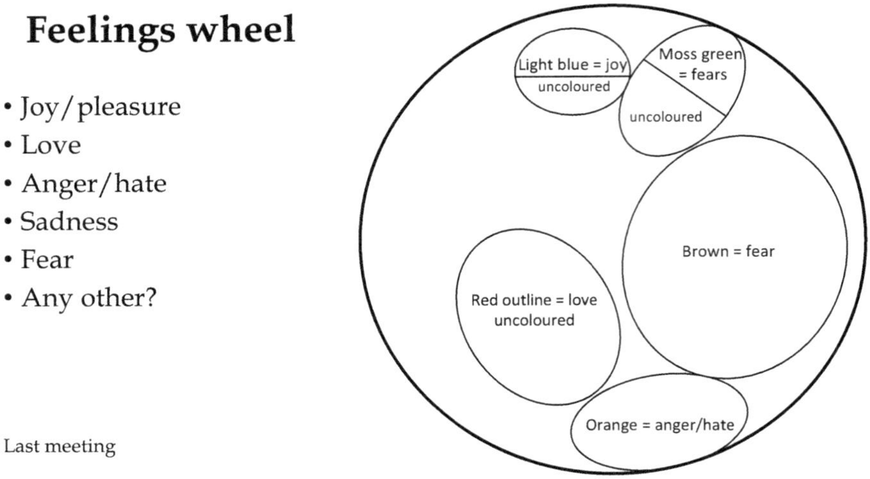

Feelings wheel

- Joy/pleasure
- Love
- Anger/hate
- Sadness
- Fear
- Any other?

Last meeting

Figure 6.8 Feelings wheel – Case 2 – last meeting

Case 3: from a case of shame to a lost case

This case was presented at the 28th Annual Conference of the International Association for Forensic Psychotherapy, in spring 2019 in Constance, Germany, under the title: "Who was offended first?"

Much has been reported about the Yezidi women kept in IS prisons in Iraq who were constantly raped and even group raped by several men from IS. During imprisonment, some of these women died, others gave birth; some, however, were released. It is also known that in 2015, a number of released women were sent to Europe and Canada in order to undergo psychological help. Most of them were placed in convents due to protection policies. Since then, less has been reported about the psychological state of these women, as most of them have refused to undergo any kind of psychological help, while closing themselves in their silent clan in the convents.

Once I was asked to assess a young woman in her 20s who was placed in one of these convents. A case of shame in the clan, as she committed child sex abuse on one occasion and was automatically socially excluded from the clan as an offender (symbolically as an IS member).

During my first contact with her, she barely expressed herself verbally. In addition to being mentally challenged, a latent aggressiveness in her became apparent to me. Hence, the core goals of my work with her were improving communication whilst allowing her to be in contact with her aggressiveness. I started seeing her fortnightly with the help of an interpreter. To improve communication, I adopted a play narrative technique, and the stories were portrayed with Playmobil® dolls in a sandbox (sometimes I also add clay). The plots of the stories were mostly connected to aggressiveness, i.e., we buried together Playmobil® dolls in the clay or sandbox. After three months, she became more alert, more self-regulating and she could express herself better verbally. Her role as an offender faded into the background in the clan and consequently her social contact improved. At this exact point, she surprised me by asking me to talk to another girl from the clan, who, according to her, needed my support – a clear indication that 'shared meaning communication' could be achieved with her.

The girl who she asked me to talk to was intending to commit suicide – a lost case for the whole clan, a girl in her early 20s who had spent the last two years lying on her bed in a darkened room, wanting only to die.

During our first contact, she came wearing black clothes with angry eyes, and I said:

> Wow such angry eyes! I can see your anger through your eyes! Indeed, your black clothes seem to express no colour, no contact, I am closed!

Then I invited her to draw her 'timeline', so that she could tell me how long she had been unhappy for. As in the case of Mr. I. (Case 2) in Chapter 5, the 'timeline' drawing had a remarkable resonance for her, as through it, she was able to build representations of her emotional experience (Bion 1965) during the traumatic events in her life. As a result, she realized that her imprisonment was not the primary traumatic event; quite apart from that, it was more connected to attachment losses before then, namely since her early teens. At a certain point in our chat, she asked me:

> Could you give me back the life I had before?

And I answered her:

> I am so sorry, but I am afraid I cannot give you back your life . . . look at the 'timeline' . . . there is no way back . . . here is the life movement (I explained to her following the process illustrated in *Chapter 5*) . . . however, we could try to look at whether there are still things in your life that could be repaired, but only if you want to.

She listened to me attentively and asked me whether she could hold her 'timeline', and I gave it to her as a gift – a gift she brought to our sessions, which she decided to attend fortnightly with the help of an interpreter. Our meetings were focused on creating a neutral space, in which her suffocated rage could be cathartically expressed in play whilst building representations of her emotional experience in words. The former was achieved by adopting creative fighting exercises, like with 33-inch Mashoonga swords made from foam (Bittner and Franieck in press; Bach and Goldberg 1976). The latter was achieved by adopting 'fairy-tale' drawings, as well as putting into words the meaning of some of her behaviour. To illustrate, every time she ignored me by leaving me to talk to myself, I usually said:

> OK! Now it is the "stuff you" moment! Actually, the way you are behaving with me now seems like you are telling me . . . stuff you! . . . OK . . . I need to accept that!

With this approach, I tried to show her not only her aggressiveness towards me (a rude and powerful way of expressing her rage) but above all how I felt impotent in situations when she refused to contact me, and I was left alone. In fact, 'feeling impotent in a situation' as well as 'being left alone' are two basic emotional experiences which women who have been raped go through. This approach always had a positive impact on her, thus also on our relationship. She always laughed after my intervention, relaxed and returned to communicating with me.

Nowadays, both young women have ordinary lives. They are working and have started families.

With time, other women from the clan decided to come and talk to me. Not all of them were able to or were less willing to experience a communication process. The women who were able to benefit from TICA were those who were still young, childless, and without a husband, or they were the older ones with grownup children and who were already grandparents. Through TICA, these women were able to express their inner struggles and their contained anger, and they were especially able to establish contact with their dark side. To illustrate, once one woman told me she had felt so lonely in the prison that she had bargained with a member of IS to do whatever he wished with her if he would fetch her best friend from the village and bring her to the prison to be near her – a desperate struggle against the feeling of 'being left alone', as well as 'being impotent' as previously mentioned. It is important to emphasize that in cases like this, the therapist must have the ability to remain unbiased, otherwise the practice of 'shared meaning communication' with the client fails in its essence.

Some personal observations

A major concern for TICA is that the therapist needs to be able to come into contact with, as well as be receptive to, the patient's feelings, wishes, and phantasies (including the traumatic ones) without being dominated by them – neither splitting, denying, nor projecting them (Cassorla 2018; Caper 1997), which requires some training. Furthermore, the permanent triangular setting requires the skill and awareness on the part of the therapist in experiencing situations where he or she will be placed as the third element

All in all, it is true that most refugees and asylum seekers suffer from psychiatric disorders caused by the adverse circumstances and traumatic events they have experienced. Nevertheless, they are all survivors, which suggests that they might have some unique psychological resources. I understand that many of them are unaware of their own potential. From my own point of view, the primary purpose of any kind of intervention is to support them to rediscover their potential, their sense of 'self'.

References

Alexandris, A., and Vaslamatzis, G., eds., 1993. *Countertransference: Theory, Technique, Teaching*. London: Karnac.
Bach, G.R., and Goldberg, H., 1976. *Creative Aggression*. London: Coventure.
Becker, R., and Bowles, R., 2001. Interpreters' Experience of Working in a Triadic Psychotherapy Relationship with Survivors of Torture and Trauma: Some Thoughts on the Impact on Psychotherapy. *In:* B. Raphael and A.-E. Malak, eds. *Diversity and Mental Health in Challenging Times*. Parramatta, NSW: Transcultural Mental Health Centre, 222–230.
Bion, W.R., 1965. *Transformations: Change from Learning to Growth*. London: William Heinemann Medical Books Limited.
Bion, W.R., 1984a. *Learning From Experience*. London: Karnac Books.
Bion, W.R., 1984b. *Second Thoughts: Selected Papers on Psychoanalysis*. London: Routledge.
Bittner, N., and Franieck, L., in press. *Psychosocial Group Work with Disadvantaged Children and Young People*. Wiesbaden: Springer Nature.
Bot, H., and Wadensjö, C., 2004. The Presence of a Third Party: A Dialogical View on Interpreter-Assisted Treatment. *In:* J.P. Wilson and B. Drožđek, eds. *Broken Spirits: The Treatment of Traumatised Asylum Seekers, Refugees, War, and Torture Victims*. New York and Hove: Brunner-Routledge, 355–378.
Burnett, A., and Peel, M., 2001. Asylum Seekers and Refugees in Britain: The Health of Survivors of Torture and Organised Violence. *BMJ (Clinical Research Ed.)*, 322 (7286), 606–609 [online]. Available from: https://pubmed.ncbi.nlm.nih.gov/11238163.
Caper, R., 1997. Symbol Formation and Creativity: Hannas Segal's Theoretical Contributions. *In:* D. Bell, ed. *Reason and Passion: A Celebration of the Work of Hanna Segal*. London: Routledge, 37–56.
Casriel, D., 1972. *A scream Away from Happiness*. New York: Grosset & Dunlap.
Cassorla, R.M.S., 2018. *The Psychoanalyst, the Theatre of Dreams and the Clinic of Enactment*. Abingdon, Oxon and New York: Routledge.
Castrechini-Franieck, L., 2014. *We Were Born on the Street, How Do Experiences of Transience and Permanence Affect Us?* [online]. Available from: https://ifpe.wordpress.com/volume-3-winter-2014/ [Google Scholar].
Castrechini-Franieck, M.L., 2017a. *Giving Deeply Traumatised Refugees the Space They Need in Which to Reconstruct the Boundary They Have Lost Between Reality and Fantasy, While They Face Language and Cultural Barriers* [online]. Available from: https://wp.me/pelHL-Ep [Accessed 2 May 2020].
Castrechini-Franieck, M.L., 2017b. Managing Narcissistic Impulse-Reminiscence and Cultural Ideal Under the Circumstances of Mass Immigration. *Psychoanalytic Review*, 104 (6), 723–734.
Engstrom, D.W., Roth, T., and Hollis, J., 2010. The Use of Interpreters by Torture Treatment Providers. *Journal of Ethnic and Cultural Diversity in Social Work*, 19 (1), 54–72.
Franieck, L., and Günter, M., 2010. *On Latency: Individual Development, Narcissistic Impulse Reminiscence, and Cultural Ideal*. London: Karnac Books.

Green, H., Sperlinger, D., and Carswell, K., 2012. Too Close to Home: Experiences of Kurdish Refugee Interpreters Working in UK Mental Health Services. *Journal of Mental Health*, 21 (3), 227–235.

Grinberg, L., and Grinberg, R., 1989. *Psychoanalytic Perspectives on Migration and Exile*. New Haven and London: Yale University Press.

Hofstede, G., and Bond, M.H., 1984. Hofstede's Culture Dimensions: An Independent Validation Using Rokeach's Value Survey. *Journal of Cross-Cultural Psychology*, 15 (4), 417–433.

House, R.J., 2004. *Culture, Leadership, and Organizations: The Globe Study of 62 Societies*. Thousand Oaks and London: Sage.

Jensen, B.S., 2013. *Treatment of a Multi-Traumatised Tortured Refugees Needing an Interpreter with Exposure Therapy, Case Reports in Psychiatry* [online]. Available from: https://www.ncbi.nlm.nih.gov/pmc/articles/PMC3580894/.

Joseph, B., Feldman, M., and Spillius, E.B., 1989. *Psychic Equilibrium and Psychic Change: Selected Papers of Betty Joseph*. London: Tavistock, Routledge.

Leanza, Y., Miklavic, A., Boivin, I., and Rosenberg, E., 2014. Working with Interpreters. In: L.J. Kirmayer, J. Guzder, and C. Rousseau, eds. *Cultural Consultation: Encountering the Other in Mental Health Care*. New York: Springer, 89–114.

Mahtani, A., 2003. The Right of Refugee Clients to an Appropriate and Ethical Psychological Service. *International Journal of Human Rights*, 7 (1), 40–57.

Maude, B., 2016. *Managing Cross-Cultural Communication: Principles and Practice*. 2nd ed. London: Palgrave Macmillan Education.

Ogden, T.H., 2004/1994. *Subjects of Analysis*. 1st ed. Lanham, MD: Rowman & Littlefield.

Plutchik, R., and Kellerman, H., 2014. *Theories of Emotion*. Saint Louis: Elsevier Science.

Prosser, S., and Bawaneh, A., 2010. When Words Are Not Enough: Psychodynamic Psychotherapy in Chronic Conflict Settings. *International Journal of Mental Health, Psychosocial Work and Counselling in Areas of Armed Conflict*, 8 (2), 146–147.

Resera, E., Tribe, R., and Lane, P., 2015. Interpreting in Mental Health, Roles and Dynamics in Practice. *International Journal of Culture and Mental Health*, 8 (2), 192–206.

Riesenberg-Malcolm, R., 1999. Interpretation: The Past in the Present. In: P.L. Roth, ed. *On Bearing Unbearable States of Mind*. London: Routledge, 38–52.

Searight, H., and Searight, B.K., 2009. Working with Foreign Language Interpreters: Recommendations for Psychological Practice. *Professional Psychology, Research and Practice*, 40 (5), 444–451.

Slobodin, O., and Jong, J.T. de, 2014. Mental Health Interventions for Traumatised Asylum Seekers and Refugees: What Do We Know About Their Efficacy? *International Journal of Social Psychiatry*, 61 (1), 17–26.

Stern, D.N., 1995. *The Motherhood Constellation: A Unified View of Parent-Infant Psychotherapy*. New York: Basic Books.

Tribe, R., and Morrissey, J., 2003. The Refugee Context and the Role of Interpreters. In: R. Tribe and H. Raval, eds. *Working with Interpreters in Mental Health*. Hove: Brunner, Routledge, 199–218.

Trompenaars, A., and Hampden-Turner, C., 1997. *Riding the Waves of Culture: Understanding Cultural Diversity in Business*. 2nd ed. London: Nicholas Brealey.

Winnicott, D.W., 1958. The Capacity to Be Alone. *The International Journal of Psychoanalysis*, 39, 416–420.

Winnicot, D.W., ed., 1971. *Playing and Reality*. S.l.: Basic Books.

Winnicott, D.W., 1990/1984. Psychiatric Disorders in Terms of Infantile Maturational Processes. *In:* D.W. Winnicott, ed. *The Maturational Processes and the Facilitating Environment: Studies in the Theory of Emotional Development*. London: Karnac and the Institute of Psycho-Analysis, 230–241.

Winnicott, D.W., 2005. *Playing and Reality*. London: Routledge.

Winnicott, D.W., 2018. The Mother-Infant Experience of Mutuality. *In: Psycho-Analytic Explorations*. London: Routledge, 251–260.

Winnicott, D.W., *et al.*, 2012. *Deprivation and Delinquency*. Milton Park and Abingdon, Oxon: Routledge.

Chapter 7

TICA in multicultural team supervision

This chapter is based on the final essay entitled "The supervisor as an 'Outsider'" which formed part of my degree to become a supervisor.

The supervisory setting and the role of the supervisor

Any supervisory process (i.e. individual case supervision, group supervision, team supervision) requires an appropriate, unbiased setting in order to facilitate the achievement of the tasks (Grinberg 1990). The supervisory setting, like any workplace, is characterized by individuals who often behave, think, and feel based not only on fully conscious desires and wishes (Gabriel and Allcorn 1999), but also on unconscious ones. Allcorn and Stein (2015) similarly emphasize that any kind of organization (i.e., private or public, small or large) has one thing in common – they are composed of people and each person will have their own understanding of their organization, which depends on how they visualize, create, and operate this organization. Thus, human nature has a pervasive influence over organizations and consists of conscious (or rational) as well as unconscious (irrational) elements; yet, rationality is what is expected in the work environment. Hence, having a good grasp of the interplay between conscious and unconscious sides in the organizational context is an essential feature for a supervisor to comprehend the dynamic established among the individuals at different levels; for instance, at the individual, interpersonal, group, and organizational levels (Allcorn and Stein 2015, p. 22). Indeed, the supervisor needs not only to consider carefully, but also to manage properly attitudes and/or drivers from the supervisor's and supervised individuals' sides that may threaten the communication from either party and put the aim of the task at risk – in particular, when problems arise from transference and countertransference matters (Grinberg 1990). After all, supervisors are not only observers of the content but are also an element of the context. Needless to say, the supervisory process differs from the therapeutic one, as the goal of the former is based on growing and not on healing, unlike the latter (Jacob 1993; Grinberg 1990) – although sometimes, supervisory process might afford a kind of healing.

DOI: 10.4324/9781003232087-10

Stein (2017) and Allcorn and Stein (2015) define the role of a supervisor in a group or in an organizational team as: a) a short-lived participant in the group or an observer, processer, and longitudinal group participant; b) an outsider (like a stranger); c) an interpreter (and filter) of conscious and unconscious elements; and d) a mediator of the group.

In any supervising process, the focus of attention should be on the communication practice, which embraces verbal, non-verbal, and pre-verbal articulations, miscommunication, language dominance, etc. (Maude 2016). Indeed, making the right decision on which method to adopt in the supervising process should be associated with the goal of facilitating communication – a challenging task. This is certainly a greater challenge for supervisors who are immigrants, as they not only need to cope with expected verbal and non-verbal language issues but also the features of communication may vary according to the different cultural backgrounds they were brought up and immersed in (Castrechini-Franieck 2017a, 2017b, 2016; Franieck and Günter 2010). In this setting, the supervisor turns into a genuine outsider. However, due to current globalization and massive waves of immigration, organizations and societies have demandingly been required to deal with different cultural norms and expectations that not only include the unfamiliar members, but also support their way of thinking and the way they communicate (Maude 2016). This is clearly noticed in the interplay and dynamic of a multicultural team. From this angle, the supervision task may also be a challenge for non-migrant supervisors, as they have been forced to find ways of handling not only the features of cultural differences, but also the aspects of cross-cultural communications, whilst reaching out to people who might be considered 'strangers' to them (Gruen 2000).

As referred to in Chapter 2, TICA is culturally an accurate approach for use in intercultural communication and in this case also for the creation of a neutral space for improving communication. Once again, communication should be encouraged via external objects, such as a moderator suitcase (a professional workshop case which is filled with an extensive array of workshop materials) and homework.

A multicultural team supervisory process

Background

The supervisory process described here took place in the field of elderly care provision, which was provided by a religious sponsor. One of its nursing homes, which comprised three departments, formed the setting. Each department had a residential area manager and a representative that reported to the board of directors.

The request for supervision arose from a recent change in the board of directors. Three months prior to the beginning of the supervisory process, the previous nursing home manager had been transferred to another nursing home run by the same sponsor, and her representative, who was previously one of the residential area managers, assumed her post. Hence, team-building was the main purpose of the supervisory process, as well as the clarification of the expectations from the board of directors, the residential area managers and the representatives.

The supervisory process comprised of a fortnightly meeting on Fridays over three months, making a total of six sessions of 90 minutes each.

Interview with the board of directors

The board of directors, Mrs. S. (the nursing home manager), and Mr. D. (the director) were waiting for the supervisor in the nursing home manager's office. With the help of the organogram copy, they started narrating the changes that had occurred in the nursing home over the past three months, after the previous nursing home manager had been transferred and the current one had replaced her. Remarkably, they highlighted more than once that although Mrs. S. had been the representative of this post in the past, she needed to apply for the post, and so did several other candidates. Despite following formal procedures, the board of directors were not sure whether employees would be able to appreciate and also to accept Mrs. S. as their new superior. Therefore, Mr. D. requested an intensive, short-term supervisory process with the three residential area managers, their representatives and the social worker. According to the board, the team was made up of people who have experienced the process of immigration, and therefore, an immigrant supervisor would perfectly suit their needs. Indeed, the board of directors felt that it was essential for them to take part in the supervisory meetings as members of the team. Mr. D., for instance, had no doubt that the presence of the board would be expected by the entire team, as the expectations of the team and the board needed to be clarified. Being aware of the multicultural features of the team and also of the risks of miscommunication, I convinced the board members to hold one or two meetings with just the team, in order to get them ready for future meetings with the board. After all, starting the supervision in the presence of the board could cause distress and make some of the team feel intimidated, therefore hindering the aim of achieving their goals.

Towards the end of the interview, I was made aware of my role in this new setting: a) I would be a short-lived participant in the group; b) I would be a mediator of the group; and c) I would be truly an outsider (Stein 2017). However, being made aware of my role had not made me feel less anxious nor less uncertain about facing the daunting challenge of supervising and building a team in the presence of superiors. At that time, I could not work out the origin of these feelings inside me. Were they related exclusively to my subconscious? Was I supposed to perform this new task as an immigrant supervisor (being an outsider)? Or were they related to counter-transference issues (non-verbal and pre-verbal communication)? On reflection, I realized that the more effective way to deal with this inner uncertainty was to wait for new inputs, while observing and undertaking the role of temporary container (Stein 2017; Allcorn and Stein 2015).

First meeting: bringing up issues that need to be resolved

Aware of some previous issues (i.e. the multicultural features of the group in connection to the supervisor's prevailing feelings of anxiety and uncertainty), I set the goals of improving communication whilst avoiding miscommunication and cultural noise (Maude 2016). For this reason, the focus of my first meeting with the team was to explore the group members' expectations of the supervisory process (including non-verbal and pre-verbal issues) whilst improving understanding and sharing information. To this end, the meeting was divided into steps and each step was to be discussed at a time:

Step 1   Introduction.
Step 2   Group's feedback about:

    a   Who had already experienced a supervisory process.
    b   What supervision means.
    c   What should be the goal of the next supervisory meeting.

Step 3   The announcement of the board's wish to attend the supervision together with the team.

A meeting room in the nursing home was reserved fortnightly for the supervision. All members of the team were already waiting in the room, namely: a social worker (Mrs. D.), three residential area managers (Mrs. P., Mr. R., and Sister I.), and one representative (Mr. S.).

Initially, the team could not understand the need for supervision. Indeed, just one third of them had already experienced a supervisory process; thus, most of them had no idea what was being discussed. Those with experience of supervisions described the process as a method applied either in situations of conflict or in situations where a team's communication required improvement. In this instance, the team faced 'cultural noise' (Maude 2016) as regards to what 'conflict' means, since for Mr. R., the meaning of conflict in his culture related to assault, while for the others, it referred to problems in communication. In fact, the team could not identify any conflict among them and/or towards the board of directors. Nonetheless, Mrs. S.'s new role in the team triggered feelings of anxiety and uncertainty from all members. Based on this, the team were able to identify some issues that needed to be discussed, namely: a) what the board of directors' goals would be going forward; b) what their expectations of 'them' (the team) were; c) whether they planned any changes to the job; and d) how 'they' should behave towards Mrs. S., who once was 'their' close colleague. At this suitable climax, the supervisor won over the team, convincing them to invite the board of directors to attend the supervision as well.

Second meeting: disturbance in the team

The meeting should have been in a different room; however, not everyone was informed about this. Thus, the supervisor, Mrs. P., and Mrs. D. went to the room that had been booked and stayed there waiting for the rest of the team. Whilst they waited, Mrs. P. started talking with Mrs. D. about how she had felt unhappy and distressed by her new demanding tasks. A month prior to the start of the supervisory process, Mrs. P. had been transferred from a house specializing in care for the elderly (where she had been working for many years) to a house specializing in addiction (the post left by the current nursing home manager, Mrs. S.). Indeed, she was terrified of the aggressive behaviour of the new clients, which she found difficult to cope with. After about 45 minutes of waiting, Mrs. S. found them chatting. Then, she asked in a harsh tone what they were doing there, as the rest of the team had been waiting for the supervisor in another room. Mrs. S. was particularly harsh with Mrs. P. and Mrs. D., as according to her, both should have known about the room change. Mrs. P. and Mrs. D. were very embarrassed about the situation. This occurrence caused tension during the supervisory process and in the team. It was the first meeting between the team and the superiors, and the method adopted during the time remaining had to be one that could offer not only a 'holding and secure environment' (Winnicott 1960), but could also facilitate the thinking process, or container-contained process (Bion 1984). In other words, it was a method that enabled thoughts to be expressed without any inhibitions – a difficult task to perform when disruptive/confusing thoughts, feelings, and behaviours such as fear or anger were present in some members of the team at the time. The approach adopted involved a combination of written information with role changes. The supervisor gave some coloured cards and pens to the team. The board of directors got blue cards, and they were required to answer openly and anonymously the question, "What do I expect from the team?" The team got yellow cards and they had to answer openly and anonymously the question, "What do I expect from the board?" The next exercise was based on role reversal. Everyone received white cards and had to answer the question: "If I were the client, what would I expect from the team and the board of directors?" The goal of using written information in an anonymous format was to improve communication among the team's members (including the supervisor as a part of this system), without anxiety, via an indirect intervention – a transitional object (Winnicott 1953). In doing so, most of the emotional impact triggered previously by disruptive/confusing thoughts, feelings, and behaviour could be contained and the remaining time would then be productive. In the end, everyone was not only focused on the task proposed, but they were also pleased with the act of expressing their thoughts without any fear. The supervisor took charge of collecting all the cards together and presenting them to the group in the next meeting in a table format.

Third meeting: improving communication

The third meeting started with a warm-up round, and everyone (no one was absent) was looking forward to receiving the list of expectations. Each member of the group got a copy of the list that comprised of two columns: on the left side, a total of 11 items from the team, and on the right side, a total of 15 items from the board of directors, which were itemized according to their frequency in descending order (Table 7.1).

Table 7.1 Expectations

Team manager expectations with regards to the board of directors	Board of director expectations with regards to team managers
1. concrete task – what needs to be done?	1. to perceive his or her responsibility as live-in area managers and representatives
2. respectful	2. treat each other with respect a. mutual respect and acceptance
3. trustworthy	3. being able to ask for help
4. working together	4. organize the area well

5. good working atmosphere
   a. among the departments
   b. between team managers and the board of directors
	5. addressing problems in dealing with each other
	   a. can, may, should, must

6. clarity
   a. more transparency
   b. openness
	6. reporting/sharing problems to the board of directors

7. honesty – when something doesn't fit, address it	7. honesty – open contact with each other
8. ability to listen and to take criticism	8. ability to listen to criticism without taking it personally a. address criticism against superiors directly to the board of directors
9. follow-up conversations	9. be open to new ideas
10. stand behind the team managers	10. creativity or constructive cooperation
11. listen to suggestions from/past experiences of team managers and possibly implement them.	11. organization of the department
	12. loyalty
	13. implementation of guidelines/agreements

	14. consider the department as a whole
	   a. co-workers
	   b. residents

	15. see us as part of the whole team

144 TICA in intercultural settings

The expectations from both sides were quite similar; however, the supervisor still had the task of discussing the content of some of them, with the purpose of clarifying miscommunications while avoiding 'cultural noise'. The team started with four expectations the team had of the board, namely: a) clear communication about the task – "what needs to be done"; b) respect – what this means – "I feel respected when my boss" . . . What respect means in relation to my colleagues as well as in relation to my work; c) trust – "how trust can be damaged"; and d) collaboration – "with whom do I have to work? – why are we working together?"

The group was divided into pairs for discussion. The board of directors was not supposed to close itself off, and so the pairs rotated after finishing their discussion of each item. This method not only aimed to introduce the group to the supervisory process, but it also offered them a chance to deal with their fears and insecurities (as they had to express themselves to different members of the group, which included the board), whilst promoting clear and unbiased communication.

For each item, they had 15 minutes for discussion. Then, they had to write their conclusions on a card and present the cards to the group for collective discussion (together with the supervisor). The dialogue was characterized by lively conversations and rich illustrations of daily practice. Nonetheless, in the end, the directors expressed their discontent. They were expected to discuss their expectations first. To ease them into things, the supervisor left them with homework. This method (the homework) not only played the role of a transitional object (keeping the supervisee focused on the work); it also freed up the time available during the supervision for discussing points in greater depth (Haynes *et al*. 2003). Hence, the team members had to read the expectations of the board, and if anything was unclear, they had to bring their question(s) to the next meeting. The board members, for their part, had to finish reading the team's expectations, and then also bring their question(s).

The supervisor left this meeting with the strong feeling that she should behave and respond in accordance to the board of directors' wishes (to be just their messenger) instead of developing a team by herself. Unexpectedly, she had the usual wish to break the supervisory process. Being aware of counter-transference issues (Grinberg 1990), she decided to face the next meeting (despite her feeling of being trapped) in order to observe and undertake the role of a temporary container (Stein 2017; Allcorn and Stein 2015).

Fourth meeting: conflict in the team emerges

The fourth meeting started with a warm-up round. The group's feedback was that by doing the homework, they were able to reflect more deeply on the work performed in the last meeting, and this was positive. The first question was posed by Mr. R. It was unclear to him as to what the following meant: "to perceive his or her responsibility as a residential area manager and representative" – what did the board expect?

Mrs. S. replied promptly by highlighting that residential area managers and representatives not only need to behave exemplary in their posts, but they also need to follow the rules, which at that moment were being violated, for instance, the 'smoking break' and 'the use of mobile phones'. All members of the team were surprised by Mrs. S.'s response.

Mr. R. replied by emphasizing that rules must be clear (above all in their meaning) in order to be followed. Mrs. S. insisted that these rules had been violated (in particular, the rule about the 'smoking break' and 'the use of mobile phones'). Mr. D. was beginning to get annoyed about this issue when Mrs. P. started a direct quarrel with Mrs. S. According to Mrs. P., over the past 20 years, she had been working in this nursing home and doing everything right, and up to now, she had never had any kind of problem. In fact, she claimed she was going to retire in five years. Hence, from now on, she was not going to start conforming to this kind of control. On the other hand, Mrs. S. played the victim's role, though in a very aggressive way, using non-verbal communication, which triggered the rage of Mrs. P. As a result, Mrs. P. started to bring up unfinished business with Mrs. S. At this point, the supervisor interrupted sharply whilst pointing out that this particular matter had nothing to do with the team, and hence, both should talk about it later in a more private setting. As the quarrel was emotionally very intense, the supervisor recognized the group's need to express their perceptions before leaving the meeting. In doing so, the role of the supervisor could be defined as: a) a mediator of the group; and b) an interpreter and filter of conscious and unconscious elements by listening intently. Aside from Sister I., the whole team saw the quarrel as a challenging though constructive situation. Furthermore, the team was very grateful for the supervisor's intervention, as she intervened at the right time. As for Sister I., she had difficulties in dealing with the quarrel, since this kind of situation would be unacceptable in her culture. However, for Mr. R., according to his culture, there had not been a quarrel, but rather a conversation – cultural noise. As regards to Mrs. P. and Mrs. S., they apologized to the group for the dispute. When the supervisory meeting was nearly over, the supervisor decided to avoid any verbal communication that could endanger the peace-making process of the group. Their apologies were amicably accepted.

Near the end of the meeting, the supervisor pointed out that what had happened in the group that day had led her to infer that there were still important issues to be discussed. Therefore, she set a different piece of homework for the board of directors and the team. Whilst the directors had to clearly list and write down the rules they expected to be followed and respected, the team members had to list the rules they were already aware of and which they had followed.

Fifth meeting: unexpected news

Mrs. S. started the meeting by communicating that Mrs. P. was sick. Mr. D. informed them that Mrs. P. would be transferred to another nursing home run by the same sponsor.

All were shocked and surprised by the news. I asked when this had happened and Mr. D. said, "Yesterday". The group sat in silence for a long time. The silence was broken by Mr. R.'s remark: "We lost a very good and very experienced colleague!" At this point, Mrs. S. complemented Mr. R., saying, "Indeed, it is a big loss, but she left this nursing home of her own freewill. Actually, due to her private life (grandchildren), she would like to have a part-time job. Nevertheless, as long as she holds the post of residential area manager, she does need to work full-time". Mr. D. added, "Indeed, this decision had no connection to what happened in the last supervisory meeting!"

The group sat in silence. Again, Mr. R. broke the silence by saying, "It does not matter; it is just sad! We have lost a very qualified and experienced professional!" Sister I. later commented, "You say that there is no connection to the last supervision, but after that meeting, I talked to Mrs. P. and she was really very angry with you. How can you say there was no connection?"

Facing the current situation, I decided to embrace the experience of the group by creating a calming, soothing, and safe individual and shared experience – a 'holding environment' – whilst undertaking the role of temporary container by absorbing disruptive/confusing thoughts, feelings, and behaviour (such as fear, loss, sadness, or anger) – a 'container' (Allcorn and Stein 2015) – an open conversation took place. The method had a beneficial effect on the group, and before the meeting finished, Mr. D. said,

> I would like you to know that I am deeply pleased with the work of all of you. I also would like to apologize for not praising you frequently. Though this does not mean I am not able to recognize the value of your work. In addition, keep in mind, please, that everything we have been talking about here is just to help our work.

I left this meeting sceptical about the reasons why Mrs. P. had left the team. However, I was convinced that the group had managed to take a step forward as regards to the team's dynamic. Interestingly, from this point onwards, the counter-transference feelings of anxiety and uncertainty disappeared.

Sixth meeting: farewell

Surprisingly, Mrs. P. came to the last meeting. According to her, she wanted to say goodbye to everyone (including me). Her presence was very important, because it was possible for the team members to express their regret that she was leaving. All remaining questions as regards to her transfer, as well as any miscommunication and cultural noise from the fourth and fifth meetings, were able to be cleared up. Indeed, the intercultural features and the development of this supervisory process could be evaluated. At the end, I carried out an anonymous survey as shown in Appendix 7.1. Its outcomes are presented in Chapter 10.

Some personal observations

The supervisory process encouraged the team's growth. The intense feelings of anxiety and uncertainty felt by me in the counter-transference were contained, put into practice (the use of a transitional object) and were finally replaced by a feeling of confidence (open and clear communication among the members). Indeed, sensitive to the multicultural features of the group, I was careful to create a neutral and secure space for clarifying communication, whenever necessary. By doing so, miscommunication and cultural noise could not only be faced, but could also be mutually accepted. In other words, 'transient shared meaning communication' could be achieved. The survey outcome in Chapter 10 clearly illustrates this.

Some limitations of the supervisory process should be noted, beginning with the fact that the clarification of the expectations between parties remained unfinished due to the short-term nature of the supervision. As for counter-transference, there still remains the question – could my previous wish (to break the supervisory process) be connected to Mrs. P.'s decision to leave the team (at the pre-verbal communication level)?

Concerning the role of the supervisor in the workplace context, I must confess that refraining from the therapeutic role and focusing on the development of the specific tasks are daunting challenges. The supervisor's task is to improve and/or clarify communication in the team and perform in such a way as to achieve the workplace objectives. In this setting, communication already exists and is influenced by previously established expectations – a restricted process. Up to this point, the use of TICA has been focused mostly on the clinical field, regarding the creation of free (new) 'shared meaning communication' in the inter-relationship between therapist and patients as well as the achievement of 'transient shared meaning communication' in ephemeral clinical settings. From this point of view, the workplace supervisory setting closely resembles the ephemeral clinical settings; hence, only achieving 'transient shared meaning communication'. Remining aware of this similarity is essential.

References

Allcorn, S., and Stein, H.F., 2015. *The Dysfunctional Workplace: Theory, Stories, and Practice*. Columbia: University of Missouri Press.

Bion, W.R., 1984. *Learning from Experience*. London: Maresfield Reprints.

Castrechini-Franieck, M.L., 2016. Remarks on Latency: Onset in Different Cultures. *The Journal of Psychohistory*, 43, 214–227.

Castrechini-Franieck, M.L., 2017a. *Giving Deeply Traumatized Refugees the Space They Need in Which to Reconstruct the Boundary They Have Lost Between Reality and Fantasy, While They Face Language and Cultural Barriers* [online]. Available from: https://wp.me/pelHL-Ep [Accessed 2 May 2020].

Castrechini-Franieck, M.L., 2017b. Managing Narcissistic Impulse-Reminiscence and Cultural Ideal Under the Circumstances of Mass Immigration. *Psychoanalytic Review*, 104 (6), 723–734.

Franieck, L., and Günter, M., 2010. *On Latency: Individual Development, Narcissistic Impulse Reminiscence, and Cultural Ideal*. London: Karnac Books.

Gabriel, Y., and Allcorn, S., 1999. *Organizations in Depth: The Psychoanalysis of Organizations*. London: Sage.

Grinberg, L., 1990. *The Goals of Pschoanalysis: Identification, Identity and Supervision*. London: Karnac.

Gruen, A., 2000. *Der Fremde in uns*. Stuttgart: Klett-Cotta.

Haynes, R., Corey, G., and Moulton, P., 2003. *Clinical Supervision in the Helping Professions: A Practical Guide*. Pacific Grove, CA: Brooks/Cole.

Jacob, T.J., 1993. Transference-Countertransference Interactions in the Supervisory Situation: Some Observations. *In:* A. Alexandris and G. Vaslamatzis, eds. *Countertransference: Theory, Technique, Teaching*. London: Karnac, 221–239.

Maude, B., 2016. *Managing Cross-Cultural Communication: Principles and Practice*. 2nd ed. London: Palgrave Macmillan Education.

Stein, H.F., 2017. *Listening Deeply: An Approach to Understanding and Consulting in Organizational Culture*. Columbia: University of Missouri Press.

Winnicott, D.W., 1953. Transitional Objects and Transitional Phenomena: A Study of the First Not-Me Possession. *The International Journal of Psycho-analysis*, 34, 89–97.

Winnicott, D.W., 1960. The Theory of the Parent-Child Relationship. *The International Journal of Psycho-analysis*, 41, 585–595.

Appendix

Appendix 7.1

Survey

Feedback on the supervision   Your feedback is important!

Overall, the organization of the supervision was satisfactory for me.

    fully agree ☐   agree ☐   agree less ☐   disagree ☐

Participation in this supervision group was useful to me.

    fully agree ☐   agree ☐   agree less ☐   disagree ☐

I am satisfied with the methods and interventions used by the supervisor.

    fully agree ☐   agree ☐   agree less ☐   disagree ☐

The supervisor wants to enable the achievement of certain goals with supervision. Which of these goals were achieved for yourself with this supervision group?
(Multiple answers possible)

Professionalization ☐	Improving the quality of work ☐
Increase motivation ☐	to keep joy in the profession ☐
Avoiding burnout ☐	Increasing job satisfaction ☐
Role clarification ☐	Rules clarification ☐

Other goals? Which ones?

What was particularly positive or helpful for you in connection with the supervision you attended? Positive or helpful?

What would you like to suggest?

Part four

TICA adaptations (variations)

Chapter 8

T-WAS – Together We Are Strong

Maria Leticia Castrechini Fernandes Franieck and Niko Bittner

What is T-WAS?

T-WAS – or *Together We Are Strong –* is the name of a three-year project on preventive work with deprived children in latency, based on weekly group interventions. The authors worked with refugee children and conducted three different groups, each from a different refugee shelter, totalling more than 70 refugee children.

As an approach, T-WAS lays emphasis on both corrective attachment experiences (Luyten and Fonagy 2014), and the processing of the group's ongoing experiences with paradoxical situations, ambiguities, and diversities – starting with the paradoxical background embodied by the group conductors per se (Trautmann-Voigt and Voigt 2019; Hofmann 2010; Westman 1996; Foulkes and Foulkes 1990, pp. 285–296) – a productive strategy for the achievement of 'shared meaning communication' with deprived children. The authors use an eclectic theoretical frame of reference for this purpose, which includes some elements of ontological psychoanalysis (Ogden 2019), pedagogy, Gestalt therapy, and creative aggression.

A detailed description of T-WAS, along with specially selected, full transcriptions of the group sessions and analyses thereof are available in the book entitled *Psychosoziale Gruppenarbeit mit benachteiligten Kindern: Paarleitung und kreatives Spiel* (*Psychosocial group work with deprived children: a pair of co-conductors, one male and one female and creative play*) to be published by Springer Nature in 2023 (Bittner and Franieck in press)

In summer 2019, T-WAS was introduced as a community-based work project at the 51st Congress of the International Psychoanalytic Association in London, United Kingdom, under the title "Mama! Papa! Where are you? Are you still there? What's wrong with you?".

Among other things, three explanatory videos on the development of the work with T-WAS were presented at the Congress. In these videos, the group conductors described how they met, the roots of their idea of eclectic group conductors and how they overcame the challenges of creating a new approach in the group work with deprived children. In the appendix for this chapter, a table with a summary of each video is provided, including its respective YouTube link and QR-codes. The films are listed in the table according to their chronological presentation. A fourth

DOI: 10.4324/9781003232087-12

video on how contact with the children was maintained during the COVID-19 lockdowns was produced later, especially for this book chapter.

Why is the focus on refugee children in latency?

M.L.C.F. Franieck (2005) has long been conducting research studies on the quality of identification with parental figures in children in latency. In Franieck's terms, "latency is a developmental period that plays a transitional role, like 'a bridge', between early childhood and adolescence (the beginning of early adulthood)" (Franieck and Günter 2010, p. 1) and can be perceived as the following.

1. *A timeframe* from 6–12 years of age which is characterized by new cognitive acquisitions, focused greatly on the learning process (i.e., the ability to become literate). The child in this period is longing to be taught and told what is acknowledged as right and good.
2. *A psychological state* describing a period of dynamic defences during which the child experiences a complex reorganization of the defensive structure of the ego, whilst actively searching for equilibrium between drives and defences. The means the child adopts to work out his or her emotional needs (i.e., aggression) is associated with cathartic games. Finally, the child needs to trust in his or her own capacities for self-assertion in order to gain peer acceptance whilst developing a sense of independence from their parents.
3. *A structural period for cultural identity formation* which therefore underpins the feeling of 'belonging'. Children also learn how to integrate and operate within the surrounding social culture outside their family context, while developing a sense of belonging to different groups. The reconciliation between a child's ideas of self and the community's recognition of them is the daunting challenge of this period.

According to some psychoanalytic authors, external factors such as war or migration can have a negative impact on the child's emotional development during the latency period. In particular, Winnicott *et al.* (2012) claims that experiencing the real violence and aggression of a war throughout the latency period can be very unfavourable, as the child does not yet have the means to classify the level of aggression that surrounds them. Grinberg and Grinberg (1989) support the view that any migration that occurs during the latency period places the child in situations (e.g. at school) that create a sense of 'being different' and make it difficult to keep up with children of the same age in language use and involvement in cultural codes. The interplay between the feelings that the knowledge already acquired is of less value in this new environment and the feeling that the knowledge yet to be acquired may prove valuable leads to inner states of tension. It can therefore trigger feelings of inadequacy, inferiority or shame, and also shake the child's belief in his or her abilities – a deep wound to the sense of 'belonging'. Given this, it is clear why latency refugee children are more likely to be at risk

Are refugee children/adolescents per se deprived?

Ruf *et al.* (2010) report that one in five children of asylum seekers in Germany is deprived. In a paper entitled "Managing Narcissistic Impulse Reminiscence and Cultural Ideal under the Circumstances of Mass Immigration" (Castrechini-Franieck 2017b), emphasis was placed on the refugees' struggle against the risk of their ego disintegration, posed by the experience of frequently living a blurry and tenuous frontier between external and internal realities – a very similar experience to their past traumatic events, as referred to in Chapter 6.

On the one hand, their inner reality is driven by archaic feelings such as fears of extinction and the loss of their identity, which is – intensified by a lack of attachment to a cultural ideal and narcissistic impulse reminiscence, as described by Franieck and Günter (2010). Franieck and Günter perceive cultural ideal as a model that serves to make each group member feel that he or she belongs to the group by identifying himself or herself with it. In this way, this cultural ideal needs to embody the 'ego ideal' of each member of the group in order to be internalized as part of each group member's self. Only in this way can it be assimilated and become part of a group self. And only in this way can each individual identify himself or herself with their ego ideal as a member of a group and at the same time subordinate their individual needs and their own interests to the group. So, the ego ideal might partially be replaced by the cultural ideal that in turn is experienced and introjected as belonging to the ego ideal (Castrechini-Franieck 2016). What each culture values as being the effective means to keep their group under control, the 'cultural ideal', is based on the adoption of just one side of what Andre As-salome referred to as the "dual orientation of narcissism" – either "in the achievement of individuality" or "the move towards fusion" (Andre Assalome 1962, p. 4).

In the case of refugees and asylum seekers accommodated in Germany, most of them come from Asia and North Africa, i.e., from countries with cultural ideals based on 'towards fusion'. In stark contrast, Germany belongs to an individualistic culture – a cultural ideal based on "the sense of achieving individuality" (Franieck and Günter 2010, p. 79). Hence, refugees and asylum seekers have been confronted with quite a different cultural ideal from the one in which they were originally embedded. The need to adapt their sense of identity to the demands of the new environment – with values differing from those in which they were embedded – triggers considerable inner conflict, such as feelings of impotence (Castrechini-Franieck 2017b)

On the other hand, the external reality shaped by political and social measures places value on work visas, professional qualifications, and language skills. These are real barriers with which the external world reinforces and increases a sense of impotence. At this point, many families of refugees feel that political and social policies have let them down. Men have lost their provider status, as women try to maintain the roles of mother and wife whilst coping with 'hopeless' and 'useless' men at home. In these circumstances, as referred to in Chapter 6, refugees have been deprived of the opportunity to mourn their losses, whilst being unable to feel attached to anything new. As a result, emptiness is the primary feeling. Consequently, emotional availability and responsivity of parents to their children's needs may decrease (Kerig *et al.* 2013).

The refugee children/adolescents are thus not only left alone emotionally but are also largely deprived of a familiar family life. In this field of tension, they can rarely find a stable framework and a sense of security in their own family. This sense of being detached may trigger failures in their ability to control their emotions, which in turn might be portrayed as problems in social conduct – "the child whose home fails to give a feeling of security looks outside his home for the four walls" (Winnicott 1991/1964, p. 228). Yet, 'outside their home' is still an alien society to the refugee children and adolescents that is likewise unable to 'hold' them properly. So, if the essential socialization mechanisms fail, how can refugee children and youth gain the stability they need for emotional growth?

The boomerang effect – dealing with ambiguities and paradoxical roles

Mass immigration in 2015 has presented Germans with a major integration challenge. The main focus of policy was initially on learning the German language. There is no doubt that language acquisition is an important factor in communication at the verbal level; however, as mentioned in Chapter 2, it is not synonymous with full cultural integration. Instead, it might cause refugees' families to experience a boomerang effect. To illustrate, in most of the refugees' families, the children/adolescents quickly learn the foreign language, owing to their ongoing cognitive development – a natural process. They also have to emotionally process their grief for the 'lost' home, but they largely rely on their parents as 'authority figures' for making decisions for them, as they have done/experienced up to now. From the parents' point of view, they as parents carry their own grief with them and equally blame themselves for the grief of their children in the new country. After all, they were the ones who ultimately made the difficult decision to leave their homeland behind forever, to set out with hope in search of a better life, with their children's futures in the new country in mind. (Grinberg and Grinberg 1989). However, the parental role of authority must not fail to comply with their traditional cultural ideal; otherwise, the cultural identity of the whole family would be called into question. This emotional pressure can cause learning difficulties and therefore poses the daunting challenge of having to acquire a foreign language. The boomerang effect occurs when the confrontation with this challenge (learning a new language) clashes with the clinging to one's mother tongue at home – a rather desperate attempt (from the parents' side) to restore their injured sense of identity, as well as to maintain their role as authority figures. In time, the refugee children/adolescents often become their parents' translators outside the home, as their parents often cannot properly master the foreign language in order to express themselves adequately in the new environment.

Again and again, refugee children/adolescents experience these ambiguous roles: their parents' dependence on them for linguistic communication and their own dependence on their parents – the authority model is threatened by a kind of role reversal.

> In this sense, a representational model of intact family structure may be held by the deprived child, which is both beneficial for the sense of permanence and safety it provides, but also a source of anguish when reality cannot measure up to it.
>
> (Castrechini-Franieck and Page 2017, p. 1586)

The demands of coping with these paradoxical roles could lead refugee children/adolescents to experience potential ambiguity and/or a sense of detachment from a cultural ideal, as described by Franieck and Günter (2010). This is a practical example of the interplay of feelings of loss and attachment – a boomerang effect in identity development through the experience of undergoing paradoxical, ambiguous roles. An additional boomerang effect occurs when refugee children and adolescents are educated by their families in a different cultural ideal at home than in the environment they have to live in (the society outside the home country). The need for orientation is challenged when they are constantly confronted with two paradoxical cultural ideals, namely "the sense of achieving individuality" (outside the home) in contrast to the "movement towards fusion" (inside the home) (Castrechini-Franieck 2017a, pp. 38–39). Their parents will certainly have already internalized and settled down their cultural ideal in the past, in their homeland. Immediately on arriving in the new country, they will try to keep it alive by raising their children according to their own traditional ideas – a natural pathway of cultural transmission. Therefore, refugee children, like all deprived children, experience a constant inner struggle against ambivalent values as they are often confronted with contradictory realities (Franieck and Günter 2010). Some of the children can show emotional resilience, which enables them to react flexibly to paradoxical situations (Hauser et al. 2006), while others perceive them as dilemmas and as a result are more likely to show adaptation problems in social behaviour as they get stuck in them.

The roots of T-WAS

The roots of T-WAS were based on similar questions posed by both authors on issues related to the emotional development of deprived children.

Bittner (1992) raised issues related to the adoption process, particularly with regard to the placement of so-called late adoptions, i.e. those that take place in the latency phase. As previously mentioned, children in this phase have a natural interest in exploring their social identity. For example, would there be a negative or positive impact on the deprived child's search for identity to not involve the birth parents (if they are still alive) in the adoption placement process?

The focus of Bittner's work was to sharpen the understanding of how to meet the needs of the deprived child. Based on the idea that the child's right to his or her own history should be central, the question arose as to how information is passed on by both the relinquishing parents and the adoption agency. Bittner argues that public agencies should have policies that effectively support the adopted child, who is searching for his or her own identity, during the adoption placement process.

Castrechini-Franieck *et al.* (2014) in turn compared three different samples of deprived children, namely those living in 'street situations', those who have been abused, and those living in extreme poverty. The overall aim of her study was to understand the following.

1   The ways in which children living in 'street situations' think, feel, and have adapted, especially in comparison to other deprived children – those exposed to extreme poverty and those known to have been abused.
2   The family and parental representations of children living in 'street situations' and children known to have been abused when they have no family.
3   The ways in which deprived children think, feel, and have adapted to the conflicting demands of society's values and the paradoxical realities of life.

Given the results of the preliminary study, it became increasingly clear that early preventive psychosocial work needs to be created for deprived children in the latency period in order to avoid possible antisocial behavioural tendencies as described by Winnicott *et al.* (2012, p. 207) and to support them on their future path.

The authors' encounter triggered the creation of T-WAS

From my point of view, such prevention work would provide these children with socially relevant experiences with parental models of representation in a safe environment with the necessary support. That is, corrective attachment experiences that take place in the latency phase could be a way to help these children find a way into society, among other things. Yet, in practice, it was unclear to me which methods would be crucial for the development of this kind of preventive work. Indeed, most deprived children in the latency phase cannot afford treatment – not even typical consultations in common mental health settings. How could one initiate such work to reach these children? I was also somehow aware that further methods would be needed that clearly go beyond the psychoanalytical approach. I had the feeling that I should enlist the help of another professional who represents a further, more pedagogical perspective (Kivlighan Jr. *et al.* 2012). The setting should be more flexible and based on a supportive environment (Winnicott *et al.* 2012, p. 112). The work should be based on growing and not on healing (a similar process to the supervision described in Chapter 7).

Nevertheless, in the years that followed, my idea initially remained latent in the background.

When I started working clinically with traumatized adult refugees in their camps, I inevitably came into contact with their children. Complaints about refugee children destroying property were an issue both at school and in the refugee camp itself – a cry for help, as Winnicott *et al.* (2012) would say. To illustrate, one of the refugee camps was in an empty hospital, and the walls of the ground floor were filled with scribbles and drawings by the children, including many sexual symbols, drawings, and expressions. It seemed like a perfect time and place to put my latent idea into action and develop a preventive psychosocial work. How should I proceed?

In 2017, I met Niko, a qualified pedagogue, at an event organized by my employer, where he offered a workshop on self-defence. His approaches were based on Gestalt therapy and dealing with creative aggression, which I found impressive. In conversation, we automatically came up with common questions, such as: what connects children in the latency phase who live in 'street situations' with those who grow up in state-supported substitute forms of education such as homes, foster families, or adoptive families?

Would the experience of broken family relationships lead to a blurred understanding of one's own concerns/responsibilities in shaping one's own family in the future? Or what effects could be expected in the further course of life, and could these lead to social or emotional problems? Would the loss or absence of a parental model of representation lead to the deprived child relying less on others and more on themselves?

That's when I opened up to Niko about my idea of preventive work with deprived children and my desire to start a group project with refugee children in the refugee shelter. Bingo! He agreed, and our teamwork began.

What ties T-WAS to TICA?

Most of the approaches that make up TICA have their roots in introspections of my experiences as a researcher relating to different communication settings with deprived children in latency. Starting at the end and working backwards, 'building a shared meaning communication' is the primary goal of this latently longed-for prevention work. The starting point of this approach is comparable to interpretation training carried out in a group setting, for example in withdrawal therapy as described in Chapter 4. But how could interpretation training be set up with deprived children in latency?

Surely, not by adopting cartoons and films. Unlike adults, children in latency mostly express themselves emotionally by discharging their feelings through cathartic action in play, as their verbal representation of their emotional experiences and their process of symbolization are still ongoing. Additionally, they need other children; hence, play in a peer group might be the accurate means for communicating with them (Hofmann 2019; Lehle 2018a, 2018b; Franck 1997;

Winnicott 1991/1964; Foulkes and Anthony 1990; Sarnoff 1987; Ginott 1979; Slavson and Schiffer 1975; Slavson 1950; Bach and Goldberg 1976).

'Shared meaning communication', as mentioned in the previous chapters, means the ability to embrace the perspectives of others to the extent that one can understand them even if one does not agree with them. So, how could deprived children in the latency period be well versed in 'shared meaning communication'?

Deprived children, as already mentioned, are mostly confronted with ambiguities and often these are perceived by them as painful dilemmas. Decisions based on "either/or" thinking can overcome them. 'Shared meaning communication' suggests that ambiguities should be seen less as dilemmas and more as choices that can be processed/managed through 'both . . . as well as' thinking. Since ambiguous and paradoxical situations will always co-exist in their lives, children must not only learn to deal with them successfully but also to appreciate them (Wiesmann 2020). To do this, they must learn how to analyze ambiguities and adapt them to their needs by maintaining their emotional balance – thus strengthening their resilience. The group work will then be about acknowledging the existence of ambiguities and consciously dealing with them in a neutral space (Winnicott 2005). For this reason, two important basic elements in the group work should be considered: corrective attachment experiences and play methods based on creative activities (Lucas 1988). The former will enable and support the children in having new and better experiences of self in relation to others (Stern 1995, pp. 122–123). It will then help the children to become more fully themselves (Ogden 2019). The latter will create a 'neutral space' for the achievement of a new understanding of the emotional barriers that end up stagnating their perception of ambiguities. Therefore, the management of conflicts that arise in the game process should also consider for repairing deprivations and losses (Winnicott *et al.* 2012).

How could the emphasis on the existence of diversities, and ambiguous and paradoxical situations, be linked to relevant experiences of parental representational models?

Enabling and supporting children in group work to have socially new and better experiences of self in relation to others also means offering them relevant experiences with parental representations. The intent here is to support them in corrective attachment experiences by creating occasions for transference and counter-transference processes during the ongoing play and object relations process. For this reason, the group should be led by a couple – a mixed-gender team representing the parental models (Slavson and Schiffer 1975, pp. 141–142). It is important to emphasize that we are not referring here to the role of co-conductors as presented by Foulkes (2018, pp. 105–106), but rather to the role of the co-therapist couple or the concept or 're-parenting' (Ballhausen-Scharf *et al.* 2021; Hofmann 2010; Moll 1997; Rahm and Kirsch 1997; Westman 1996). As parental models, the two experienced leaders (Cividini-Strani and Klain 1984) will actively lead the group together, just as parents would normally take direction of a family. In addition to the parental representational role of the conductors, the couple taking charge of the group would also represent different ways of being as individuals, including cultural orientation, male and female views of the world, educational experiences, migration experiences, and personal preferences – a vivid and concrete way of providing deprived children with related experiences of diversity (Trautmann-Voigt and Voigt 2019; Hofmann 2010; Westman 1996). In other words, the conductors per se display a mix of attitudes, behaviours, ideas, and characteristics, and in this sense, we can speak of ourselves as eclectic group conductors. 'Eclectic group conductors' can be perceived as a new approach in group work that intentionally uses the interplay of personal differences while conducting a group and putting the conductors' skills into action. This is more about using a resource in a relaxed and child-friendly way than worrying about the group conductor's own abilities to act, or whether their authority will be challenged. The latter is usually based on the view that children could get confused by different information, making it difficult to lead the group (Foulkes 2018; Slavson 1950). And it is also the idea that the quality of the relationship with the children is endangered if they come into contact with contradictions, as if this would weaken their trust in the group's leadership. At this point, it becomes clear that the way the eclectic group conductors deal with contradictions is closely observed by the children and has a decisive influence on how the children get an idea of how to deal with ambiguities. The basis for this is our own certainty that we can actually offer the children corrective attachment experiences.

The focus is not only on the relationship between the children and the conductors but more importantly on how the group conductors interact with each other. Both should work together in moderating the group and show a form of object relationship that includes an appreciative handling of the differences. Then there is a tangible offer to make both socially relevant experiences of parental representations and 'shared meaning communication', which has an encouraging effect on the children and stimulates them in their own development.

In the case of T-WAS, our differences are very clear: I, a foreign psychologist with an ontological psychoanalytic background and coming from a collectivist culture; and Niko, a native educator and martial arts teacher with a Gestalt therapy background connected to the approach of "creative aggression" and coming from an individualistic culture.

A brief description of T-WAS

T-WAS features

The features of T-WAS can be summarized as follows, based on Bittner and Franieck (in press).

- *Indication:* there was none. Yet again, the groups were centred on growing and not on healing. Hence, the conductors were unaware of any kind of psychological problems among the children;

- *Grouping:* advertising posters with meeting dates, the venue, and pictures of children fighting with Batacas (Bach and Goldberg 1976) were fixed on the walls of the refugee shelters;
- *Group composition:* children from 6–13 years old. We started with separate boys and girls groups, so each group was held fortnightly. But in time, the children made it a mixed-gender group on their own accord, as everyone's goal was to meet weekly;
- *Group structure:* the groups were open; that is, new members were able to join at any time (Heinemann and Horst 2009; Ginott 1979);
- *Group size and features:* there was no size restriction. The number of participants ranged from 6–24 children, and they were from different cultural backgrounds, i.e., Afghanistan, Africa, Syria, Iraq, and Iran;
- *Frequency:* once a week when mixed-gender group or fortnight when boys/girls group, on the same weekday, at the same time, over two years. A total of 70 meetings. Each group meeting lasted 90 minutes;
- *Venue:* in the refugee shelter, in the shelter's biggest empty room or outside it, in a nearby park;
- *Material*: The usual materials used in child therapy, such as dolls, drawing or painting utensils, or writing boards were not available. There was also no material for developing motor skills, such as building materials. Instead, we used games with just few materials, focusing on the creation of a 'neutral space' as referred to by Lucas (1988) and well illustrated in Figure 8.1.
- *First and further meetings:* we were just there in the room, without any expectations, just waiting for the children, without knowing how many of them would come or even what we would play, without knowing either which kind of conflict we would need to deal with (Bion 1984);
- *Theoretical background:* in addition to those that make up TICA, some approaches from play education and Gestalt therapy.

T-WAS phases and the group meeting's structure

T-WAS is made up of three progressive phases, namely the following.

1. *Group formation* (first half year): building relationships and establishment of a 'holding' (and secure) environment, in addition to a 'potential space' (Winnicott *et al.* 2012), are the core goals of this phase, as illustrated in Transcription 1.
2. *Consolidation* (a full year): focuses on establishing the group's structure and strengthening relationships through object relationships and creative eclectic experiences, as illustrated in Transcription 2.
3. *Farewell* (last six months): strengthens the resilience of the children and helps them to integrate the experiences (e.g., constructive separation, dealing with gender roles, dealing with different cultures and cultural ideals), as outlined in Transcription 3.

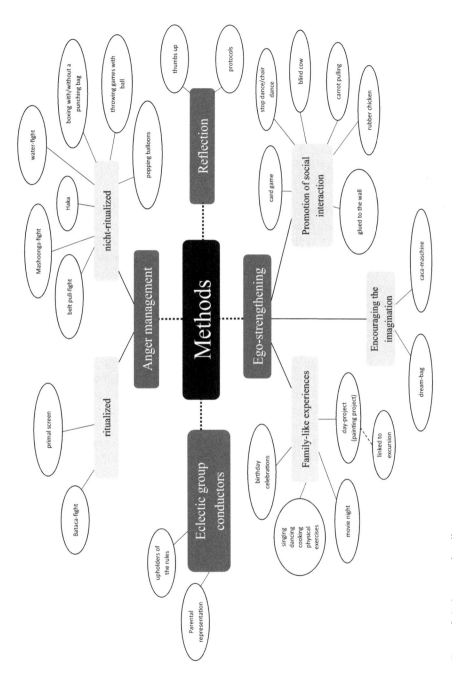

Figure 8.1 Approach-pillars

166 TICA adaptations (variations)

For each phase, there are particular play activities that support the achievement of the phases' goals, as referred to by Bittner and Franieck (in press).

The planning of a group meeting essentially includes three time slots: the welcome time slot, the game time slot and the closing time slot.

1. *Welcome time slot:* Interaction with the children is initiated by initial activities together – putting the chairs in a circle, filling out the attendance list, etc. Then, we sit down and start chatting about everyday things, as is common in a family. It is also a time for communicating organizational matters (e.g., changes in the schedule). In chatting, we get clues about the children's states of mind in the 'here and now' (Riesenberg-Malcolm 1999; Perls 1969), as shown in Transcription 2.

2. *Playtime:* This starts with a ritual (a supervised and regulated cathartic activity) that enables (and encourages) the collective release of anger in the group (Haar and Wenzel 2019; Hofmann 2019; Blom 2006; Lucas 1988). As we see it, aggression and frustration should be processed right at the beginning of the group and in the group as a general feeling. This is especially important with children when inner tensions do not yet have a conscious point of reference because of a lack of symbolization. In our case, we had adopted the 'Bataca-Fight' as our 'starting ritual' (Bach and Goldberg 1976, pp. 217–219). In this, the group conductors try to put their anger into words when demonstrating the Bataca-Fight, to connect the cathartic action with verbal symbols of their feelings – that is, to give meaning to the cathartic action, as illustrated and explained in Transcription 2. At the end of the starting ritual, we always ask the same question, "What do we want to play now?" At this point, the children can easily engage in the creative games, and they are free to choose what they want to play. If the children agree on a game, we continue as shown in Transcription 3. If not, we play the card game (as described in more detail in Transcriptions 1–2), and the winner has the right to choose the game for the whole group.

3. *Farewell time slot*: This lasts about 10–15 minutes and includes a reflection combined with a "closing ritual" (Haar and Wenzel 2019; Hofmann 2019; Lehle 2018b; Hofmann 2010; Blom 2006; Lucas 1988; Foulkes and Anthony 1990). The reflection is triggered each time by the same question: "How was the group today?" Each child just needs to give a thumbs up (if happy), give a thumbs down (if unhappy), or put their thumb in the middle (if OK). This gives everyone a chance to express their feelings about how the group is doing, considering the fluctuation in the size of the group. Towards the end, the conductors give their feedback to summarize and conclude any disagreements that may have arisen during the reflection time, as shown in Transcriptions 1 and 3. They also recall important information that was shared during the welcome phase. At the end of the meeting, there is a closing ritual that allows for a regulated cathartic expression of all the frustration experienced

in the group session. In our case, we adopted the 'primal scream' (Casriel 1972) – we stand in a circle, all hold hands and shout "Haaaaa!" together, then the chairs are cleared away and goodbyes are said.

T-WAS setting limits

Setting boundaries in group work with children is a controversial topic in the literature; different views lie in the definition of 'allowing' (Ginott 1979). For instance, Foulkes and Anthony (1990) suggested setting as few limits as possible; Lehle (2018b) recommended a setting that provides support and security with clearly defined rules and agreements; Blom (2006) perceived boundaries and limitations as necessary, as they provide structure and security for the child; and Woods (1993) underlined the care that must be taken in setting limits, so that they do not become an expression or an acting out of the leader. If this is the case, then this can trigger anxiety in the members of the group.

In T-WAS, due to its characteristics and aims, a clear and structured setting was implemented to support in-group relationships as well as to train the children on not crossing the line.

T-WAS follows the following four main principles.

1 Establishing a group atmosphere through the following 14 basic and concise group rules. The 14 basic rules were written on a poster, and this was clearly visible at each meeting. In Transcription 1, the effect on the group is quite clear. Although these rules seem to have an overly regulatory character, this clearly expresses that we care about rule clarity. Through strict rules, the children learn to deal with frustrations, which in turn can stimulate the children's coping with life and reality by recognizing and accepting their own limits – a way to teach them to use their aggressive energies constructively (Bach and Goldberg 1976, p. 55).

   a   Speak only German
   b   Be punctual
   c   Do not insult others
   d   Do not spit
   e   Do not hit others
   f   Do not yell/shout
   g   No physical altercations
   h   Do not threaten others
   I   No mobile phones or personal toys
   j   No eating, drinking, or chewing gum
   k   Anyone who comes to the group must stay until the end
   l   Anyone who breaks the rules will receive a warning
   m   After three warnings, the person in question must leave the group (is excluded) – in this case, there are always individual discussions that take

place either immediately after leaving the group or shortly before the start of the next group, depending on the current group's dynamics

n   Listen to Niko and Leticia [the last rule was added by the children themselves]

2   The children can refer to the conductors by using the second personal pronoun (an informal form of 'you'), as well as by calling them by their first names, Niko and Leticia.
3   All decisions concerning the group should be made democratically, with room for discussion and the exchanging of ideas. The role of the eclectic conductors is to present different points of view for discussion, encouraging the children to reflect.
4   The children should also assume a number of responsibilities for the group's organization. To illustrate, they should arrange the chairs in a circle in the room before the group starts and put them back when the group has finished. The organization of the birthday party as shown in Transcription 2 is another example of this.

T-WAS approaches

T-WAS made up of four approach-pillars, as follows:

1   *Eclectic conductors working together:* this is undoubtedly the most important pillar: to offer the children socially relevant experiences with positive parental representation models along with supporting them in trying out constructive experiences with ambiguities in a playful way. The presence of both group conductors at all meetings was thus essential. If one of them could not be present, the group was cancelled.
2   *Anger management:* can be perceived as supervised and regulated cathartic play/games that aim to decrease the non-symbolic rage or excitement of the group. There are ritualized and non-ritualized activities. The former belongs to the group meeting's structure and the latter may be utilized if the group is still impulsive or excited after the 'start ritual'.
3   *Ego-strengthening:* through community experiences with different foci:

   a   Promoting social integration
   b   Stimulating the imagination
   c   Family-like experiences

4   *Reflection:* takes place in the following two ways:

   a   With the children and their thoughts about the current group experience in each case
   b   With the gradual disclosure of the conductors' thoughts. At this point, we discuss different perceptions of ourselves, our roles as group conductors, conflict situations in the group (and with each other) and offer further

points of reference for the children (Ballhausen-Scharf *et al.* 2021; Hofmann 2010; Westman 1996; Cividini-Strani and Klain 1984)

The specific plays/games and features that characterized each of the approach-pillars are well illustrated in the Figure 8.1, pp. 165.

Group's transcriptions

In order to get a better idea of T-WAS in practice, we selected group transcripts from each of the progressive phases of T-WAS and from three different groups of children. Each transcript is subdivided into a description of the current group context and the progress transcript. Our explanatory thoughts, as well as the subsequently added explanations of individual procedures and our concluding remarks, are written in italics.

Transcription 1: Niko's day

Context: This transcription refers to the T-WAS group formation phase – exactly two months after we started the group. It is a boys' group in refugee shelter 'S' that took place fortnightly on Tuesdays from 5:30–7:00 pm. A total of 10 boys took part in the group on this day: El (11 years old), Ha (10), Ra (10), Ba (12), Ab (9), A (9), Di (9), Sa (12), A (10), and Na(8).

We arrived a quarter hour late because of traffic. When the children saw us, they were pleased and ran to us at the car and greeted us with a lot of shouting. Then they went with us to the group room and already started telling us one or two stories about what had happened in their week. Once in the room, the boys began to prepare the room by making a circle of chairs and moving the tables aside. At this point, two boys gave back their consent forms for the use of photos. We sat down and got everything ready to write down their names. One boy suggested reading the names off the list and they would then say if they were there or not. That's how we did it. Two more boys wanted to go back to their homes and get their consent forms after Leticia asked who else had forgotten theirs. We waited for the two to come back before starting the group . . . *Although we were already late, we decided to wait for the two boys to hold their consent as they showed a sense of responsibility, which should be appreciated by all.* . . . During this time, the group was quite restless. Two of the ten boys start provoking each other with expressions: 'cocksucker' and 'faggot'. Niko addressed this and referred to the rules. The situation remained uneasy.

None of us had a clear idea of how to react.

Ba started reading out the rules as if to support us.

What we can notice is untreated anger, which is released into the room quite openly. Our first reaction is to refer to our group rules; that is, to establish a holding environment. At this point, our hesitation creates an opportunity for a response to come from within the group, so it is sometimes worth waiting to allow this to happen. If we were to become immediately instructional, the children would be more likely to feel oppressed and avoid self-activity. Thus, it is significant to formulate and express the reference to the rules in such a way that the children feel included. This is all the more the case because we have worked out the rules together and they can thus be understood as group rules by everyone for everyone. That this is the case is made clear by the reaction of Ba, who (in our place, one could see it that way) adopts a closer reference to the rules and thus takes a step towards the solution or potential space. As Winnicott would view things, the unprocessed anger is transferred into a first opportunity for processing, which is done by the group.

Finally, we decided to begin with the start ritual, the Bataca-Fight, without paying further attention to the insults. We did the small round, but we didn't explain what this meant because it was so turbulent.

Any explanation at this stage would not be understood by the children as their attention capacity is limited due to their untreated anger.

We just started and the children could quickly grasp what a small round means . . . . *In a small round, each child fights only once. This child asks another one, who can say yes or no. If he* or *she says yes, then in a small round for both children, the Bataca-Fight is over.*

There were two challenging moments during the Bataca-Fight. On one occasion, Niko sat between two boys who kept talking to each other in their mother tongue, which disturbed the whole group; thus, we needed to intervene by reminding them of the rules. On another occasion, the leave-taking between two other boys did not work out. They always avoided each other, i.e., they did not show each other the respect that was intended by the high-fives as a form of greeting. Yet again, we needed to intervene by explaining the purpose of the leave-taking and asked the boys to repeat this as long as it worked. Then came our usually question: "What do we want to play now?"

The group wanted someone to be glued to the wall . . . . *'Glued to the wall' is a team exercise for building trust and sometimes required a high level of rulemaking because the person who was glued to the wall entrusted himself/herself to a defenceless position, which the group conductors had to protect. The unfamiliar setting opened up new spaces of experience, and the verbalization of the experience came into its own. In this way, the latent fields of conflict, such as mutual prejudice, attempts at mutual humiliation, mechanisms of exclusion, and feelings such as fear and mistrust could be addressed gradually.* . . . . and to play the card game beforehand. The winner of the card game then got to be glued.

Short description of the card game

Everyone sits in a circle of chairs. A stack of cards composed of four types of symbols: acorn, heart, leaf and balloon are used. These symbols are introduced so that they are understood by everyone. Everyone gets a playing card and keeps it in their hand, noting the symbol and which chair they are sitting on. Then, the cards are given back. Now the game leader reveals one card at a time and names the symbol of the card. All children with the corresponding symbol may move one seat to the right. If someone is sitting there, you have to sit on their lap. If several people are sitting on top of each other, only the top child may slid;, the others are blocked, even if their symbol is drawn. Once everyone has slid, the game leader reveals the next card. The winner is the first person to get back to his or her starting chair.

This card game is basically a game of chance, as its outcome is not influenced by mental or physical abilities. However, it has a cathartic character, as it often leads to situations in which there is prolonged and strong physical contact. In this blockade, each player has to work out his own frustration, in a fun and familiar way. On a symbolic level, it is an approach that allows us to process feelings of powerlessness in the face of reality. No wonder this has been one of the children's favourite games in all the groups and they really respected the outcome of the game. We never had any difficulties with the game itself being questioned, but there were many attempts at cheating (e.g., sliding one seat further than allowed) that were worked on and resolved in the group. This helped us a lot in relationship building.

Bittner and Franieck (in press)

The mood was pretty good after the card game. Leticia and Niko had stated beforehand that the game is only fun if everyone sticks to the rules and does so better than the last time. Some of the youngsters confirmed this. Ra showed great behaviour, and also told Leticia that he wanted to behave well this time and not be sent out again, a small sense of achievement. In the card game, there was a little unrest only towards the end, but the boys were able to regulate this themselves afterwards. The fun of the game prevailed, that's for sure. Niko won.

As Niko is not having his best day today, he is a bit unsure whether to get glued. Leticia noticed this and encouraged him to have a go at this new experience.

After Leticia' support, Niko changed his mind and was looking forward to being glued for once. At first, the room became quieter the more Niko was glued. Only a few boys could be active while gluing, and the others were not busy, and so, a few of these boys walked over the tables that were on one side of the room and started to pull each other's trousers down.

On the transference level, this chaotic situation during the game can be perceived as analogous to a situation in a refugee family, as described on pp. 157–158. The presence of a disempowered father (here Niko), who is stuck to the wall, and a helpless mother (Leticia) who tries to lead the group while her partner is unable to help her, represents an imbalance that triggered insecurity and consequently encouraged the boys to push the boundaries and enact antisocial tendencies.

When Ha and Ba then announce that they were now going to pull away the chair on which Niko was standing, the room became very quiet. This is the moment when it becomes clear whether the tape will hold and the person who has been taped will stay on the wall or fall off.

Of course, we make sure that the tape sticks well and are ready to protect the person, i.e., to catch them if the tapes don't hold. As in this case with Niko, the question as to whether the adhesive tape can hold the weight of a person is much more critical for an adult and also represented a new experience for the whole group. On the level of parent representation, the game makes clear that we share the same experiences with each other, especially challenging ones. The gluing game represents an example of offering a neutral space in which we act as play partners on an equal footing.

Niko stayed glued to the wall and pictures were taken (Figure 8.2).

Niko was scared and made a frightened face, and said "I can fully understand that this is really thrilling".

During the thumbs-up (evaluation round), almost everyone was satisfied with how the group meeting had gone.

"It was a super experience to finally find myself glued to the wall!'" said Niko. Then, El clearly stated that he didn't like it when his trousers were pulled down, whilst others complained that it had been loud. Finally, Niko and Leticia said that they found the arguments towards the end senseless and that they thought it was a pity. Unfortunately, the group needed to come to an end, and we didn't have time to work on complaints, as we had wished to.

In our experience, in the first year of any group, there are always instances of avoidance towards the end of the group, which indicate that there are still open gestalts, unprocessed issues with regard to leave-taking and separation.

During the final ritual, the 'primal scream', everyone was together, holding hands and letting out a powerful collective scream. At the end, they were all holding hands and the shouting was quite strong.

Evaluation discussion between the group conductors

Leticia reported back to Niko that he had been different today than usual. Niko said that he had had a busy day, being with a group of children for a period of seven hours in one go and he had been the only person leading the group, so he had had to take care of every little thing and that had taken a lot of energy. Leticia told Niko that she had noticed that, so she kept encouraging him and also teasing him a bit to get his energy levels back up. Niko said he had not been offended. During this process, we always try to remain aware of our observer role in the communication field which is created between the group conductors and the children, as described by Segal (Caper 1997).

Concluding remarks

From our point of view, the boys struggled to establish a relationship with us and to develop a group identity; for example, Ra tried to control himself because the

T-WAS 173

Figure 8.2 Glued to the wall

last time he was with us (after he had disobeyed the group rules three times and received three warnings for doing so), he had to leave the group. The boys did not feel completely safe with us, as the behaviour of pulling down their pants makes clear. With slightly antisocial tendencies, they nonetheless tried to use the 'neutral space' we offered.

Transcription 2: Leticia's birthday – a reunion with brownies

Context: This transcription refers to the T-WAS group consolidation phase – in the seventh month, after a 10-week winter break in 2019. This winter break was unusually long, as Niko had to undergo an operation on his foot and was convalescing for more than a month. Meanwhile, Leticia went on home leave. We had told the children about this at the start.

This group is a group of girls in refugee accommodation S, which took place fortnightly on Tuesdays from 5:30–7:00 pm. A total of eight girls took part in the group on this day: Hi (10 years old), Ni (10), Dij (6), Fa (11), El (9), Pa (9), Ne (10), and De (10).

We arrived on time and were welcomed by all the children of refugee shelter S before reaching the group room, even though it was the girls' group day. Pa, as always, was very excited, Ni could hardly get herself together. They hugged us warmly like "Mum and Dad are back!" Then they went to get the others, so that in the end, we were all together again.

As the group started, some girls teased Niko saying: "Niko, you have gotten older!" And praised Leticia: "Leticia you have kept young and pretty!" and everyone laughed whilst Leticia kept teasing Niko.

After an extended period of the group being together, we were obviously making jokes and teasing in all directions, involving all group members equally. It was similar to a situation in a family where there is a tolerant domestic atmosphere.

Then, the chairs were arranged in a circle, and we started with the 'Welcome' phase, asking the question: "How am I doing today?" The girls were curious and wanted to get the question answered by us first. Niko started talking about how happy he was not only because he was meeting the group today, but also because he would be able to jog again. Leticia told of her wonderful time on Brazil's beaches. Ni told how New Year's Eve was horrible due to fireworks, as their noise reminded her of rockets. Also, Pa explained she had been in Stuttgart downtown but would have preferred to have stayed at home, as it was too loud for her. Several girls referred to the same situation.

We did not go into the experiences reported about the loud fireworks and exploding rockets on New Year's Eve. We showed our interest and expressed understanding, and of course we got goosebumps while listening, because the comparison with war situations was obvious. But it wasn't our aim to deepen this analogy in order to recapitulate war memories and to mirror traumatic experiences to the girls. The helplessness expressed by the girls that they had experienced during the war could also correspond to a helplessness that they experienced with us because the break was so long, and they were unable to influence this situation.

At the end, the girls expressed clearly their wish to have a group session without any arguments.

They don't want a fight. Is this an unconscious idea that they might be afraid of their own anger? Our aim remained focused on offering 'external stability' in the 'here and now', for which the 'starting ritual', the Bataca-Fight, offers the opportunity as we understand it. There, accumulated anger from past and current experiences can be expressed and digested in contact with other children and us. Especially in the consolidation phase, what is established in the ritual is already very helpful. We supported the dimension of powerlessness by, as group conductors, accompanying our expressions of anger with words, as described below.

We then started with the Bataca-Fight. The first fight was Leticia against Niko. Both started teasing each other as an old man against a pretty woman.

Then, whilst fighting, Niko started saying to Leticia: "I'm angry because you were on the beach in the sun, and I was in the horrible hospital!" . . . and Leticia replied: "You are an old man and because of you, we had to cancel some meetings".

This got the girls excited, and they identified with the situation because what they observed was the expression of our anger based on feelings of powerlessness – feelings that can be experienced in situations of separation or war.

When our fight was over, we suggested that all the girls could fight against us (always alternating between Leticia and Niko) and that they could also express their rage towards us verbally, like we did.

We initiated the offer of doing the Bataca-Fight against us, with cathartic intention, and in addition, through verbalization, to deepen the awareness of this, that our actions had been triggered by anger and feelings of impotence, and that this anger is allowed to be there, that it is allowed to be expressed and that it should be accepted by the world around them as belonging to them, in the sense of self-empowerment.

Everyone agreed to the fight against Leticia and Niko. Hi, pointed out that she would rather fight against Pa, but when Niko teased her by saying: "What is going on? I am just an old man!"

At that moment, it was not clear to us why she refused to fight with Niko. Was it because she was afraid of her own aggression, or because she resisted? By playfully picking up on her teasing from the beginning of the group, Niko showed Hi that he can take and hold her aggression in a controlled way and is also able to give it back in a creative way (Oaklander 2001; Bach and Goldberg 1976). *By going through this digestion process herself, she is taking her own learning steps. So, her reaction to Niko's teasing showed us that she understood the mechanism.*

She started to laugh and agreed to fight against him and did it with lots of energy.

It was a successful Bataca round. All the girls hugged us tightly at the end of the fight. Then we asked: "What should we play now?"

Niko asked for game ideas and the card game quickly met the approval of most. We also agreed that the girl who won would then decide what to do next. De wanted to shuffle and deal the cards, which she did very well. It was a fun round and Ni won and suggested the game 'human memory'. After three rounds, the girls were satisfied. Even when Dij (a 6-year-old girl) cheated her partner in the first round of the game, due to her naïveté, the girls were still in a good mood.

Then came the question once more, "What should we play now?" and it came to a vote between two games: 'stop dance' and 'rubber chicken'. The former won and we played two pieces of music (twice "Despacito" and once "Fireworks"). Leticia danced to 'Despacito' more with pelvic movements, as it is Latino music.

Leticia's dance triggered a reaction from Pa, who then asked Leticia what she had worn on the beach . . . *In Leticia's counter-transference, her role as a representation of female sexuality became clear* . . . Thus, Leticia casually answered: "Oh, I was in a bikini!"

Meanwhile Hi, Ni, Dij, and Fa tried out hip dancing with Leticia. Interestingly, at the beginning, Fa was not willing to participate because of a headache; however, after Leticia's invitation to dance together, she became fully involved.

At this point, when Fa did not want to dance, Leticia was a supportive counterpart for her – a task that belongs to a mother.

Everyone had a great time dancing, including Niko.

Fifteen minutes before the end of the group session, we started the leave-taking phase. We not only had some important information to share with the girls (i.e., the group meeting calendar for 2019 and the dates of the birthday parties), which we could not discuss in the 'welcome' phase (due to the reunion), but we also wanted to celebrate Leticia's birthday with brownies she had baked herself. After the organizational matters, we started the celebration, and there was an unspoken cooperation in the organizing of Leticia's birthday celebrations, e.g., Hi prepared the napkins and Dij swept the floor. We had a nice time eating brownies together.

To conclude, we sat in a circle again to talk about: "How was the group today?" Everyone raised their thumbs and was pleased. During the end-ritual, everyone shouted loudly!

Evaluation discussion between the group conductors

After the long break, we were both quite relaxed, which also affected the mood in the group. We could immediately see that we were in a consolidation phase. We were able to easily continue the quality of contact we had achieved before the break.

Concluding remarks

At the beginning of the group, a field of tension opened up – the group's long break connected to the children's powerlessness in the face of this circumstance, as well as the analogy of New Year's Eve, which awakened feelings of impotence experienced during the war. On the child's level, this led to a playful processing, which in our opinion was expressed in the tension opposition of 'Niko is old' and 'Leticia is beautiful'. The ambiguity could be taken up playfully in chats and processed further through variations of the play methods (e.g., the verbalization offers in the Bataca-Fight). All in all, the reference to the object relations (the contact to us) was in the foreground of this group meeting. So, without avoiding the tensions, we were able to share new, creative experiences with each other that supported the bonding quality.

Transcription 3: Niko's punishment

Context: This protocol refers to the farewell phase of the T-WAS group – four months before the end of the group. This was a mixed-gender group, meeting at the T refugee shelter, which took place weekly on Wednesdays from 5:30–7:00 pm. A total of seven participants: five boys: Z (9 years old), Ad (11), H (12), Sa (14), S (14); and two girls: Sh (14), M (7).

Wednesday, 4:15 pm: Leticia met H on the street while he was on his way to the library. H told Leticia that he could not come to the group meeting today because he had a lot of homework to do. Leticia showed him her disappointment and added that the last group was a lot of fun. H confirmed this by saying that his brother, who was at the last group, told him all the details. Then H quickly said goodbye to Leticia and added that maybe if he finished his homework, he would be able to come to the group.

At 4:30 pm, S came to Leticia's office door to tell her that he had to go shopping with his mother, so he would be about 30 minutes late for group. He asked Leticia if that would be OK. Leticia told him that it would not be a problem to be late to the group as he had given the reason for his late arrival in advance.

As usual, the door of the group room was opened at 5:15 pm and Z came into the room. He said that he actually had football training that day but would rather stay here in the group. He talked about his daily routine while drinking Coke from a water bottle.

At 5:30 pm, Ad arrived. He had a stomach ache because he had drunk too much Coke and had to go to the toilet quickly. Then Sa arrived with the information that Sh would also be coming. Then Sh and S arrived together. Sa had to go to football training later and asked if he could stay until 6:00 pm and then leave early. Leticia said "Yes".

The importance and significance of the beginning of this group session became clear on two different levels: the factual level and the emotional level.

On the factual level, the children/young people refer to the schedule of the group. They know exactly when the group starts and how long it lasts. After one and a half years of the group's existence, most of them had internalized the times.

On the emotional level, they are now beginning to actively address and justify individual needs and demands that lie outside the group. They feel free and safe to share their normal personal dilemmas. Behind this is also their intention to have contact with us, even if this is only possible for less time than the group lasts.

In this context, they show us that they care and are becoming proactive, which expresses their sense of responsibility and acceptance towards the group setting, as well as their attachment towards us (the eclectic group conductors). This phenomenon that the children display is what Winnicott (2012) would probably call 'the capacity for concern'.

In terms of our response to their needs as group conductors, at this stage of the group's maturation, it is appropriate to interpret the group rules flexibly and sensitively in order to honour the concern revealed to us without reinforcing the children/young's dilemmas.

The group started and Leticia informed the children that Niko would be late today. He would not arrive until around 6:00 pm. Then Leticia, Ad and Sa started talking and thinking about an appropriate punishment for Niko because of his lateness. Everyone was enthusiastic about the idea.

In a group phase of greater familiarity with each other, it is naturally very interesting for children to claim rule, as adults normally do. Granting themselves this status is an act of self-empowerment initiated by the group conductor and appropriately received by the children. In this case, the whole group, without the male group conductor, takes on the role of the 'determiner' to playfully 'punish' the latter. In this way, the whole group can practise/experience a change of roles that is free from inner tensions without having to experience the ambiguity again, as it appears in situations where they have to play the role of 'translator' for their family.

The group decided that Niko would have to dress up as a woman and put on make-up as a punishment.

On the one hand, the children take up the idea from the last group lesson (the 'dress-up' film); apparently, they had enjoyed it a lot and continued to find the idea of dressing up interesting. The fact that Niko is supposed to dress up as a woman is a rather unusual request on account of the taboo of dealing with homosexuality/transsexualism in East Asian cultures. In the context of the group's progress so far, we can, however, observe that the children are evidently quite free to use the neutral space that we have been reliably offering to them.

But what could we do in the 15 minutes until Niko arrives? First, we watched the 'dress-up film' from last week and it went down well; everyone had fun watching it. After the film, we moved onto our 'start ritual', the Bataca-Fight. We did a small round: Sh/M, Leticia/Ad, S/Sa and H/Z without any problems. The children then wanted to listen to music, which S coordinated. Meanwhile, the dream bag was opened, and preparations were made to prevent Niko from escaping. Niko would have to take off his trousers and put on a skirt and the children prepared the corner behind the steel cupboard for this by pulling a wardrobe forward. Niko then arrived 20 minutes late in a in a manner similar to a father returning home later than expected. He greeted everyone and jokingly asked if he could still join in.

Then the children quickly explained to him what he had to do now and he joined in, changing behind the steel cupboard as if prepared. Then he was made up by all the members of the group. S was fooling around a bit and painted him without paying attention. Niko was unsettled because some were also giggling.

Here, a similar situation as in Transcript 1 when Niko was glued to the wall can be seen: The male group conductor finds himself in a dependent position. When being made up, he is at the mercy of the children's 'painting skills'. Although the children's reaction is still 'antisocial', it is directed towards the object (Niko) and not towards group (society) as in Transcript 1, when the trousers were pulled down and the situation was additionally sexualized without any concrete reason.

At this point, Niko said he trusted Sh the most – she could apply the make-up safely. Finally, only Sh was allowed to take part; otherwise, it would have become too chaotic. As planned, Sa left around 6:00 pm, reminded by Leticia that he is supposed to say goodbye to Niko as well, which he gladly did (Typical mother and father behaviour!). Sh finished the make-up while the other boys also dressed up a little. Niko still wanted tissues for the breasts and Sa and Ad picked some out and Niko stuffed them into his top. Niko was excited to see if he could scare the boys with his boobs . . . and it worked perfectly. Niko was clowning around, strutting around and wanted to be asked to dance by some of the boys – but none of them dared to do so. Sh, on the other hand, danced with Leticia and Niko together. Sh wanted Niko to have a bigger bum and got some tissues for Niko to stuff under his skirt and suggested he do it himself, but of course it didn't work so Sh suggested that Niko put one leg on a chair and wiggle his hips there. Niko tried it, but it wasn't that great. Niko kept making female gestures, but due to his high heels, Niko had some difficulties. The boys also wanted to look under Niko's skirt and sometimes dared to lift it. It was really fun.

Niko enjoyed the task and played along in his female role, with natural enthusiasm, but also laughing a lot at himself. This surprised and partly overwhelmed the children. They were able to experience impartiality in dealing with this matter and some were busy imitating Niko's individual gestures and interpreting them in their own way, while others were amazed with open mouths or simply nervous.

Then we cleaned up together as the children wanted to play something else, namely rubber chicken or zombie ball. Niko changed his clothes while 7-year-old M helped fill the suitcase again like a grownup. H wanted to help Niko take off his make-up, but Niko chose to do this by himself. Our time was coming to the end, and thus we came together in a circle to say farewell. But first, we wanted to talk about Halloween, and what we could do to celebrate it. Ad had the idea of watching a film while eating popcorn. The latter was particularly important to him. He also remembered last year's Halloween when Leticia and Niko were dressed up and couldn't speak because of their vampire teeth. That was really a special group session. Then everyone gave their suggestions for films, like Ad: *Pokémon*, H: *Jumanji*, and Leticia: *The Goonies*. Meanwhile, Niko looked on YouTube for the films and we watched the trailer for *The Goonies*. Ad then said he would like to ring the doorbells outside, but we pointed out that we would be celebrating Halloween on Monday, and not on the actual day of Halloween. Z was more of a pain, making loud noises from time to time and also getting hissed at by Ad. Ad pushed for a quick decision on the film, but we put this off until next time. Without doubt, everyone wanted salty popcorn; only Niko wanted sweet. We postponed this decision, too, for now.

The need to participate in generating ideas for what should happen in future group sessions was quite high. The idea that changing roles leads to self-empowerment for the children is, in our opinion, directly confirmed in today's group session. The identification of the children with the group as a place where they can contribute and have a voice became clear.

As to our question "How was the group today?", everyone was satisfied; only H and Sh showed some signs of not being so satisfied due to Niko's femininity, which they perceived as contradictory (too real). Leticia confronted them by saying that all Niko's provocations were part of the game and that they had also enjoyed them and had joined in. H and Sh were able to realize that, too. Meanwhile, Sa had contact with two boys outside the window, which disturbed everyone.

As to our end-ritual, we formed the closing circle with shouting and goodbyes. Then the children quickly left the room, without any problems. H came back to make it clear again that he would like salty popcorn. Z got his bottle and Ad his jumper.

Closing call and goodbyes, no big hoopla, nothing extra, everyone just leaves. We had never experienced it so relaxed. (For a long time, our experience at the end of each group was that the children did not put the chairs back but threw them as a way of expressing their anger due to the end of the group).

The fact that Niko was able to accept the two role changes (no longer being a group conductor and instead playing a woman) was a vivid experience for the children of role flexibility on the one hand and self-confidence in the gender role on the other. During both changes, Niko showed ease and impartiality instead of panic or discomfort. In our opinion, this contributes to supporting resilient behaviour.

We hope that the transcripts were able to clearly illustrate our approach, the stages of group formation, and the differences between the groups. Despite their differences, in the end, most of the themes in the three groups were quite similar and related to feelings of powerlessness and dealing with dilemmas. The children's expression of these feelings and how they deal with them in the group clearly depends on the respective group formation phases and the trust in their bonds with us. Confidence building always has two poles, holding the reliable group framework in order to offer security within it and keeping the neutral space open for development and expansion, filling it creatively.

As regards the outcome of T-WAS, most of the children that attended the group meetings regularly became less disturbed, and hence, their school performance also improved. Chapter 10 presents some remarks from organizations that followed our work.

All in all, T-WAS showed itself to be an effective approach for antisocial preventive purposes with deprived children.

Some personal observations

As a final point, we would like to highlight the features and variations between TICA and T-WAS.

- TICA was developed for work with adults (individual or group work), while T-WAS was developed specifically for group work with children in the latency age;

- TICA is a developed approach to facilitate the course of communication with vulnerable/at-risk patients suffering from personality disorders and/or addiction and/or trauma. T-WAS is a preventive work for children in the latency phase, against the increase of antisocial behavioural tendencies;
- TICA uses an external/transitional object as a means of creating a playful space between the therapist and the vulnerable/at-risk patients, while offering representations for their emotional experiences through the creation of 'shared meaning communication'. Due to the psychological characteristics of the patients, the work should not be based on object relations but mainly on a transitional space. Similar to TICA, T-WAS also aims to achieve 'shared meaning communication', but its means are mainly based on the development of object relations in-group, associated with the transitional space created through creative games.

All in all, TICA and T-WAS have the same starting point – the development of 'shared meaning communication' based on the offer of a transitional/neutral space – though their means, as well as their target group, are not the same.

References

Andre As-salome, L., 1962. The Dual Orientation of Narcissism. *The Psychoanalytic Quarterly*, 31 (1), 1–30.

Bach, G.R., and Goldberg, H., 1976. *Creative Aggression*. London: Coventure.

Ballhausen-Scharf, B., et al., 2021. *Gruppenanalyse mit Kindern und Jugendlichen: Ein Leitfaden zur Kompetenzentwicklung*. Goettingen: Vandenhoeck & Ruprecht.

Bion, W.R., 1984. *Attention & Interpretation*. London: Maresfield Reprints.

Bittner, N., 1992. *Sozialpädagogische Problem bei der Vermittlung von Fremdadoptionen: Zur Entwicklung und Diskussion Offener Adoptionsformen*. Diplomarbeit: Universität Tübingen.

Bittner, N., and Franieck, L., in press. *Psychosoziale Gruppenarbeit mit benachteiligten Kindern: Paarleitung und kreatives Spiel*. Wiesbaden: Springer Nature.

Blom, R., 2006. *The Handbook of Gestalt Play Therapy: Practical Guidelines for Child Therapists*. H. Schoeman, foreword. London: Jessica Kingsley Publishers.

Caper, R., 1997. Symbol Formation and Creativity: Hannas Segal's Theoretical Contributions. In: D. Bell, ed. *Reason and Passion: A Celebration of the Work of Hanna Segal*. London: Routledge, 37–56.

Casriel, D., 1972. *A Scream Away from Happiness*. New York: Grosset & Dunlap.

Castrechini-Franieck, M.L., 2016. Remarks on Latency: Onset in Different Cultures. *The Journal of Psychohistory*, 43, 214–227.

Castrechini-Franieck, M.L., 2017a. Wohin gehöre ich eigentlich? *JuKiP – Ihr Fachmagazin für Gesundheits- und Kinderkrankenpflege*, 6 (1), 36–39.

Castrechini-Franieck, M.L., 2017b. Managing Narcissistic Impulse-Reminiscence and Cultural Ideal Under the Circumstances of Mass Immigration. *Psychoanalytic Review*, 104 (6), 723–734.

Castrechini-Franieck, M.L., Günter, M., and Page, T., 2014. Engaging Brazilian Street Children in Play: Observations of Their Family Narratives. *Child Development Research*, 861703.

Castrechini-Franieck, M.L., and Page, T., 2017. The Family Narratives of Three Siblings Living in a 'Street Situation' Since Birth. *Early Child Development and Care*, 189 (10), 1575–1587.
Cividini-Strani, E., and Klain, E., 1984. Advantages and Disadvantages of Co-Therapy. *Group Analysis*, 17 (2), 156–159.
Foulkes, S.H., 2018. *Group-Analytic Psychotherapy: Method and Principles*. London: Routledge.
Foulkes, S.H., and Anthony, E.J., 1990. *Group Psychotherapy*. 2nd ed. London: Routledge.
Foulkes, S.H., and Foulkes, E., 1990. *Selected Papers of S.H. Foulkes: Psychoanalysis and Group Analysis, Edited and with a Brief Biography by Elizabeth Foulkes*. London: Karnac Books.
Franck, J., 1997. *Gestalt-Gruppentherapie mit Kindern*. 1st ed. Freiamt: Arbor-Verl.
Franieck, L., and Günter, M., 2010. *On Latency: Individual Development, Narcissistic Impulse Reminiscence, and Cultural Ideal*. London: Karnac Books.
Franieck, M.L.C.F., 2005. *Mental Representations of Parents and Family Structure of the First Grade Elementary School Children from Two Countries. Brazil and Germany: Similarities and Differences*. PhD Thesis, Universität Tübingen.
Ginott, H.G., 1979. *Gruppenpsychotherapie mit Kindern: Theorie und Praxis der Spieltherapie*. Frankfurt aM: Fischer.
Grinberg, L., and Grinberg, R., 1989. *Psychoanalytic Perspectives on Migration and Exile*. New Haven and London: Yale University Press.
Haar, R., and Wenzel, H., 2019. *Psychodynamische Gruppentherapie mit Kindern*. 1st ed. Stuttgart: Kohlhammer.
Hauser, S.T., Allen, J.P., and Golden, E., 2006. *Out of the Woods. Tales of Resilient Teens*. Cambridge, MA, London: Harvard University Press.
Heinemann, C., and Horst, T.V.D., 2009. *Gruppenpsychotherapie mit Kindern: Ein Praxisbuch*. 1st ed. Stuttgart: Kohlhammer.
Hofmann, E., 2010. Gruppenanalytische Arbeit mit Kindern: Eine Gruppe wird 'geboren': Stufen im Prozess zu einer ambulanten Kindergruppe. *Gruppenanalyse*, 20 (1), 53–81.
Hofmann, E., 2019. Nach-Denken über eine gestaltende Kinder- und Jugendlichengruppe in einem Erstaufnahmezentrum für Asylsuchende. *Gruppenanalyse*, 29 (1), 7–20.
Kerig, P.K., and Alexander, J.F., 2013. Family Matters: Integrating Trauma Treatment into Functional Family Therapy for Traumatized Delinquent Youth. *In:* P. Kerig, ed. *Psychological Trauma and Juvenile Delinquency: New Directions in Research and Intervention*. London: Routledge, 122–140.
Kivlighan Jr., D.M., London, K., and Miles, J.R., 2012. Are Two Heads Better Than One? The Relationship Between Number of Group Leaders and Group Members, and Group Climate and Group Member Benefit from Therapy. *Group Dynamics: Theory, Research, and Practice*, 16 (1), 1–13.
Lehle, H.G., 2018a. 'Egotraining in Aktion': Das Spiel in der psychoanalytischen Kindergruppentherapie. *In:* B. Traxl, ed. *Psychodynamik im Spiel: Psychoanalytische Überlegungen und klinische Erfahrungen zur Bedeutung des Spiels*. Frankfurt aM: Brandes & Apsel, 133–158.
Lehle, H.G., 2018b. *Freiräume des Spiels: Psychoanalytische Gruppentherapie mit Kindern und Jugendlichen*. 1st ed. Frankfurt aM: Brandes & Apsel.
Lucas, T., 1988. Holding and Holding-On: Using Winnicott's Ideas in Group Psychotherapy with Twelve-to Thirteen-Year-Olds. *Group Analysis*, 21 (2), 135–149.

Luyten, P., and Fonagy, P., 2014. Mentalising in Attachment Contexts. *In:* S. Farnfield and P. Holmes, eds. *The Routledge Handbook of Attachment: Assessment.* London: Routledge, 121–140.
Moll, M., 1997. Thesen zur gruppenanalytischen Arbeit mit Kindern. *Arbeitshefte Gruppenanalyse*, 12, 22–31.
Oaklander, V., 2001. Gestalt Play Therapy. *International Journal of Play Therapy*, 10 (2), 45–55.
Ogden, T.H., 2019. Ontological Psychoanalysis or 'What Do You Want to Be When You Grow Up?'. *The Psychoanalytic Quarterly*, 88 (4), 661–684.
Perls, F.S., 1969. *Ego, Hunger and Aggression: The Beginning of Gestalt Therapy.* New York: Vintage.
Rahm, D., and Kirsch, C., 1997. *Integrative Gruppentherapie mit Kindern.* Göttingen: Vandenhoeck & Ruprecht.
Riesenberg-Malcolm, R., 1999. Interpretation: The Past in the Present. *In:* P.L. Roth, ed. *On Bearing Unbearable States of Mind.* London: Routledge, 38–52.
Ruf, M., Schauer, M., and Elbert, T., 2010. Prävalenz von traumatischen Stresserfahrungen und seelischen Erkrankungen bei in Deutschland lebenden Kindern von Asylbewerbern. *Zeitschrift Fur Klinische Psychologie Und Psychotherapie – Z Klin Psychol Psychother*, 39, 151–160.
Sarnoff, C.A., 1987. *Psychotherapeutic Strategies in the Latency Years.* Northvale, NJ: Aronson.
Slavson, S.R., 1950. *Analytic Group Psychotherapy: With Children Adolescents and Adults.* New York: Columbia University Press.
Slavson, S.R., and Schiffer, M., 1975. *Group Psychotherapies for Children.* A Textbook of S.R. Slavson and Mortimer Schiffer. New York: International Universities Press.
Stern, D.N., 1995. *The Motherhood Constellation: A Unified View of Parent-Infant Psychotherapy.* New York: Basic Books.
Trautmann-Voigt, S., and Voigt, B., eds., 2019. *Mut zur Gruppentherapie! Das Praxisbuch für gruppenaffine Psychotherapeuten: Leitfäden Interventionstipps Antragsbeispiele nach der neuen PT-Richtlinie.* Stuttgart: Schattauer.
Westman, A., 1996. Cotherapy and 'Re-Parenting' in a Group for Disturbed Children. *Group Analysis*, 29 (1), 55–68.
Wiesmann, C., 2020. Konflikt in einer multikulturellen Kindergruppe – eine gruppenanalytische Perspektive. *Gruppenpsychotherapie und Gruppendynamik*, 56 (1), 33–45 [online]. Available from: https://link.gale.com/apps/doc/A618128979/AONE?u=anon~7cead0e&sid=googleScholar&xid=c4183899.
Winnicott, D.W., 1991/1964. *The Child, the Family, and the Outside World.* London: Penguin.
Winnicott, D.W., 2005. *Playing and Reality.* London: Routledge.
Winnicott, D.W., et al., 2012. *Deprivation and Delinquency.* Milton Park and Abingdon, Oxon: Routledge.
Woods, J., 1993. Limits and Structure in Child Group Psychotherapy. *Journal of Child Psychotherapy*, 19 (1), 63–78.

Appendix

Appendix 8.1

Appendix 8.1 Short films produced for the presentation at the 51st Congress of the International Psychoanalytic Association in London, United Kingdom

Film	Plot summary	YouTube link
1. The Beginning	The authors chat about how they met, what their previous expectations of the collaborative work were, and how they overcame the daunting challenges of setting up the T WAS group. One can sense how they easily deal with their amazing diversity.	https://youtu.be/NFWki0OhUb0
2. Roles & Conflicts	The authors chat about their role as a pair of group conductors who embody different representations, e.g. male/female, father/mother, native/foreigner. They make it clear how they deal with the interplay of their personal differences and put them into action in conflicts within and outside the group.	https://youtu.be/aAAEkIfIPTM
3. Conflict & The Eclectic Pair Conductors	This film is a sequel to the film Roles & Conflicts. The authors talk about another intense conflict situation in the group. They explain how they experienced the effectiveness of their role as eclectic pair conductors and how that had an integrating effect on the children.	https://youtu.be/wSawfIUd4Vs
4. The Lockdowns This film was produced later specially for this book.	From weekly phone calls and letters, to the production of weekly amateur short films, this video is about the author's struggle to keep one children's group alive and the difficulties they had in building a new one - all of this set in the context of the first and second COVID 19 waves.	https://youtu.be/7EXt6MQG2iw

Chapter 9

TICA in the COVID-19 pandemic

Maria Leticia Castrechini Fernandes Franieck and Niko Bittner

The COVID-19 lockdown restrictions have posed an enormous challenge for all of us. We had to abandon face-to-face contact and replace it with technologically supported virtual encounters. Particularly in my work with traumatized refugees who live in refugee camps and do not have the same technology as we do, with limited access to digital media and little competence in using it, the restricted channel of communication has had a huge impact on the work with individuals and especially on group work involving children. In such uncertain times, and yet still aiming to keep a safe framework for all, my colleague and I have had to quickly develop new approaches. From letters, emails, phone calls (or video conferences) with patients and interpreters in individual settings to producing films for the children's group, we once again found the motivation and the 'Hope' (Havel and Hvížďala 1991, p. 181) despite the restrictions. As stated in the Introduction to this book, "Hope is definitely not the same thing as optimism. It is not the conviction that something will turn out well, but the certainty that something makes sense, regardless of how it turns out". Yet again, TICA and T-WAS had to be adapted, this time to COVID-19 lockdown restrictions.

Letters and/or emails

When patients were inaccessible by phone or even when they were in withdrawn psychiatric treatment, emails and/or letters were sent to them for the purpose of maintaining communication and a connection with them despite all the COVID-19 lockdown restrictions. Although I initially received no response to this old-fashioned, time-consuming, and costly method of contacting patients by letter, patients later expressed how pleased they were when it was delivered to them. They felt as though they had not been forgotten. To illustrate, I refer to a case concerning a man in his mid-30s from Asia suffering from schizophrenia. He had to stay in withdrawn therapy in a psychiatric hospital for six weeks due to experiencing hallucinations following a suicide attempt. Communicating with him was actually unfeasible, as mobiles were not allowed in the psychiatric hospital, nor were personal visits permitted due to COVID-19 infection risks, nor were phone calls possible. Therefore, I started to write letters to him once a week.

I did this mostly at the same time as his usual session time with the help of the interpreter. I also made it clear in the letter that I was writing to him during this time slot. The content of the letters was similar to a conversation with him from my side. I included my thoughts about how he might be doing, my wish to get in touch with him, and above all, I shared the daydreams (Cassorla 2018) which had been triggered in me by his absence. That is, I intended to express in words all the pictures, feelings, and sensations trigged in me by his absence. After his release, he told me that the letters had helped him to connect his thoughts to the 'here and now', which from my point of view, suggests a therapeutic effect.

Telephone (video) counselling

Since telephone counselling means talking to a therapist, whilst hearing only the therapist's voice (sometimes together with the voice of an interpreter), it is also important to create a holding setting (Winnicott 1955) in which the patient can feel safe. This is the reason why most patients have weekly one-hour call appointments on the same day and at the same time. Most of the patients were waiting for my call and were able to talk for an hour. However, some patients had difficulties talking on the phone, and in these cases, I called them two or three times a week to talk to them for just a few minutes. To illustrate, I will present the following three cases.

Case 1: hope

The first case refers to a married man in his early 40s with four children, who is a university graduate. In his country of origin, homosexuality is not allowed and if discovered, the person receives a death sentence – this is the reason why he fled. We started the counselling sessions shortly before the COVID-19 pandemic, so we were able to meet in person three times; after that, the counselling was always done by phone, as in his camp there were lots of COVID-19 cases. In the beginning, he had difficulties in accepting calls and talked to me for no more than 15 minutes. I then started to call him three times a week, sometimes even just to ask him: "How are you doing?". Over time, he started to talk more and more, and I was able to reduce the phone calls to once a week. According to him, he felt calmer when he listened to my voice. Once he said: "I feel like a baby that is listening to Mom's voice". His case was complex. As a homosexual, he had been persecuted and had to abandon his wife, children, and partner without notifying them.

Working with him by phone was quite challenging and had demanded reverie (Bion 1984) und mutuality (Winnicott 1992/1987, 2018) abilities on my part. During our calls, I noticed a constantly strange voice, as though he were sleeping or under the influence of narcotics. After a couple of phone calls, he revealed that he had drunk at least a bottle of vodka or whisky combined with sleeping pills. This behaviour got worst when he received the news that his asylum appeal had been rejected, because of the EU Dublin Agreement. He started to drink more and to have suicidal thoughts. At this point, I had to work carefully on the theme of finding differences and similarities between the reality of deportation (exclusion) and all the other experiences of exclusion that he had gone through during his life due to his sexual orientation. Every conversation ended with me encouraging him that, despite all the adverse circumstances, he had survived until today and fought for his identity. However, this fight for identity was and would continue to be a constant in his life, no matter where he decided to live. With time and after some phone calls, he stopped drinking and thinking about suicide – later he started to exercise his body and to work. Also, the core topic of our phone calls gradually became more about his future, his identity and his possible decisions, considering his deportation and all the pros and cons. More simply, the main goal was how he could find his 'Hope' (Havel and Hvížďala 1991).

More recently, after four weeks of holidays, he did not attend his call session, which was quite uncommon, and I could not reach him by phone anymore. Therefore, I emailed him to tell him that I could not reach him and that I wanted to know whether he was OK. Days later, I received a response in which he told me that during my holidays, he had decided to return to his home country on a freewill basis (instead of being deported), as his father was close to passing away and was also asking to see him. His father's wish moved him deeply and he realized that that it was of considerable importance for him to see his father before he died and before he himself was deported. He ended the email saying: "Having sessions/appointments with you really help me to stabilize my life. I really appreciate it!"

From the fragile man, the victim of society, the 'unwelcome', the 'black sheep', the 'Outsider' or as he defined himself, 'the baby who was listening to his mom's voice', he took the lead for his own life and accepted the positive side of being an 'Outsider'. I could see this as he was able to find his 'Hope'. Indeed, he was able to reflect and to realize that perhaps he could try to come to Germany sometime again in the future, although on a more secure basis, since he had not been deported.

Case 2: motherhood

Case 2 is a 23-year-old woman from Africa with a diagnosis of depressive schizophrenia. In her case history, she left her home country in Africa at the age of 17 to escape military service. On her journey to Europe, she travelled through other countries in Africa and spent a few years in Libya. In Libya, she was treated like a slave and was also raped almost daily. She got pregnant there and suffered a miscarriage due to further sexual abuse. This period in her life was very traumatic.

Since arriving in Germany, she had been acting very depressed with suicidal thoughts. Indeed, she had often been in withdrawn psychiatric treatment. At the end of 2019, she fell pregnant by an ex-boyfriend from her country, who she had met in Germany again. At the beginning of the pregnancy, she was both very sad and angry. She realized that she would have to go through with the pregnancy without the support of her family (mainly from her mother). Her feelings towards her pregnancy were very conflicted.

Due to the COVID-19 pandemic, we were unable to continue meeting in person, so I decided to call her twice a week as she usually did not talk for long on the phone. Each time I called her, she sounded very pleased and wanted to talk about her pregnancy, as well as the birth. The calls continued even during the time she was in hospital for the birth. Then came a phase when she was exhausted because the newborn baby did not sleep all night, and she asked me to stop making calls for a while. I respected her wish but suggested that I might call her once a month just to see if everything was all right with her. She agreed to this.

Recently, I spoke to her. Her baby is now 10 months old, and she seemed to be a completely different person, more communicative, more alive, and happier. Motherhood has helped her to recover her identity and find her 'Hope'. She was also very grateful to me and the interpreter, as according to her, "you have always supported me on my dark path in life, and I will never forget that". Thus, she is currently no longer taking any psychiatric medications. This is a good example of how life can surprise us both in good ways and bad ways. My role in this case was just 'to be with her along her pathway' by calling her twice a week – not more than this.

Case 3: someone was reborn in the COVID-19 pandemic

Case 3 is a 30-year-old woman from Africa, married to a white man from another African country, who is 16 years older than her and with whom she has five children. She has been discriminated against since childhood due to her black skin. According to her, however, the gravest forms of discrimination happened in her husband's country, where she was attacked several times on the street. This was the reason she fled to Europe. When I accepted the case at the beginning of the COVID-19 pandemic, the woman was unable to leave her room because of fear. She was invited to a telephone interview and after that, she wanted to keep up the counselling through phone calls with an interpreter. I called her once a week and she had always spoken on the phone for at least 60 minutes. Her strong emotions regarding the issue of discrimination were clearly noticeable and, in my opinion, led to her having a blind spot in her perception of the world when it came to this issue. The focus of my work with her was to address the relationship between the role of the victim and the role of the tormentor. During the phone calls, she often projected her emotional chaos onto the interpreter so that the interpreter began to mirror her emotional excitement (this issue will be explained further in some personal observations). After three months of talking on the phone, we met once, and because of our meeting, she left her room for the first time and tried to come to my office alone. After five months of counselling, she was able to have a normal life and was more stable, thus we decided to end the counselling with a commitment that she could return anytime if she felt weak and alone again. This was my first case in the COVID-19 era, which was based solely on phone calls. In the meantime, I have handled other cases based on calls.

Video calls, which make communication smoother than simple phone calls, depend heavily on the quality of the internet connection, which can be frustratingly poor at times. In this case, you must find a way to deal with your own frustration.

Producing films for T-WAS

When the COVID-19 broke out in the middle of March 2020, we suddenly needed to stop the groups for children in the refugee camps due to COVID-19 lockdown restrictions. Group S was in the farewell phase, whilst Group B was in the group formation phase. In April, shortly before Easter, we sent each child in Group S a photo (Figure 9.1) of us taken during the last group session (when we all celebrated Niko's birthday). In the card, we expressed how we were missing the children and how we were hoping to meet them again soon. We did not send a photo to Group B, as there was not yet a strong bond between us and we had had just one group meeting.

From the beginning of May until the beginning of the summer holidays in 2020, we started to maintain regular contact with the children from both groups through a sequence of letters, phone calls, and films. The work with Group B, which started in June, was more challenging because we were still 'Outsiders' (strangers) to them. We had to introduce ourselves to them and we did this with films (Bittner and Franieck in press).

We called the children weekly at the times when group meetings would 'normally' have taken place and sent two letters beforehand. One of them reached the children the day before the phone call, the other one the day after. The content of the former letter was always connected to our wish to call them and we also sent them our short film, as illustrated in Figure 9.2.

The content of the latter letter was always connected to the feedback about our call and also to the announcement of the next short film, as illustrated in Figure 9.3.

The letters were kindly delivered by the social workers in charge for the refugee camps. Immediately after the phone calls, we sent the children short amateur films, small video clips we had produced ourselves, with us as the protagonists, via WhatsApp.

As regards to WhatsApp, for each child, we had obtained consent forms from the parents, who showed us a lot of support. In a way, they were an active part of the communication, as they provided their own cell phones and sometimes chatted with us.

The topics of the films were kept humorous and were intended to keep the contact light and inspire joy. With this light-hearted approach, the children were able to watch us develop from small children to the adults we are today. In other films, we gave information, e.g., about cooking our favourite food, and the children

TICA in the COVID-19 pandemic   191

Figure 9.1 Leticia and Niko

were encouraged to try cooking. Sometimes it was also about giving answers to questions posed by us and the children were able to win a gift like in a raffle. Sometimes we played funny games or even danced or sang together. This was not about our dancing or singing skills, but about creating a transitional space in our communication with the children. Although we didn't always hit the right note

Hello dear children!   Monday, 29th June 2020

Tomorrow is children's group time again!

We will call you again .

The next film is prepared. There are actually two films.

One shows us training in the forest.

The other is made up of funny pictures of us.

We hope to speak to some of you tomorrow.

Do it well!

Just in case: Leticia's phone number is 0176-18107150.

Leticia   and   Niko

Figure 9.2 First letter to the children

Hello dear children!   Wednesday, 1ˢᵗ Juli 2020

Here we are   again!

Yesterday we sent you two films.

Some also gave us a thumbs up. Thanks.

We think it's a shame that there are still so few who gave us the phone number and the declaration of consent.

Show the films to each other. Then you will get something from us !!! We have already prepared a surprise for next week.

If you want to call us. Here is Leticia's number: 0176 18107150

With lovely greetings

Leticia and Niko

Figure 9.3 Second letter to the children

or get the right tone, sometimes appearing a bit clumsy, we showed ourselves as approachable individuals with different qualities – as mentioned in the previous chapter, this is after all a core characteristic of 'eclectic group conductors'. The main aim was to communicate to the children that we were missing them and were thinking of them in during the COVID-19 pandemic. In other words, we wanted to reassure the children that we were still there as 'eclectic group conductors' and at the same time show them that we were making an effort to keep in touch with them – a vivid example of how to deal with the ambiguities created by the COVID-19 restrictions in this case. It is true that this approach was more connected to entertainment than to assisting the children with corrective attachment experiences and play methods based on creative activities; still, it could at least help them with dealing more constructively with loss/separation processes and experiences.

After the summer break, from September to October, we came together again in the refugee camps. Since COVID-19 rules severely restricted indoor gatherings, we met outside, usually in the nearby park. There were always between 10 and 20 children in each group, and we played the whole time outside despite the fresh autumn air. As regards to Group B, we were surprised by the resonance of our letter and film approaches; despite communicating with the children at a distance, we had been able to build a bond through our correspondence. From November until mid-December, lockdown restrictions applied once again, and we returned to phone calls, letters and films as a way of keeping in touch. The groups ended before the second strict lockdown in December. Immediately before that, we had still been able to say farewell in individual meetings with the children.

In Appendix 9.1, there is a table with a summary of each video, including the respective YouTube links and QR-codes. The films have been listed in the table according to their chronological creation, together with the information for which group they were produced.

A total of 19 video clips were produced: Four of them exclusively for the children of group S (in the farewell phase) and three of them exclusively for the children of group B (in the formation phase); the remaining 12 films were created for both groups. Among the four T-WAS videos presented in Chapter 8 (whose links and QR-codes can be found in Appendix 8.1), the fourth of these with the title *The Lockdowns* highlights the development of contact building with the children in the COVID-19 lockdowns.

Some personal observations

On the phone calls

Counselling on the phone is very demanding, as the counsellor has to pay attention to all the small details during the conversation, such as a slight difference in the patient's voice like in Case 1, or even a small noise in the background. To illustrate, one day, when I called a patient, I could not talk to her due to an annoying bird noise. Then, I asked her what was going on and she said that she had birds at home and that the female bird had died overnight and the male bird would not stop squawking. Then she started saying what a bad person she was, as she had assumed she was not a good caregiver and that was the reason why the female bird had died. The theme of the call for a couple of minutes was based on this representation of her emotional experience (Bion 1965) – not being a good caregiver. She then began to talk about the moment when she had taken the dead female bird out of the cage with its nest. At that moment I asked, "Nest"? The patient answered, "Yes". Then, I asked her if she had looked inside the nest. She said she had not been able to touch the bird. Then, over the phone, I encouraged her to lift the bird and see if there was anything under it. She did and was surprised to see that there was an egg. I then asked her to put the nest and egg back in the cage as the male bird would probably calm down. With that said and done, as soon as she put the nest back in the cage, according to her, the male bird flew to the nest and sat on the egg and calmed down. Indeed, the bird noise had stopped. Then, we started to talk about the difference between her fantasy and reality, as the bird had actually died due to the egg and not due to mistreatment. Another important theme that day was her fear-motivated reluctance to check the nest. This short segment of a phone call is a good example of how the therapist's attention could move a set of daily problems, closely related to the representation of the patient's emotional experience. Returning to the previous point, conducting a one-on-one session by phone call creates some problematic issues. Specifically, the counsellor cannot talk about deep issues until he or she is sure that the patient feels safe in communicating with him or her – or put another way, when the therapist is sure that he or she has been able to create a 'holding setting'. The last 15 minutes of the phone call should be reserved for strengthening the client's ego, as well as for giving the client feedback about the session. Here, above all, the therapist should not leave any unfinished business, just like in pretrial detention setting (see Chapter 5).

The work is even more challenging if an interpreter is needed. In this case, the patient may try to project all his emotional disorganization onto the interpreter, as referred to in Case 3 and also due to their connection as described in Chapter 6. It is therefore necessary to prepare the interpreter for this task and this can be done through a joint feedback session between the therapist and the interpreter at the end of each individual session. Here, the therapist should listen with interest to the interpreter's free associating, a kind of daydreaming communication (Cassorla 2018).

In acute crises, it is also necessary to provide support for interpreters and social workers, who are in charge of the cases, on how to deal with patients' disorganized behaviour. In this way, it is possible to maintain both the counselling setting and its goals. Likewise, it is possible to protect the client. Without doubt, it is a demanding and timing-consuming job that takes double the amount of time than in-person sessions. So far, this kind of work has turned out to be constructive for all parties involved and has subsequently been highly appreciated by all sides.

On producing films for T-WAS

Children need real contact, personal relationships, and real people to grow with them, and this cannot happen through films (Oaklander 2001). Due to the COVID-19 lockdown restrictions, we could not offer the children the opportunity to move on from the conflicts they had encountered or even to find 'external stability' in us (Winnicott 1991/1964). Furthermore, some children simply moved away, and we were unable to say farewell. That is to say, we were unable to keep offering a neutral space for experiencing diversities, nor could we offer 'socialization training', and we could not assist the children with corrective attachment experiences by creating transference/counter-transference conditions that promote a new and better experience of one's self in relationship with others – the core objectives of T-WAS, as stated in Chapter 8, could not be achieved in this way. Due to this restricted work setting, we sadly decided to end the children's group work in the middle of December. However, we are quite sure that this time, the children could work out a new kind of separation from what they had lived when they needed to leave their country (Bittner and Franieck in press).

References

Bion, W.R., 1965. *Transformations: Change from Learning to Growth*. London: William Heinemann Medical Books Limited.

Bion, W.R., 1984. *Learning from Experience*. London: Maresfield Reprints.

Bittner, N., and Franieck, L., in press. *Psychosoziale Gruppenarbeit mit benachteiligten Kindern: Paarleitung und kreatives Spiel*. Wiesbaden: Springer Nature.

Cassorla, R.M.S., 2018. *The Psychoanalyst, the Theatre of Dreams and the Clinic of Enactment*. Abingdon, Oxon and New York: Routledge.

Havel, V., and Hvížďala, K., 1991. *Disturbing the Peace: A Conversation with Karel Hvížďala*. 1st ed. New York: Vintage Books.

Oaklander, V., 2001. Gestalt Play Therapy. *International Journal of Play Therapy*, 10 (2), 45–55.

Winnicott, D.W., 1955. Metapsychological and Clinical Aspects of Regression Within the Psychoanalytical Set-Up. *The International Journal of Psycho-analysis*, 36, 16–26.

Winnicott, D.W., 1991/1964. *The Child, the Family, and the Outside World*. London: Penguin.

Winnicott, D.W., 1992/1987. Communication Between Infant and Mother, Mother and Infant, Compared and Contrasted. *In:* D.W. Winnicott, *et al.*, eds. *Babies and Their Mothers*. Reading, MA and Wokingham: Addison-Wesley, 89–104.

Winnicott, D.W., 2018. The Mother-Infant Experience of Mutuality. *In: Psycho-Analytic Explorations*. London: Routledge, 251–260.

Appendix

Appendix 9.1

Appendix 9.1 Short films produced during COVID-19 (first and second waves)

Short Film	Plot summary	YouTube link
1. 'FITNESS IN THE FOREST' (Group S)	In this amateur video, both group conductors, Leticia & Niko, demonstrate several physical workout exercises in the forest, which the children could try out in the park near their camps.	https://youtu.be/5Xr6Helq62s
2. 'LETICIA & NIKO GROWING-UP' (Groups S & B)	During the first COVID 19 wave, the group conductors, Leticia & Niko, start producing the first amateur video for the children. It shows portraits of them in chronological order of their growing up and thus creates a small visual biography. A charming video that won the hearts of the children.	https://youtu.be/VWiKplw78oE
3. 'LETICIA & NIKO FACEMOR-PHING' (Groups S and B)	The group conductors, Leticia & Niko, playfully morph their faces in a second amateur video. An odd video.	https://youtu.be/UZ1LssoiiRw

TICA in the COVID-19 pandemic 199

Short Film	Plot summary	YouTube link
4. 'NIKO DUNKED' (Groups S)	This amateur video answers questions about Niko, one of the group conductors. After the children had received these questions in the form of a letter a week earlier, Leticia, the other group conductor, now gives the answers in a funny way. . . . it gets a bit dirty on Niko's face.	https://youtu.be/iLvRKYY2O8s
5. 'NIKO'S COOKING TIP' (Groups S)	In this amateur video, one of the group conductors, Niko, introduces one of his favourite dishes - a typical Austrian dish called "Kaiserschmarrn" (a sweet, sliced pancake with sultanas). He teaches the children step-by-step how to prepare it.	https://youtu.be/AtDJbYv-5e4
6. 'LETICIA'S COOKING TIP' (Groups S)	In this amateur video, one of the group conductors, Leticia, reveals the secrets of her chocolate cake, which she has often baked for the children's birthdays. In a playful way, she teaches the children how to bake their favourite cake themselves.	https://youtu.be/_hXxK0xyzWk
7. 'LETICIA DUNKED' (Groups S and B)	Niko, one of the group conductors, answers in a funny way the questions about Leticia, the other group conductor. These questions had been sent to the children by letter a week before. Leticia gets a bit dirty in the face. This time there is a reward for those who have answered the most questions correctly.	https://youtu.be/1mvm-QyhH48
8. 'LETICIA'S QUESTIONS' (Groups B)	This amateur video shows the group conductor, Leticia, asking the children questions about herself, which they are asked to answer by indicating true or false. In this initial phase, we had hardly had any contact with the children in this new group and were keen to get to know them.	https://youtu.be/Br6CSF_hHTA

(Continued)

200 TICA adaptations (variations)

Appendix 9.1 (Continued)

Short Film	Plot summary	YouTube link
9. 'NIKO'S QUESTIONS' (Groups B)	This amateur video shows the group conductor, Niko, asking the children questions about himself, which they are asked to answer by indicating true or false. In this initial phase, we had hardly had any contact with the children in this new group and were keen to get to know them.	https://youtu.be/a0qxw8SecIU
10. 'LETICIA & NIKO DUNKED' (Groups B)	This amateur video is a sequel to the 'Leticia's and Niko's Questions' films and answers the questions about the two group conductors, Leticia and Niko. The questions are part of a competition and were sent to the children a week earlier in two separate amateur videos (in each video a group conductor asked questions about themselves). Now each group conductor gives the answers to the questions about the other group conductor, in a very amusing way. . . . it gets a bit dirty on the faces of Leticia and Niko.	https://youtu.be/g9hBdWauqT8
11. 'FAVOURITE STATUE' (Groups B)	This amateur video shows three sculptures from the plastic artist Goertz. One week earlier, the children got a letter asking not only for their impressions of the sculptures, but also requesting they choose and give a name to their favourite one.	This short film is not available on You Tube, due to copyrights issues
12. 'GUESSING GUITAR SONGS' (Groups S and B)	This amateur video resolves a song guessing game. The children had been asked by letter a week earlier to put the titles of six songs in the right order. The two group conductors played the songs without subtitles (i.e. without a solution), Niko on the guitar and Leticia singing. This video now shows the solution, namely with subtitles. The two group conductors behave comically and sing out of tune.	https://youtu.be/Ql_nqncaKis

Short Film	Plot summary	YouTube link
13. 'WATER FIGHT' (Groups S and B)	This amateur video shows the group conductors, Leticia and Niko, having a water fight on a playground. The water fight was the traditional farewell game for the group before the summer holidays. The aim of this video was to remind the children of this ritual.	https://youtu.be/ UDcf0NB4re4
14. 'HAVE A GREAT SUMMER HOLIDAYS 2019; (2020)' (Groups S and B)	This is the last amateur video before the summer holidays in 2020. The two group conductors, Leticia and Niko, bid the children a warm and playful farewell into the summer holidays. They assure them that they will continue to be there for them after the holidays, even if it is not clear whether this will be in person or in the form of weekly calls, letters and videos.	https://youtu.be/ bCrJXSnvCDI
15. 'SWITCHED VOICES JOKE' (Groups S and B)	The first amateur video produced after two months of face-to-face group meetings in autumn 2020. Each group conductor, Leticia and Niko, tells a joke, although their voices were switched. The aim of this video was to make the children laugh, even though we could no longer meet due to the new COVID-19 second wave restrictions.	https://youtu.be/ IUrzfr7m9Lk
16. 'CLOWN & WITCH' (Groups S and B)	This silent amateur video was produced for Halloween. It tells the story of the witch (Leticia, the group conductor) who tries to trick the clown (Niko, the other group conductor). The poor clown has no chance and ends up in the poop.	https://youtu.be/ TTGerP245dl

(Continued)

202 TICA adaptations (variations)

Appendix 9.1 (Continued)

Short Film	Plot summary	YouTube link
17. 'JERUSALEMA' (Groups S and B)	This is an amateur dance video produced to create a guessing game. A week before, the children had received a letter with the following questions: 1. what is the name of the dance? and 2. what did Leticia and Niko eat during it? The winner(s) would be rewarded with a popsocket, and the children put in a lot of effort.	Due to copyright issues, the music had to be removed from the video. https://youtu.be/ a21DVUipy5U
18. 'SPORTS AT HOME' (Groups S and B)	In this amateur video, both group conductors, Leticia and Niko show several amusing sports that the children could try to do at home during lockdown, either with their parents or siblings.	https://youtu.be/ UcZtJVRCkQQ
19. 'CAKE FIGHT' (Groups S and B)	This is the last amateur video produced before the end of the groups. In this video, the group conductors, Leticia and Niko, perform an amusing and classic cake fight. The children were delighted with this video, which made it one of their favourite ones.	https://youtu.be/ AUwgckB0F14

Part five

Reflections on TICA

Chapter 10

Outcomes and limitations

In the course of the book, I have highlighted how communication with 'highly vulnerable/unbearable patients' in different settings could be supported and assisted by TICA, along with how preventive psychosocial group work with deprived latency children to avoid an increase in antisocial behaviour can be achieved by means of T-WAS. However, all that has been portrayed so far has been based on representations of my emotional experiences (as an 'outsider' therapist) in the relationship with these patients and children, which is quite personal (Bion 1965). More people were also indirectly involved with them, i.e., in the forensic setting: care officials, social workers, service providers in the multicultural setting: social workers, interpreters; in the children group setting: representatives from other children's organizations. So, these people may also hold representations of their emotional experiences with the patients and the children. Finally, the patients themselves (and participants in the supervision context) have their own representations of their emotional experiences of the communication process undergone, which should be fully appreciated. Hence, most of this chapter reports third-party appreciation (and/or criticisms) related to feasible improvement of patients' behaviour patterns (collected via voluntary statements), patients' communication through drawings, and supervisory participants' surveys.

Outcome of TICA from third parties

Institution director's feedback

Institution director (psychiatric hospital and pretrial detention)

> In the withdrawal therapy, I followed three or four of your cases that I was more closely in contact with. What attracted my attention in a positive way was that these patients felt personally accepted compared to other ones. That is why I wanted you to go to the pretrial detention centres because I always knew that you got along well with people and that was the most important thing to me. I wanted someone who could understand the prisoners and you can understand them emotionally. I just had this impression.

DOI: 10.4324/9781003232087-15

At the beginning of your work in the pretrial detention centres, there was a split among the staff. Some were worried as you wanted to get all information about the prisoners, and in pretrial detention centres, one should be more impartial. There were two or three critical cases, however, where I perceived that you had difficulty in adapting your work from withdrawal therapy to crisis intervention. I well recall our conversation about this issue when I told you that you should not work on the genesis of their crime, as there had been no verdict yet. After that, I noticed a change in your work. And since then, I have received feedback from some prisoners that they liked to talk with you, and I noticed that they were also more open and thoughtful. Without doubt, others were more reserved. Anyway, your struggle to adapt your work from withdrawal therapy to pretrial detention was clear to me. Beyond that, another very positive point refers to the weekly conference with the staff to assess suicide risks. In it, you were able to bring information about the interplay of cultural issues that helped us to better understand some prisoners' behaviour patterns, along with how to deal with them in a more appropriate way. It was very helpful for me and for the staff. To be honest, we usually don't get this kind of information from German psychologists because they can't assess it.

Institution director (pretrial detention)

The psychological service works alongside other specialist services active in criminal prosecution under the legal mandate of the prosecution (and also protection of the general public from crime and preparation of the prisoner for a life of social responsibility without crime) and in this function, fulfils an important role.

In cooperation with other services, the psychological service is responsible for explaining and assessing the psychiatric disturbances of prisoners, introducing and executing measures with those experiencing crisis-point reactions to being detained. The psychological service is also responsible for the work with suicide prevention. The psychologists offer opinions on criminal prognostic assessments and work on the prosecution planning, as well as on the treatment of deficits in personality development and on the social behaviour of prisoners.

In this regard, the psychology service also serves an advisory function for prisoners, e.g., concerning continuing psychotherapeutic measures which are very important for the prisoners for unloading and for further development.

Furthermore, the psychology service acts as a point of reference for officials, regarding, for example, the handling of problematic prisoners. In addition to the duties named, the psychology service delivers internal, theme-specific training for prison staff and engages in questions about the organization's development.

The main subject areas of the criminal prosecution should ideally be overseen by a team of different professional services and professionals. They should also be worked upon in such a way as to present as multi-layered a picture of the personality of the prisoners as possible and they should lead to the necessary methods of treatment. In this regard, the psychology service makes a very significant contribution. Therefore, for tasks to be completed in a sensible and goal-focused way, a modern criminal prosecution service should not be without a psychology service.

Feedback from the staff from the withdrawal therapy

A care official at the psychiatric hospital

My role at the station was that of a staff member – deputy ward manager of the therapy ward. During the time that Mrs. Franieck worked with us, I was particularly impressed by the fact that for the very first time, the patients spoke very positively about a therapist because Mrs. Franieck created a positive environment, which was based on her personal life experiences. The other therapists before her, all of whom were fresh out of university and therefore had little lived experience and only had specialist knowledge acquired from books, had great challenges in creating a positive environment, and other therapists did not always succeed as well as Ms Franieck did from the very beginning. As an eyewitness, it was also clear that these harsher men in prison coped very well with Mrs. Franieck's clear approach; she always approached people and always thought about the good things she could bring to the people, so that she could always reach them at a level where she could take care of them. I think that in all the 18 years I have worked in withdrawal therapy, the members of Mrs. Franieck's group made the best progress in this form of therapy. Whether this was acquiring social skills or being in a group, good progress was made and yes, it is also now easier for me to deal with them personally. Without doubt, there were difficulties with Mrs. Franieck's patients, but dealing with these problems was easier because the patients had strategies and simply got the tools from Mrs. Franieck and were able to confront their problems and get a different perspective on how the other person thinks, how the other person feels, and why they themselves have a problem and what they can do about it. These are important strategies for later life, after prison and after therapy.

Often, there were conversations with patients after an individual session or after the group session, or later after imprisonment when patients contacted me, and they were very positive about the whole thing and the fact that they had worked with Ms Franieck. Sometimes it was a very difficult learning process, but they also said that it was easy for them to deal with problems and with their previous lives, as the approach was suitable for finding solutions, for dealing with problems, for coming to terms with daunting issues and there was a lot of gratitude and a lot of relief. As I said, at the beginning, it was a difficult path, but when the path was gone and the patients were able to look back and see the path they had worked out together in therapy with their therapist, which had now gone, and were then able to find the solution, they were all very happy. There was positive feedback even later, years later, when I was so happy that they had gone through therapy with Ms Franieck and it really helped, and they still benefit today from the solutions suggested and these thoughts about using long-term therapy.

I really enjoyed working with Ms Franieck in the team because she comes from Brazil – of course, a completely different culture – and as I said, because of her life experience, she looked at things from a completely different point of view to the rest of the team and was able to take a very good position and was always able to apply her group therapy among the respective patients and then, in my eyes, she always got along very well with them, and was always able to challenge them.

Working alongside the services, she was always very good at communicating and it was simply very fruitful to listen to her opinion and have the benefit of her expertise and she was always there for us, always had a question, not only for the therapy participants, but also for the officials. Mrs. Franieck was a very important point of contact.

Feedback from the staff of the pretrial detention centres

Service provider

There were different reactions from the prisoners, but the first reaction that I noticed was something completely new for the prisoners – suddenly they were confronted with a psychologist who was basically looking to initiate conversations. Previously, things had been different because it had been the prisoner who had wanted a conversation with a psychologist. Now, things had changed – the psychologist was looking for a conversation with the prisoner and it was basically something new for the prisoner and was not necessarily always positively received. Most of the prisoners received this positively. In the meantime, it had become clear to the prisoners that there was a psychologist, who had approached them, and I had the feeling that the prisoners were also able to open up to this. For the service here, I have noticed that it has certainly had positive effects because we have learned things from the psychologist about a prisoner that we had not even suspected before, which means that it has definitely helped us in our daily dealings with the prisoners. Personally, of course, it has also helped me because I have suddenly noticed that I have different ways of looking at and describing a prisoner, and I think that the psychologist as an instrument in the pretrial detention centre' is a good thing and a good way to make the prison more positive.

Deputy service provider

Several prisoners express that they feel pushed to talk to the psychologist, in order to be granted their release from the observation period. Conversely, there are also prisoners that express how surprised they were when they realized the positive emotional effect of their conversation with the psychologist. They feel they were able to talk freely with someone about their difficult issues.

The psychologist's participation in the team meeting gave us new insights in how to deal with the prisoners (not just with those suffering from mental illness). We have learnt not to take some of their behaviour as aggression directed towards us as a person, but as behaviour that belongs to their dynamic. The staff have developed more understanding and hence the prison has become calmer. Of course, there are several colleagues that don't like the psychological services (which is quite normal); nevertheless, over the years most of them have realized that the psychological service is not so bad. As long as the psychological service helps the prisoners, indirectly it also helps us.

Operations – leader

Many prisoners come back to work quiet and withdrawn after the sessions. It is evident that many of them are thinking about what has just been discussed with them. Some, however, do not understand what it all meant. On other occasions, the prisoners often come to me and want to hear confirmation again of what was said to them, and then, they consider things differently than they did before. There are, of course, prisoners who block everything out straightaway, saying "What rubbish".

Many changes for the better, becoming more open and calmer. Others, on the other hand, stay the same, worrying but keeping things to themselves. Many feel ashamed when they have to go to the psychologist – I tell them "Go – it can't do any harm". See the case of H.R. – the sessions even helped him. His aggressive behaviour has improved 100%.

After the sessions, one often does not come into contact with the prisoners. As reported [previously], the prisoner sometimes only feels more at ease after some days when he has thought about things again. Their behaviour after the sessions is certainly not more difficult, hence nothing goes against the psychological sessions. It cannot actually do the prisoner any harm – either he stays the same or his behaviour improves, but I would not say it gets any worse.

Social worker 1

After the sessions with the psychologist Dr. Franieck, the prisoners in question were always in a better position to cope with their situation. It was easier to hold target-focused sessions. Likewise, passive and direct aggression seemed less intense. Contact with the prisoners in question was then more relaxed, in my opinion.

Furthermore, after the sessions with Dr. Franieck, the prisoners found it much easier to develop realistic ideas about the future again.

After sessions with Dr. Franieck, prisoners who seemed potentially suicidal were once again stable with regards to the danger of possibly committing suicide. After contact with Dr. Franieck, the act of coming to terms with their crime was able to take place in a more appropriate way than before.

With regards to suspected suicidal tendencies in prisoners, after contact with the psychologist, there was great opportunity to evaluate the nature of the risk of a possible suicide. It became clearer which indicators should be shown particular attention in order to recognize potentially suicidal thoughts.

After sessions with the psychologist, a better tactic for managing contact with particularly distressed and aggressive prisoners was established.

Likewise, through consultation with Dr. Franieck, it was possible to obtain a clearer picture of the severity of the prisoners' psychological problems, which differed greatly when compared to the average prison population. This also made it possible to manage prisoners and their symptoms better.

Through the mediated paired sessions, it was possible to direct the conversations in a promising way and potentially deflate any existing conflict between the partners thanks to the earlier discussion with Dr. Franieck.

Social worker 2

Yes, changes are clearly visible after the sessions with the psychologist. On the one hand, there are prisoners who do not want to speak any more with the psychologist, but nevertheless, after the sessions, these prisoners often seem calmer in the sense of experiencing a mild 'aha-reaction', whereby something has become clear to them. There is also the occasional angry prisoner, in whom changes in behaviour have not been visible to me. On the other hand, there are many prisoners who are calm after the session and who appear to be thinking about something. Something has perhaps become clear to them or they are able to accept something as a given. Their behaviour gives me this impression. In the sessions, they are then mostly more open with me too and it is easier to direct things. Many prisoners are then also grateful for any further sessions with the psychologist.

Yes, our sessions at the conference have an effect on my behaviour. I feel surer of myself; I can ask questions and receive answers which help me to generate insights better. I can therefore respond with more understanding and caution, but also more carefully and/or clearly.

I also found the psychologist's handling of non-German prisoners particularly pleasant and helpful – the conversations about these prisoners make me feel more self-assured. I am learning a lot.

Official

With some, it was possible to see changes in behaviour after psychological sessions – in particular, with traumatized or schizophrenic prisoners (the black man, who always saw ghosts, you probably remember).

It was possible to see that the prisoners were able to handle their 'problem' themselves better, which helped us in our day-to-day job. The black prisoner (mentioned [previously]) recognized his problem thanks to her help, but still pressed his alarm during some nights out of fear.

In the session, he said "I know that only I can see the ghost, but I am still scared of her".

There were many other things we were unable to observe because there was often not the time for an intensive session. Problematic cases usually remained problematic cases during their time in prison. Regarding suicidal prevention, despite all of the sessions, two deaths were sadly reported. I do not think that anyone in the world can truly see into another person's mind, especially when there are knee-jerk reactions. But I am sure that through the attack on the topic of suicide, many further deaths were prevented since the prisoners called for help in time. Therefore, considerably more prisoners were placed into emergency psychiatry than before! I think this was because psychological help was finally available onsite, being led by 'civilians' rather than officials. I also think that this contributes a lot to the 'spiritual opening-up' of prisoners.

At the conferences in the past, I can only remark that regarding the variety of services, which were finally discussed, with information being exchanged, specialist services are often cut off from each other and valuable information is therefore easily lost.

I think that through the exchange of information and views, a prisoner was often considered in a different light, approached with more care, or also, from time to time, shown more attention.

Nowadays, I consider the conferences as a valuable opportunity to exchange experiences and opinions – without them, far too much information simply gets lost in our day-to-day roles. Through information exchange, we can, however, be sure that no one else will fall by the wayside.

To conclude, I would like to comment that at the conferences, it was also possible to quietly mention the diagnosis you (Dr. Franieck) had announced so that it was easier for the supervisor to understand some 'decisions'. We are of course trained in psychology, but we are not professionals. Perhaps tips with regards to handling difficult prisoners would be very helpful.

Feedback from the Dutch trainees in the pretrial detention centres

On Monday 13th June 2016, we were welcomed in the pretrial detention by Dr. Castrechini-Franieck. As students of the clinical forensic psychology programme at the University of Tilburg (the Netherlands), this was a unique opportunity for us to get a better insight to the psychological intervention that is offered in German prisons. In the context of our education programme and our internship, we have visited many different prisons and forensic clinics in the Netherlands and have learned about the methods and interventions that are applied there. Being able to experience and learn about the prisons and forensic interventions in Germany has given our knowledge an extra dimension.

Not only was the visit to the prisons and the people we have met during these visits unique and very [educational], but the method also that Dr. Castrechini-Franieck applies was very instructive, as well. The method, in which she uses cartoons to let the prisoners open up about their feelings, which is especially helpful since this is often quite hard for them, has been advocated by our internship supervisor. The opportunity that has been given to us to talk with Dr. Castrechini-Franieck about this method and being able to experience how this method is brought to practice has been very helpful to us.

The visit to the pretrial detention centre has been of great value for us and has definitely enriched our internship; therefore, we are very grateful to Dr. Castrechini-Franieck and the staff for giving us this opportunity. Dr. Castrechini-Franieck is so passionate about her work in the prison, which is reflected in the contact she has with the prisoners. They really open up to her, which results in a good working environment that is indispensable for any change or progress made by the prisoners.

Feedback from the social workers at the refugee psychological centre

Social worker 3

For over ten years, I have been working in a counselling centre for traumatized refugees. In this time, I have gained many insights to the therapeutic activities of all kinds of therapists of various orientations and an in-depth insight to the work with severely traumatized people, who, to some extent, found it difficult to open up and/or found it difficult to enter into therapy.

Through observation and analysis of this group of people, I have recognized just how important the relationship is between therapist and client – therapy can only commence when trust is established between both parties.

Ms Franieck has the gift of being able to create a trusting and empathetic environment. She built relationships with her clients very successfully.

In her sessions, she aimed to include new stimuli using a variety of therapeutic methods and thereby made it easier for clients to identify their problems and thus find a way of dealing with these problems in the long term.

She radiates openness and warmth and can therefore touch the hearts of people.

It was lovely to watch how clients were pleased to see Dr. Franieck again as they entered the counselling centre.

Time and again, I was also able to witness highly emotional situations when it was time to say goodbye.

Dr. Franieck not only demonstrated great openness towards the clients; her manner towards colleagues was also filled with openness and empathy.

She offered to discuss individual cases. In so doing, I witnessed how quickly and with such intense empathy she was able to identify with other people's situations and as a result was able to give suitable advice.

Social worker 4

About me: I am a certified social worker, and I have been working with refugees in various contexts since 1989. For a large proportion of this time, one of my areas of focus was psychological therapy for traumatized refugees and their relatives.

About the group of people: In my experience, not every refugee and also not every victim of torture develops a form of post-traumatic distress. People process the consequences of their experience of extreme threat differently. Trauma can be experienced directly, but also indirectly via relatives, and therefore, it can still have an effect across generations.

In the counselling sessions, refugees described the feelings of fear and helplessness as being their constant companions whilst they were fleeing. They described their experiences during their flight as being frequently 'worse' than the reasons for their flight in the first place.

A sigh of relief after arriving in Germany was often followed by disillusionment – the uncertainty about the security of their stay, as well as a variety of problems in everyday life, e.g., in the shared accommodation, led to complex disorders.

The psychiatric (and physical) effects of the traumatic experiences, which I witnessed in the sessions, were always the refugees' attempts at managing the act of coming to terms with the trauma. In so doing, symptoms arose on an individual basis, with a variety of traits, often in connection with disturbances in their emotions, changes in their self-perception and in social relationships.

During my work with traumatized refugees, I have also worked from time to time in a team with Dr. Franieck, and thereby got to know her specialist work.

On the client level: I did not take part in Dr. Franieck's meetings or sessions. I can, however, provide feedback on my impressions of the clients from before and after the conversations with Dr. Franieck.

I often opened the door for Dr. Franieck's clients and showed them into the waiting room before the start of their meetings. When arriving, many of them seemed to be harassed, worried, beside themselves, agitated, nervous, pale, out of breath, tense, 'as if on the run', their eyes to the ground, their shoulders hunched.

When the doors to the treatment rooms opened again (after the meeting), these people came out transformed: relaxed (even their facial features), walking freely, standing tall, with 'colour in their cheeks'. They made eye contact with me – some smiled at me, saying goodbye.

On a personal level: To learn about my style of work, Dr. Franieck attended so-called pre-appointment sessions, which I held with clients. Her questions (which followed) gave me an opportunity to critically analyze and assess the course of these sessions and my reasons for organizing them in the way I did.

Dr. Franieck's feedback on some specific points was given in the form of open questions. I treated this form of feedback as a highly valuable invitation to uncover my inner "motivations" and their effects on the way I conducted my sessions (as well as the effects on the client).

One example: The fear of (also) becoming a perpetrator by conducting the session in an "insensitive" manner.

> Leading question 1: who do I protect – the client or myself? What from?
> Leading question 2: taboo – seen against the backdrop of the social issue of 'Germany as a perpetrator country' (relating to the Nazis)

On a team level: work with traumatized people leaves its mark on those in a supportive role and on advisers, too; providing long-term treatment and mentoring to traumatized victims can have an effect on the health and wellbeing of colleagues. Such consequences can affect professional and volunteer helpers in equal measure, since these people often become involved in all aspects of the problems. One refers to this as secondary traumatic stress – trauma 'is infectious'.

Every two weeks, Dr. Franieck offered a round of talks under the working title "Time with Leticia" as a modified form of unloading. Here, individual cases of intervention could likewise be requested, such as sessions for questions or sessions on the dynamic of traumatic stress and its consequences.

As a representative of the professional group of social workers in the team, I have realized that this offer of intervention has become for me, as a 'non-therapist', a vital resource for analyzing my own professional practice. It has also become important in relation to my personal sensitivity (and opinions) in my work with traumatized victims, their relatives and in my work with colleagues.

Feedback from the social workers at the social psychiatry centre as regards psychologically ill refugees

Social worker 5

> Communication is made more difficult by the lack of language skills, which in my opinion also has an effect on relationship building.

Ms Franieck always tries to bring a relaxed attitude into the therapy sessions and to address the client directly. However, this is always disrupted by conversations between the professionals and by the fact that the interpreter acts as a speaker.

Ms Franieck is very careful in respecting the client's boundaries and in giving him the opportunity to decide for himself what he wants to reveal. At the same time, she always creates hypotheses that help her to re-establish a relationship with the client. For example, the assumption that the client feels alone and also abandoned by the professional staff. Result: The client receives a piece of paper from her reminding him of the next appointment. Small gesture, big effect.

It is clear that Ms. Franieck is actively working on a relationship and also examining it on a meta-level, which I do not think the client can get involved in yet. At the moment, he is taking the therapy sessions because the psychiatrist he trusts said they would be good for him. Furthermore, I could observe that body language is very important in the sessions. For example, consciously adopting an open body language and asking the client to mirror it. This level of communication is direct and does not go through a third person.

Feedback from the interpreters

Kurdish interpreter

Assessment of your working practice

- You are always friendly.
- You laugh with the people as a sign of your empathy.
- You create a trusting atmosphere in which clients feel at ease.
- Without addressing your clients' problems directly yourself, you subtly lead the clients to each respective problem, giving them the opportunity to talk about them of their own accord.
- Through stories about your own life experiences, you bridge the gap between therapist and client. This creates trust and sympathy.

Arabic interpreter

She leads the discussion in a quiet and purposeful way, normally mentioning this or that point about the client which she had read about beforehand. It is rather interesting to work with her. She talks to the clients without the intention of finding a solution for their problems, or of giving them hope that she will help to solve a problem.

It is interesting how many clients at the beginning of the first meeting have almost decided not to come anymore. After 50 minutes, most of them change their mind and agree to another appointment.

I have learned to look at people in my environment differently, without prejudice, but also with a bit of analysis.

My job as an interpreter is to overcome the language barriers between people with different languages.

Despite the fact that I should remain neutral, I believe that my character, behaviour, and appearance could have an effect on the clients; I have experienced in many cases how I can have a calming effect on the clients.

I am not aware that the meetings burden me, but some behaviour on the part of the clients means it is difficult to communicate with them on a certain level, despite my professionalism, if it does not correspond to my understanding. Furthermore, the habit of people from the Middle East in not ending their sentences and expecting me to understand them and to complete them, which in turn is against the language intermediary Codex, demands a lot of strength from me.

Persian interpreter

I am a sworn interpreter in Afghan languages (Dari and Pashto), and I also interpret the Iranian language Farsi and the Pakistani language Urdu. I have been working in counselling centres for over 15 years. In my work with different psychologists, I am pleased to say that I have of course been able to gain much experience.

I first met Dr. Franieck in May 2016. We had about eight clients between us. I felt immediately as though she understood me.

When our work together was interrupted by circumstances out of our control, many of our clients were sad and disappointed. They told me that after such a long time [that] they finally felt understood. They felt understood after only a few sessions and were on the right path to slowly building up trust – a few of our clients were also no longer attending.

Like many other psychologists, she has her own methods. In addition to other materials, she works with paper and coloured pens, which is well received by the clients. The people for whom I interpret often have difficulties expressing, explaining, and describing their feelings.

They have never heard anything about 'the psyche' before, and sometimes in their mother tongue, they have difficulties understanding the things we are talking about. In this regard, Dr. Franieck knows how to approach these hard-to-reach people, and here, it could often be seen that the clients were beginning to understand themselves. Dr. Franieck attempts to interpret life experiences and the unpleasant events in the drawings.

She receives confirmation from clients time and again. They feel as though Dr. Franieck understands them, and this helps the patients to open up more and more. Dr. Franieck also makes every effort to understand the cultural heritage of the clients, and I am more than willing to help with this. Sometimes, (when we have time), we spend half an hour discussing the clients and the meeting.

I was very impressed by the fact that Dr. Franieck never makes many notes but manages nonetheless to remember every detail about each client and is very well-prepared at every meeting, recalling the issue we had last spoken about.

Dr. Franieck is also very friendly, honest, and precise, and this makes my work much easier. She also had the gift of quickly understanding people and being able to advise, treat and support them accordingly. In my eyes, she is certainly a successful psychologist, and I wish her much success and great joy in her work.

Somali interpreter

I have been interpreting for Dr. Leticia Castrechini-Franieck as a Somali interpreter since 2019. In a few sentences, I will give my view of your being there as a psychologist:

You meet your clients very kindly and are not hasty but talk very superficially at first. By the second or third appointment, you gain the client's trust and [he or she] then feels comfortable with you. You respect the different cultural differences of each client.

I have interpreted for two of your clients so far, and they have told me that they always felt relieved after their visits with you.

I appreciate your work very much because you try to help everyone.

Tamil interpreter

Dr. Franieck's personal, forthright approach stood out in contrast to that of many other therapists in my experience. She engaged directly with her client, challenged his position frequently, and expressed candid opinions. The client did not appear to be disconcerted by this. With time, he or she returned less often to his or her preoccupation with his or her burdened past, and he or she began to initiate a few questions on how to manage the present.

Outcome of T-WAS from third parties

Social workers from the refugee camps

Team from refugee Camp S, where a group took place

We would like to thank you as a team for the successful children's group project in our accommodation. And we do this with one laughing eye and one crying eye.

Since the beginnings in July 2018 with separate boys' and girls' groups to the last dates in December 2020 as a children's group (in which the latter gender has become secondary in terms of numbers), a lot has changed. And through close contact with us, we have always been involved in current developments or topics.

We would like to emphasize that both of you have overcome the hurdles that the pandemic has presented you with since the beginning of this year with great resourcefulness. Temporary visiting bans, limited group sizes in the rooms, more difficult contact possibilities due to lack of telephone/internet, etc., have complicated many things.

Therefore, we would like to thank you in particular for the fact that in times of the pandemic you 'stayed with' the children with great commitment and were the only reliable partner 'from outside' for a long period of time, who kept contact throughout and actively influenced the children's group experience.

Team from refugee Camp B, where a group took place

At present, 45 children and adolescents live in refugee camp B (after the recent conversion to 7 m²), about 20 children belong to the target group of T-WAS. Unfortunately, we have had to observe above-average aggressive behaviour among the children in the past years, which is why an early connection to T-WAS was sought. Despite massive efforts (reminders, accompanying the children to the group in the T refugee camp, parent talks, [etc.]), we did not succeed in permanently connecting at least our 'most difficult' cases to the children's group in refugee camp T, which is why we already asked for an offer in B at the beginning of 2019.

After a long wait, Ms Franieck and Mr. Bittner were finally able to start the children's groups we had long hoped for at the beginning of 2020. Right from the start, almost all children of the corresponding age group were present at the first group. The feedback was extremely positive, and the children were very keen to continue. Then, COVID-19 regulations and the first lockdown put an abrupt end to this. With a lot of effort, Ms. Franieck and Mr. Bittner kept in touch with the children via WhatsApp and videos, riddles and phone calls and, as soon as it was possible, were on site again in person. During lockdown, the T-WAS children's group was a joyful change, and the transition to the 'real' group eventually went smoothly.

Based on the children's feedback, we have the impression that offering this group is gratefully received. Even between the sessions, the children talk about and reflect on the processes, contents, and dynamics during the group. Boundary violations become clear to the children, as does (in) appropriate aggressive behaviour from others and from themselves. Even at the few group events, the children already seem to gain a deeper understanding of the behaviour of all participants and increasingly begin to distinguish "good" from "bad" behaviour.

As professionals on site, we welcome the enormous commitment of Ms. Franieck and Mr. Bittner for the children of refugee Camp B. and are extremely curious to see how the children will develop in the future course. We consider the T-WAS children's group to be an irreplaceable service and are very grateful that it can take place here.

Guests from children organizations

Social worker, NGOs

R. reported after each group meeting to be extremely pleased with the activities and is flourishing properly. She is looking forward to the next one at the end of each session, which, in my opinion, encourages her in everyday life. She looks more confident and enjoys having a session with the group only for herself. With her nine siblings, she sometimes gets lost at home and is therefore all the more pleased about the group's attention. It is very important that the group continues to meet regularly so that positive developments can be consolidated.

Art therapist, Child Protection Centre

When I arrived in the refugee camp, many children welcomed me in the group room. They waited excitedly until the group started at 5:30 pm. The mood was energetic and sometimes very turbulent. It was noticeable that the group was familiar with each other and had a sense of community. A reliable framework was created, in which the children could interact playfully with their peers and the consistent, adult caregivers (leaders). The children interacted in the social group and were able to learn that each personality has the right to be respected. Despite the daily obligations and the individual migration history, it would certainly be helpful for every single child to be able to take advantage of such support more often.

Outcome of TICA from supervisory participants

Before finishing the supervisory process, I developed a short survey, for the purpose of confidentially assessing the participants' satisfaction, as pointed out in Chapter 7.

According to the survey's results, most of the supervision tasks were achieved:

- question 1: 14% fully agreed, 86% of the group members agreed;
- question 2: 29% fully agreed, 71% of the group members agreed;
- question 3: 29% fully agreed, 71% of the group members agreed;

FEEDBACK ON THE SUPERVISION Your feedback is important!

Overall, the organization of the supervision was satisfactory for me.

fully agree ☐   agree ☐   agree less ☐   disagree ☐

Participation in this supervision group was useful to me.

fully agree ☐   agree ☐   agree less ☐   disagree ☐

I am satisfied with the methods and interventions used by the supervisor.

fully agree ☐   agree ☐   agree less ☐   disagree ☐

The supervisor wants to enable the achievement of certain goals with supervision. Which of these goals were achieved for yourself with this supervision group? (Multiple answers possible)

Professionalization ☐   Improving the quality of work ☐

Increase motivation ☐   to keep joy in the profession ☐

Avoiding burnout ☐   Increasing job satisfaction ☐

Role clarification ☐   Rules clarification ☐

Other goals? Which ones?

What was particularly positive or helpful for you in connection with the supervision you attended? Positive or helpful?

What would you like to suggest?

Figure 10.1 Survey

- question 4: Professionalization: 29%; Improving the quality of work: 0%; Increase motivation: 29%; To keep joy in the profession: 43%; Avoiding burnout: 0%; Increasing job satisfaction: 57%; Role clarification: 71%, Rules clarification: 86%; Other goals: Clarify wishes and expectations from both sides;
- question 5: 1) more openness of colleagues, 2) more appreciation of each other, 3) being able to address more conflict, 4) open conversation, 5) team has grown, 6) new information, 7) the exchange, 8) the organization of supervisors – how it was managed; 9) seeing my position clearly and be assured of my decision;
- question 6: 1) To keep the team meetings going, 2) A few lively discussion sessions.

According to the outcomes, not only were the goals of the supervision able to be achieved, but the participants were also satisfied with their experience of the TICA they experienced.

Outcome of TICA from patients

Patients' card drawings on three different occasions in a withdrawal therapy context

When my nose was operated on, I needed to be away for three weeks and leave the Dalva group with homework (analyzing films). Surprisingly, they made a get well soon card for me (Figure 10.2), both individually and as a group, and asked the staff to post it to my private address while I was recovering. At that time, most of them had already undergone nearly nine months of treatment.

They tried to draw 'me' in convalescence holding a voodoo doll. The voodoo doll symbolized one of our last discussions as a group before my operation. The theme of the discussion was religion and in the group, I highlighted some religions that believe in reincarnation or spiritual contact after death or with dead people. At that point, as always, I posed lots of questions for reflection and they were impressed with my knowledge of this matter. Mrs. M. started to say that I could work with voodoo dolls. So, the card was related to our last group meeting. What surprised me most was that they drew the Dalva logo on the top with its name – confirmation of their group identity. As referred to in Chapter 4, the Portuguese word 'Dalva' means the first star one can see in the sky when the day ends, and night begins. As regards the picture, all members of the Dalva group offered their ideas and Mr. R. drew it.

Two months later, at Christmas time, when most of them had already undergone nearly 11 months of treatment, I received Christmas cards from them during our last group meeting before going on holiday for three weeks (Figure 10.3, Figure 10.4). This was when they got their last homework, as referred to in Chapter 4.

222 Reflections on TICA

Figure 10.2 Get well soon card

Outcomes and limitations 223

Figure 10.3 Santa Claus

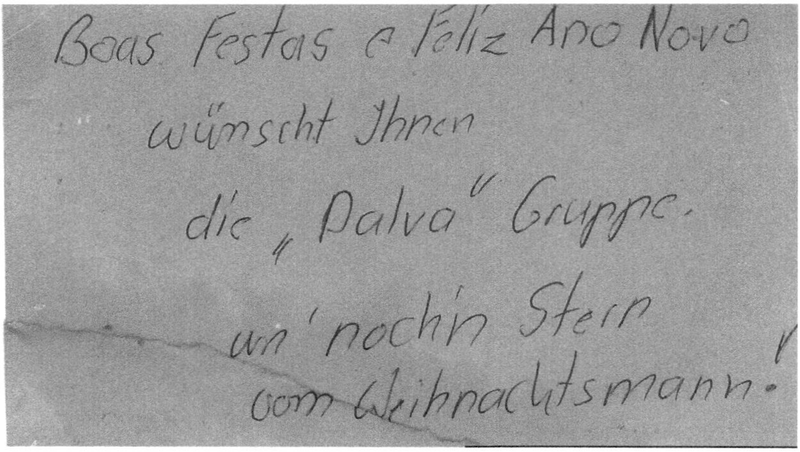

224 Reflections on TICA

Figure 10.4 Boas Festas

Once again, the Dalva Star was noticeable in the card, though now as a Christmas star. Inside the card, they wrote in Portuguese the words "Merry Greetings and Happy New Year (*Boas Festas e Feliz Ano Novo*) wish you the Dalva group and also a star from Santa Claus". According to them, they found out the Portuguese translation of the sentence after asking the care official to search for it on the internet. Yet again, the Dalva members selected ideas and Mr. R. did the drawing. I was moved by their wish to communicate with me in my mother tongue, even though they only wrote five words. Behind the verbal communication, there was the emotional intention of surprising me and making me feel pleased, which I certainly was. When one reflects on their gesture, it shows that they have learned to consider other people's perspectives, which implies that 'shared meaning communication' was achieved. The same had been previously stated by the care official:

> [W]ithout doubt, there were difficulties with Mrs. Franieck's patients, but the way to solve the problems was easier because the patients had strategies and simply got the tools from Mrs. Franieck and were able to deal with their problems and get a different perspective, considering what the other person thinks, how the other person feels and why they themselves have a problem and what they can do about it.

A month later, somehow the Dalva Group found out the date of my birthday. As mentioned in Chapter 4, in such a big institution, the staff has access to some information on the therapist's private life, like the date of their birthday, and there is no way of controlling this. So, they surprised me with a birthday card (Figure 10.5).

Figure 10.5 Birthday card

All the Dalva members and also the staff signed the card inside. Due to data protection, I am not permitted to show the signatures. At this point, the patients had already received the news about the end of my contract, as well as that fact that I should be leaving the station in a month's time, this is the reason why they wrote "in Memory of Dalva". Yet again, the intention of their emotional communication was to surprise me and to make me pleased. In Winnicott's words, their gesture could also be perceived as their 'ability to concern' (Winnicott *et al.* 2012).

Patients' farewell gifts in withdrawal therapy context

A month later was the farewell. The Dalva group members and several patients of the other group made a small donation in order to buy me a farewell gift: a vase of small white orchids on a stand in the shape of three hearts (Figure 10.6). According to the patients, as soon as they saw the heart-shaped stand they said: "this is perfect for Mrs. Franieck; the hearts are just like her!" Since then, orchids have been blooming every year in February (the month I stopped working at the prison).

Figure 10.6 Orchid

Outcomes and limitations 227

In addition, I received two more farewell gifts with optimistic messages from two patients of the other group (Figure 10.7, Figure 10.8). One message says: "I wish you the best in your life. Keep strong. One way closes, another way open" and the other message says: "never lose hope or passion for life". The former was from a patient, an immigrant from Africa, who felt very much discriminated against in the prison due to his skin colour. As I was the one who could

Figure 10.7 Flower

Figure 10.8 Fairy

speak English quite fluently, we used to have short daily chats on the floor, which according to him made him feel more welcome. The latter was from a patient who was a member of the Dalva group for the first four months of his treatment, but was transferred to my colleague's group, as the psychiatric director assumed I would be unable to follow his German. According to him, he had made this picture whilst participating in occupational therapy at the beginning of his treatment, without knowing to whom he could give it. When he got the news, I was leaving the centre, he thought that giving it to me would be perfect. Whether the patient related his time in the Dalva group to the time he had made the picture and then with me is unclear.

I was certainly overwhelmed by the generosity of all of the patients. Indeed, my last working day in the withdrawal therapy was completely different from my first day, as described in Chapter 1. I left there still with the feeling of being an 'Outsider', though I was not sceptical anymore. The Dalva group and I had grown up with the help of TICA, and surely, one can offer, develop and reach a form of 'shared meaning communication', as long as one really wants to.

Summary

In this book, I tried to share with the reader (myself in the role of an 'Outsider') the representations of my emotional experiences (Bion 1965) within the challenging clinical work with 'highly vulnerable/unbearable' adult patients in the forensic setting, as well as with traumatized adult patients in the intercultural one. Although the two settings may give the impression of being divergent, they are in fact connected to each other as processes associated with the psychological dynamics of aggressor/offender vs. traumatized/victim are intrinsically linked. They are complementary and remain essentially unchanged in both settings. Based on this premise, the primary focus of the work with these patients has been on the 'Transient Interactive Communication Approach' (TICA), which in turn provided the foundation of T-WAS ('Together We Are Strong'), psychosocial group work with deprived latency children aiming to achieve a decline in antisocial tendencies in the preventive field.

Whilst expressing the representations of my emotional experiences to the reader, an attempt emerged on my part to draw attention to several issues for reflection in the clinical work, as to:

- how to deal with our blind understanding of communication levels (verbal, non-verbal and pre-verbal), including the intercultural one;
- the challenge of learning, as well as training on the job, the meaning of some theoretical concepts like: 'maternal reverie', 'container-contained model', 'α and β elements' of Bion (1984a, 1984b); 'transitional object and transitional phenomena', 'mutuality', 'holding', 'deprived child', 'cultural experience' of Winnicott (2018, 2005, 1953); 'analytic triad' of Ogden (2004/1994); 'analyst's daydreaming' of Cassorla (2018) and Katz et al. (2017);

- the challenge of learning how to deal with ephemeral encounters and their sadly inevitable frustrations, alongside the responsibility of not leaving any unfinished business with the patient/client;
- the courage to apply psychoanalytical knowledge to the social context or community one, whilst being aware that the approaches applied are quite different from the psychoanalytical ones;
- the challenges of learning how to cope with triangular settings, including the one as being your own observer in the relationship with the patient and/or with the group members and fellow conductor (Caper 1997);
- the acceptance and the awareness of one's own role as an 'Outsider', whilst perceiving it positively;
- the challenges of learning how to keep oneself neutral whilst communicating with 'highly vulnerable/unbearable' patients without shielding oneself of feeling empathetic towards him;
- the difficulty of how to reach our emotional balance whilst in contact with such highly vulnerable patients;
- The ability to be creative and playful in the group work whilst setting boundaries as a group conductor;
- the ability to conduct a group together with a partner, whilst developing object relations and corrective attachment experiences with group members;
- the ability to deal with our own lack of awareness and further misunderstandings related to the representation of our own emotional experiences.

Throughout this reflection process, the following two key concepts could be introduced.

1 "Shared meaning communication": one's ability to understand each other's perspectives well enough to accept them, albeit one may not agree with them – the basic pillar of TICA.
2 "Eclectic group conductors": a new approach in group work that intentionally uses the interplay of personal differences when conducting a group and putting the conductors' skills into action – the essential pillar of T-WAS for the achievement of 'shared meaning communication' with deprived children in latency.

Limitations

The most critical limitation to TICA as well as to T-WAS is connected with the 'wave of a psychotherapist's unconscious bias in their contact with 'highly vulnerable/unbearable' patients or with deprived children', which is mostly triggered by transference and counter-transference issues. Yet again, in practice, a precondition for the therapist would be the need to have undergone personal training analysis and/or being closely supervised. As previously referred to, the therapist needs to engage in interactions with 'highly vulnerable/unbearable' patients or deprived children and building 'shared meaning communication' with them, though this requires resources that go beyond the books. It implies one's ability to allow oneself to undergo a primitive emotional state in the interaction with these patients (in both settings: individually and in the group) without the fear of losing oneself; without being dominated by patients' wishes, phantasies or traumas; and whilst keeping one's own sanity on top of one's professionalism. Metaphorically speaking, it is like diving deep into a dark ocean without knowing where one is; it is like trying to reach the deepest point of it but never forgetting and always being aware that one has to hold enough oxygen in their lungs to rise to the surface again.

Some personal observations

Personally, I have long been working with TICA and T-WAS, and with time, I have noticed that I have changed the way I perceive people, and also the world – that is to say, I keep playing the role of an 'Outsider'. As referred to in Chapter 2, I have had contact with more than 3000 prisoners, 300 traumatized refugees, and 250 deprived children. I have drawn on paper and in my mind, so many time-lines and feelings wheels – most of them very weirdly and bizarrely. I have heard things that one may think are the stuff of films, but they were very real. I suppose I have lost the diagnostic perception that a counsellor has to perform in the first interview according to what the system expects from us. That is to say, of course the knowledge is there, and I can run a diagnostic, though I refuse to do it, as it would not help me to remain neutral in a communication session with a new patient/client. Today, what matters to me is to develop TICA and T-WAS further (i.e., the next challenge will be to build and conduct an open, voluntary, and low-threshold psychosocial group with highly vulnerable adolescent refugees who are threatened and/or affected by social disadvantage and who are not or only insufficiently reached by other social work offers – the group will take place in the open air). Nevertheless, sometimes when I think about TICA and T-WAS, I ask myself "What are you doing, Leticia? Does that make sense?". Perhaps at these times I am regressing to the toddler Leticia and feel I should not have tried to run along the footpath alone. But then again, when I meet new 'highly vulnerable/unbearable' people and/or deprived children/adolescents, the wish to understand them and communicate with them grows inside me. Perhaps here, I sense the toddler Leticia that was just playing in a potential space (Winnicott 1953), whilst testing her limits – that feeling of being alive.

To conclude this book and the communication between us, I would like to say some more words:

"Departure and encounters"

For some moments
We have been together
Me. . . . in the author role

You . . . in the reader role
We don't know each other!!!
But what does it matter?
We have just talked to each other . . .
The writing was our encounter . . .
Our thoughts were our speech
Now it is time to say goodbye . . .
But if by chance
You could understand my doubts . . .
See me in your doubts . . .
Then we have met each other before . . .
And I am delighted to tell you:
"It was great to see you again!!!"

Some of your personal observations

(Please use this blank page for your thoughts.)

References

Bion, W.R., 1965. *Transformations: Change from Learning to Growth*. London: William Heinemann Medical Books Limited.
Bion, W.R., 1984a. *Attention & Interpretation*. London: Maresfield Reprints.
Bion, W.R., 1984b. *Learning from Experience*. London: Maresfield Reprints.
Caper, R., 1997. Symbol Formation and Creativity: Hannas Segal's Theoretical Contributions. *In:* D. Bell, ed. *Reason and Passion: A Celebration of the Work of Hanna Segal*. London: Routledge, 37–56.
Cassorla, R.M.S., 2018. *The Psychoanalyst, the Theatre of Dreams and the Clinic of Enactment*. Abingdon, Oxon and New York: Routledge.
Katz, M., Cassorla, R.M.S., and Civitarese, G., eds., 2017. *Advances in Contemporary Psychoanalytic Field Theory: Concept and Future Development*. London and New York: Routledge.
Ogden, T.H., 2004/1994. *Subjects of Analysis*. 1st ed. Lanham, MD: Rowman & Littlefield.
Winnicott, D.W., 1953. Transitional Objects and Transitional Phenomena: A Study of the First Not-Me Possession. *The International Journal of Psycho-analysis*, 34, 89–97.
Winnicott, D.W., 2005. *Playing and Reality*. London: Routledge.
Winnicott, D.W., 2018. The Mother-Infant Experience of Mutuality. *In: Psycho-Analytic Explorations*. London: Routledge, 251–260.
Winnicott, D.W., et al., 2012. *Deprivation and Delinquency*. Milton Park and Abingdon, Oxon: Routledge.

Index

Page numbers in **bold** indicate a table on the corresponding page.

achievement-ascription relationships 13
adoption placement process and refugee children 159–160
affect attunement 18, 120
aggression 27, 45, 55, 132–133, 155, 161, 166, 175
Allcorn, S. 19, 138–139
anger management 168
Anthony, E. J. 167
anti-aggression training 40
antisocial behavioural tendencies 160
approach 105–106; *see also* TICA (transient interactive communication approach); T-WAS (Together We Are Strong)
Arabic language 16
As-salome, A. 14, 157
assertiveness 13
asylum seekers, language issues for 117
attachment 155, 160
attunement 18, 29, 120

Bagdad Café (film) **66**, 72
Bataca-Fight 166, 170, 175
Battle at Kruger (film) **56**
Bion, W. R. 17, 19
Bittner, N. 159–160, 163–164, 166
Blom, R. 167
blz2 (film) **59**
"Brennender Baum" (cartoon painting) 53–54
Bucket List, The (film) **67**, 73
bullying 129

cartoons: "Brennender Baum" (cartoon painting) 53–54; optical illusion 31, 46–49, 51–52

Casriel, D. 122
Castrechini-Franieck, M. L. 14, 16, 156, 157, 159, 160, 163–164, 166
Centre Stage TV CCTV9 **63**
Child Friendly (film) **59**
Codex (language intermediary) 216
cognitive behavioural therapy (CBT) 116
collectivism 14
commercials: Butterfinger **61**; Graffiti - Pfizer **61**; McDonald's **57**
communication 15–20; building through optical illusions 47–49, 51–52; and drawings 91–96, 122; framework 90–91; language communication level 15–16, 109; pre-language communication level 17–20; pre-verbal 18–19, 119; primitive 17–20; transitional objects for 30, 94; verbal 16, 18, 109, 115, 118, 119, 120, 140, 145, 224; *see also* intercultural interactional communication
confidence building 180
confidentiality 91
container-contained process 142, 146
coping 159
Corona *see* COVID-19 pandemic, TICA in
corrective attachment experiences 34, 122, 155, 160, 162–163
counter-identification 17
counter-transference 17, 119, 144, 147, 162, 176
COVID-19 pandemic, TICA in: author's observations 194–196; letters and/or emails 186–187; producing films for T-WAS 190–191, 194; telephone (video) counselling 187–190
creative aggression 155, 161

Index 235

creative games 166, 181
creative thinking 17
crisis interventions 87–88
cross-cultural community 10–11
cross-modal imitation 18
culture: cross-culture 10–11, 18; cultural codes 156; cultural experience 15; cultural ideals 14–15, 118, 157, 158; cultural identity 118, 156, 158; cultural mediation 118; cultural noise 16, 18, 19, 30, 141, 145; cultural orientation 163; cultural transmission 159; defined 11–12; values 157; *see also* intercultural interactional communication; multicultural team supervision, TICA in

Dalva-case study 64–65, 72–80
daydreaming 17, 109, 125, 187, 195
decision making 44
depression 116
deprived children 34, 157–158; *see also* T-WAS (Together We Are Strong)
Devil's Advocate, The (film) **70**
disillusion 117
drawings and communication 91–96, 122
dual orientation of narcissism 14, 157

early discharge 39
eclectic group conductors 163, 168, 194
ego: cohesion 117; disintegration 117, 157; ideal 14, 157; strengthening 168
Elephant Birth in Bali (film) **56**
Elephant Man, The (film) **71**
emails for counselling 186–187
emotional availability 158
emotional barriers 162
emotional disorganization 195
emotional training 40
Empire of the Sun (film) **71**
emptiness in refugees 158
ephemeral setting xxi, 88–89, 92, 94, 96, 99, 103, 105, 107, 111, 115
exclusion 39, 46, 118, 129, 170, 188
experience of self 94, 103, 116, 131, 175
external environment and child's emotional development 156
external objects 15, 19, 30, 55, 120, 139

fantasy and fact, difference between 30
fears of extinction 157
feedback 80, 144, 166, 190, 195; from Dutch trainees in the pretrial detention centres 211–212; from group members 42; in group sessions 79–80; from institution director 205–207; from interpreters 215–217; from social workers 212–215; from staff from the withdrawal therapy 207–208; from staff of the pretrial detention centres 208–211
feelings' wheel: case 1 125–129; case 2 129–132; case 3 132–134; interpretation of the drawing 124–125; introduction to task 122, 124
feminine values 12
films for interpretation training **56–63**
Fliegende Blätter (German humour magazine) 47–48
Fly Bird Fly (film) **59**
Foulkes, E. 11, 19, 46, 78
Foulkes, S. H. 11, 19, 46, 78, 167
frustration 109, 166–167
future-oriented behaviours 13

gender egalitarianism 13
genetic issues and perceptions 51–52
genetic predispositions 14
Germany, dealing with mass immigration 157–159
Gestalt therapy 155, 161, 164
GLOBE survey 13
Grinberg, L. 17, 156
Grinberg, R. 156
group: self 157; settings, limits in 167–168; therapy 40, 46
group conductors 40, 170, 172, 176, 178–179; eclectic 162–163, 168, 194; therapist as 46–47
group identity 55; closed 77; establishing 46–47, 64–65
Günter, M. 14, 157, 159

Hall, E. T. 12
Hamden, C. 13
Hofstede, G. H. 12–13
holding environment 18, 47, 146, 169–170, 195
hope xviii, xxi, 27, 65, 78, 88, 186, 187–189
hospital director, role in withdrawal therapeutic treatment **43**
House, R. J. 13
humane orientation 13

ICD-10/DSM categorization xviii, 49
idealization of therapist 78–79

identity: loss and migration 157; sense of 157, 158; social/cultural, of refugees 116
imitation 18
impotence 28, 157, 175, 176
independence 12
individualism-communitarianism 13
individualism *vs.* collectivism (IDV) 12, 13–14
individualistic culture 157
individual therapy 40, 42
in-group collectivism 13
in-group mental operations 19
in-group relationships 167
INPES Free Hugs **61**
Inside Out (film) **71**
institutional collectivism 13
interactive communication approach 32
intercultural encounter 18
intercultural interactional communication: communication 15–20; cultural dimensions theory 12–14; culture, defined 11–12; intercultural communication, defined 12; overview 9–11; psychoanalytical perspective and previous perspectives 14–15
intercultural society 10
interdependence 12
interpersonal experiences 118
interpretation training 30, 161–162; building communications through optical illusions 47–49, 51–52; establishing the therapeutic setting 52–54; exploring short films 54–55, **56–63**, 64
interpreter(s) 189, 195; feedback from 215–217; role in therapeutic setting 117–118; supervisor as 145
Interview with the Vampire (film) **71**
Intouchables, The (film) **71**
intrapsychic experiences 118
ironic mirror image approach 105–106
Ishihara test 51–52

Japanese language 16

Katz, M. 17
King's Speech, The (film) **70**

Ladyhawke (film) **67**, 73
language: acquisition 158; common 7; and communication 15–16, 109; domination 16; fluency 16; issues for refugees 117; representation by 15–16, 17; and sense of self 158–159; use and childhood 156
Last of the Mohicans, The (film) **70**
Last Samurai, The (film) **70**
latency, refugee children in 156
leave-taking in group sessions 170, 172, 176
Lehle, H. G. 167
letters for counselling 186–187
long-term *vs.* short-term orientation 13
Lucas, T. 164

masculine values 12
masculinity *vs.* femininity (MAS) 12
maternal attunement 18
maternal reverie 9, 17, 127
Maude, B. 11
mediator, supervisor as 145
mental health 39, 117–118
Mester, G. 53–54
migration, effect on child's latency period 156
Ministry of Social Affairs – Lebanon – Animals (film) **60**
miscommunication 16, 141, 146
mourning processes, coping with 117
multicultural society 10
multicultural team supervision, TICA in: author's observations 147; background of supervisor 139–140; interview with board of directors 140–146; supervisory role 138–139, 141–142, 145; supervisory setting 138–139
mutuality 18, 29, 120, 187

narcissism: dual orientation of 14; narcissistic impulse reminiscence 14, 157
narrative exposure therapy (NET) 116
national cultures: dimensions of 13; values 12
Nell (film) **71**
neutral-emotional relationships 13
neutrality of therapist 79
neutral room *see* neutral space
neutral space 164, 173, 180, 196
non-verbal communication 16, 119
nursing staff, role in withdrawal therapeutic treatment **43**

object relation 34
occupational therapist, role in withdrawal therapeutic treatment **43**
occupational therapy 40, 41
Ogden, T. H. 19
ontological psychoanalysis 155
optical illusion cartoons 31, 46–49, 51–52
'Other,' the xix, 15, 17, 18, 25; *see also* communication
Other/Wise: The Online Journal of the International Forum for Psychoanalytic Education 115
'Outsider,' the xix, 15, 17, 18, 25, 188; *see also* communication

parental representation of emotional experiences 34, 160, 162–163, 168
pastor, role in withdrawal therapeutic treatment **43**
pedagogy 155
pendants 33, 109–111
perceptions and interpretations of therapist 49, 51
performance orientations 13
personality building 15
personality disorders cases: case 1, blurred distinctions 96–99; case 2, childhood abuse 99–102; case 3, irony of fate 102–104; case 4, depressed young man 104–107; case 5, symbolic expressions for communication 107–111
phantasies 8, 29, 117, 122, 134
playful space 46–49, 51–54, 77, 168, 175–180, 219
Playmobil® dolls 88, 132–133
play narrative technique 132–133
Plutchik's wheel of emotions 122
post-traumatic stress disorder (PTSD) 116
potential space xv, 15, 19–20, 24, 29, 32–34, 46–49, 51–54, 65, 88, 103, 164, 170
power distance (PDI) 12, 13
powerlessness 175
pre-verbal communication 18–19, 119
primitive communication 17–20
prison director, role in withdrawal therapeutic treatment **43**
privacy of therapist 78–79
psychodrama 40
psychological regression 18

psychologists, role in withdrawal therapeutic treatment **43**
Psychosoziale Gruppenarbeit mit benachteiligten Kindern: Paarleitung und kreatives Spiel (*Psychosocial group work with deprived children: a pair of co-conductors, one male and one female and creative play*) 155
Publi Tv – niños con cáncer (film) **60**
punctuality in group sessions 80

quality of life 40

Rain Main (film) **71**
reflections on T-WAS 168–169; *see also* feedback
refugee children in latency 156; dealing with ambiguities and paradoxical roles 158–159; refugee children/adolescents per se deprived 157–158; *see also* T-WAS (Together We Are Strong)
relapse prevention 40
relaxation training 40
representation: of emotional experiences 8, 134, 161, 181, 205, 229, 230; by language 15; of parents 34, 160, 161, 162–163, 168; verbal xix, xx, 6, 33, 47, 161–162
resilience 34, 64, 94, 159, 162, 164; *see also* COVID-19 pandemic, TICA in
resonance reactions 19
responsivity of parents 158
reverie 9, 17, 127, 187
risk assessments 87–88
Ruf, M. 157

Sand Art Love 2008 **63**
Sandro del Prete 49
Satir 9
Segal, H. xv
self-assurance training 40
self-destructive behaviour 55
self-empowerment 178, 180
self-esteem 55
self in relation to others 162
self-symbolization 117
sense of belonging 156
sense of detachment 159
sense of identity 157, 158
sense of impotence in refugees 157–158
sense of self 94, 103, 116, 131, 175

shared language/shared meaning 46–47, 72
shared meaning communication 29, 46–47, 72, 161–163; *see also* TICA (transient interactive communication approach)
short-term therapy with traumatized refugees: author's observations 134–135; building 'shared meaning communication' 119–120, 122, 124–125; case 1, love burns 125–129; case 2, overcoming a taboo 129–132; case 3, from a case of shame to a lost case 132–134; psychological situation of refugees 116–117; social situation of refugees 115–116; triangular constellations 117–119
social behaviour and adaptation problems 159
social competence training 40
social conduct of refugee children 158
social/cultural identity of refugees 116
social culture 156
social workers 195; at the refugee psychological centre 212–214; role in withdrawal therapeutic treatment **43**; at the social psychiatry centre 214–215
specific-diffuse relationships 13
sport 40
Stein, H. F. 19, 138–139
Stern, D. N. 18
storytelling 19
street situations 3, 25–29, 88–89, 91, 96, 160–161
Suzuki Bikes Dog Walking (film) **58**
symbolization 15–16, 17, 30, 117, 166

taboos, dealing with 178
Take the Lead (film) **70**, 73
team-building and supervisory process 140
team constellation 42, 44
team members, roles in withdrawal therapeutic treatment **43**
telephone (video) counselling 187–190
Terminal, The (film) **69**, 73
therapists: attention of 194–195; idealization of 78–79; neutrality of 79; occupational, role in withdrawal therapeutic treatment **43**; as the 'Other' xix,15, 17, 18, 25; privacy of 78–79; role in the triangular constellation 118–119; unconscious bias of 230–231
Thun, Schulz von 9
TICA (transient interactive communication approach): case in a forensic setting xix–xv; case in an intercultural setting xv–xxi; COVID-19 pandemic 34; developing 'shared meaning communication' 30–32; forensic withdrawal therapy 32–33; introduction xviii–xix; observations on 29–30; preventive work with deprived children 34; short-term multicultural team supervision 33–34; vignette 25–29; work with traumatized refugees 33
TICA, outcome from third parties: Dutch trainees in the pretrial detention centres, feedback from 211–212; institution director's feedback 205–207; interpreters, feedback from 215–217; from patients 221, 224–225, 227, 229; social workers, feedback from 212–215; staff, feedback from 207–211; from supervisory participants 219, 221
TICA and perspectives on interactive communication: from a business/organizational perspective to a genetic one 11–14; on communication 15–20; relating the psychoanalytical perspective to the previous perspectives 14–15
TICA in pretrial detention: author's observations 111; case 1, blurred distinctions 96–99; case 2, an abused little boy 99–102; case 3, the irony of fate 102–104; case 4, depression 104–107; case 5, disguised patient 107–111; drawings 91–96; risk assessments and crisis interventions 87–91
TICA in withdrawal therapy: creating a potential space 46–49, 51–54; establishment of common transitional object 65, 72–73; exploring short films 54–55, **56–63**, 64; Theseus group-case study 44–46; from Theseus to Dalva-case study 64–65; withdrawal therapeutic community context 39–42, 44
timeline method: and communication setting 88–91; and drawing 91–96

Together We Are Strong (T-WAS) *see* T-WAS (Together We Are Strong)
transference 122, 162, 171
transient interactive communication approach (TICA) *see* TICA (transient interactive communication approach)
transient shared meaning communication 88–91, 99, 107, 147
transitional objects for communication 30, 94
transitional space 30, 76, 94, 116, 181, 191
triad/triangular xv, 9, 117
Trompenaars, F. 13
trust building 170
T-WAS (Together We Are Strong) 34; approaches 168–169; author's observations 180–181; creation of 160–161; dealing with ambiguities and paradoxical roles 158–159; features of 163–164; focus on refugee children in latency 156; group's transcriptions 169–180; introduction 155–156; limitation to 230–231; phases and the group meeting's structure 164, 166–167; producing films for 190–191, 194; refugee children/adolescents per se deprived 157–158; roots of 159–160; setting limits 167–168; and TICA 161–163
T-WAS, outcome from third parties: guests from children organizations 219; social workers from the refugee camps 217–219
Twohy, M. 52–53

uncertainty avoidance (UAI) 12, 13
unconscious communication 18
unconscious primitive ego function 14
universalism-particularism relationships 13

verbal language 16
verbal/non-verbal information 15
verbal representation xix, xx, 6, 33, 47, 161–162
verbal thinking 15
video counselling 187–190, 194
vulnerable patients *see* TICA (transient interactive communication approach); T-WAS (Together We Are Strong)

"Wallpaper" (cartoon painting) 52–53
Watzlawick, P. 9
WhatsApp 190
Winnicott, D. W. 15, 18, 20, 116, 156, 160–161, 178, 225
withdrawal therapeutic community: core pillars of the treatment 40–41; exclusion criteria for the treatment 39; goals 40; treatment step programme 41–42, 44
Woods, J. 167
work in prison 40

You, Me and Dupree (film) **68**, 73

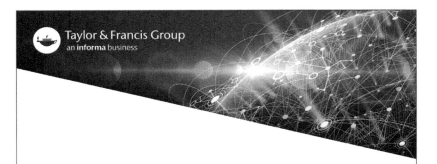

Taylor & Francis eBooks

www.taylorfrancis.com

A single destination for eBooks from Taylor & Francis with increased functionality and an improved user experience to meet the needs of our customers.

90,000+ eBooks of award-winning academic content in Humanities, Social Science, Science, Technology, Engineering, and Medical written by a global network of editors and authors.

TAYLOR & FRANCIS EBOOKS OFFERS:

- A streamlined experience for our library customers
- A single point of discovery for all of our eBook content
- Improved search and discovery of content at both book and chapter level

REQUEST A FREE TRIAL
support@taylorfrancis.com